Diverted

High Flyers and Frequent Liars

Mark S. Mogel

NOTE TO READERS

This book is based upon thousands of e-mails and instant messages, scores of television, radio and print interviews, interviews with key participants, government and court documents, and my copious notes and memory.

Readers may notice discrepancies herein in regard to certain facts such as the amount of time that American Airlines Flight 1348 was on the tarmac in Austin, Texas on December 29, 2006. Until September 2007, most news accounts of the incident cited a duration of eight hours or more. In September 2007, the Inspector General for the U.S. Department of Transportation released a report that set the duration as nine hours and sixteen minutes. That is the duration I use throughout this book.

Readers may also notice, at times, a three-hour difference between instant message timestamps and the time of day discussed within those messages. This is due to the difference between the East and West Coast time zones.

All quotes from blogs, instant messages and e-mails written by Kate Hanni or me were reproduced verbatim including spelling and grammatical errors. The only alterations made were to modify certain expletives, and to remove extraneous text and unnecessary personal information. I also redacted the names of third parties who might otherwise be unduly harmed by their inclusion in this story. The [sic] convention was employed only where third-party e-mails or news articles contained errors that were reproduced verbatim.

Some of the URLs listed in the bibliography were no longer valid on the date this book was published. Readers can find higher quality color photographs of those included herein on my Facebook page.

THIS IS THE story of the part I played in a three-year journey to change the world of commercial aviation for airline passengers – and what a strange and turbulent journey it was.

CONTENTS

PROLOGUE

THE HEADLINE IN the *Napa Valley Register* read, "Real estate agent assaulted in vacant home." The article described an incident that was reported on the afternoon of June 21, 2006:

> Kate Hanni said she received a call on her cell phone from a
> man saying he was interested in looking at property she had
> listed in the 100 block of Berna Avenue in Napa. … Hanni was
> alone in the house turning on the lights when a man wearing a
> ski mask entered the home, according to Napa police.[1]

According to the article, police said that Hanni escaped by biting the assailant on his hand, and that she was taken to a local hospital where she was treated and released.

Six months later, on December 29, 2006, Hanni boarded American Airlines Flight 1348 in San Francisco with her husband and two sons. The family was headed to a vacation resort in Alabama with a stopover at the Dallas-Fort Worth International Airport.

As Flight 1348 approached Dallas at around noon, a broad line of severe thunderstorms was passing through central Texas. Tornado warnings were issued. Air traffic controllers closed the Dallas airport. Unable to land in Dallas, the flight landed at Bergstrom International Airport in Austin, Texas.

Due to the severe weather, which continued throughout the afternoon, over 120 other flights that had been bound for Dallas were also forced to land at Austin and other airports in the southwest region. It was the largest disruption in air service since 9/11. Both American Airlines and the regional airports where the flights landed were unprepared to deal with the crisis. Many of the smaller regional airports were running scheduled incoming and outgoing flight operations, and there weren't enough gates available to accommodate all of the unexpected jets.

Throughout the afternoon, the weather in Dallas alternately cleared and worsened. During the clear periods, some flights were able to resume their trips to Dallas. That led other flight crews to believe that they too would get clearance to complete their trips. For many of them, and thousands of passengers who sat on those airplanes, it was a clearance they would never receive.

The severe weather eventually reached Austin. Lightning pounded the airport – preventing airplanes from taking off and ground personnel from moving about safely. As more hours passed, snacks and water became scarce. Lavatory toilets were filled to the rims – the stench of human waste flowed throughout airplane cabins. Parents ran out of formula and diapers for their babies. Police were called to break up a fight on one of the jets. An ambulance was called to another to assist a diabetic with a colostomy bag. A small dog defecated in the cabin of yet another, which led to a cascade of vomiting passengers. It was a nightmare.

Nine hours and sixteen minutes after American Airlines Flight 1348 landed in Austin, its captain, without permission, maneuvered his airplane to a gate and let the passengers deplane. Kate Hanni, the real estate agent from Napa, stepped off of that airplane and into commercial aviation history.

Within three years, Hanni will have successfully lobbied the federal government to issue regulations that would threaten airlines with a fine of up to $27,500 per passenger for tarmac delays of over three hours. Airlines would be required to change how they reported tarmac delay statistics. Bumping compensation would be increased, and airlines would be required to provide full and accurate ticket pricing on their websites.

High-level government officials would meet with Hanni to discuss aviation-related subjects ranging from baggage fees to pilot fatigue. She would become a popular media commentator on airline safety, security and consumer issues.

Within a six-month period in 2006, she had survived a terrifying assault and had endured a nine-hour and sixteen minute tarmac stranding. Three years later, she had done what no one else could or would do, what many would say was impossible. She had turned her anguish and anger into advocacy. She had taken on the commercial airlines and their powerful Washington lobbyists and had beaten them. News reports would herald Hanni as the woman who forever changed the way that airlines treated their customers – a determined woman who led a national coalition of grassroots activists to fight for and attain basic human rights for airline passengers.

Four years after Hanni's tarmac stranding, ABC *World News* anchor Diane Sawyer would wrap a lengthy tribute to Kate Hanni's extraordinary accomplishments asking, "Who says one person can't change a lot in this country?"[2]

APRIL 2010

Let's do this

THREE YEARS AND four months after Kate Hanni walked off of the airplane in Austin, Texas, I was sitting at my dining room table with a reporter for a travel industry publication.

"Are you okay?" the reporter asked. "You don't look good."

Mike Fabey had driven from Virginia to my home in Collegeville, Pennsylvania to interview me for an article he was writing about Hanni. I wasn't okay. My head felt like it was going to explode or implode, I couldn't tell which. I was dizzy, short of breath, sweating – thought I might be having a heart attack.

"You might have to take me to a hospital, Mike," I said.

By now, Kate Hanni was a nationally known consumer advocate, considered by many in the public, the government and the news media to be a heroine for airline passengers.

Six months earlier, Hanni had filed a lawsuit against Delta Airlines and another company. She alleged that they engaged in a conspiracy to hack into her e-mail account and computer. Their motive, according to documents she filed in court, was to sabotage her organization's ability to advocate for federal airline passengers' rights legislation – legislation that had not yet been enacted. In addition to the lawsuit, an FBI investigation had been launched on behalf of the federal government. The story was national news.

A week after the lawsuit was filed, Mike Fabey had written an article in which Hanni alleged that the former information technology director for her organization, me, was the prime suspect in the hacking conspiracy. Hanni had also told Fabey that she had always been fearful of me and that she was worried about her physical safety. She wrote to him, "I understand there will always be people who will try to destroy us. ... Sorry I'm so emotional. I'm just living in a lot of fear right now."

Now in April 2010, six months after Fabey's article was published, an e-mail written by a detective for the Napa County California Sheriff's Department had been posted in a publicly accessible online court docket for the Delta lawsuit. The detective's e-mail alleged that: "suspect Mark S. Mogel" had hacked into Hanni's home computer network, that I was in possession of a video in which Hanni "exposes herself sexually," and that I threatened to give the video to a reporter – presumably unless Hanni paid me off. The subject line of the detective's e-mail was "Extortion Investigation." The theme of the e-mail depicted me as being obsessed with Hanni.

Fabey had seen the detective's e-mail on the court docket and called to ask me about it. I told him that the computer hacking, sex video, extortion and obsession allegations paled in comparison to something else I was told a few days earlier; that Hanni had alleged that I drugged and raped her in a hotel room near Washington, D.C. in April 2008.

Fabey asked if I would be willing to meet with him to discuss all of this in person. I had agreed.

My heart attack symptoms hadn't just started when Fabey arrived from Virginia that morning. I had been ill for months. I also had severe, constant acid reflux and unprecedented rashes on my arms. The rashes would appear for a couple of hours and then disappear, only to return. Following a recent battery of medical tests, my doctor had told me that all of these symptoms were physical manifestations of extreme stress.

Those symptoms had become even more acute in anticipation of Fabey's arrival at my house, and after he walked through my kitchen door I felt as though I might have only minutes to live. Part of me regretted that I had agreed to talk to him, that I had made a colossal error in judgment. Another part of me thought that it was time to put an end to the insanity once and for all.

"Do you need to go to the hospital now?" Fabey asked.

"No, let's do this," I said.

"How did you get involved with Kate Hanni?" he asked.

"It all started over three years ago ...," I said.

FEBRUARY 2007

Hi, this is Kate Hanni

ON FEBRUARY 1, 2007, one month after Kate Hanni walked off of that airplane in Austin, Texas, I was sitting in my living room recliner, working on a business project. My laptop computer was suspended over my legs by a polyethylene tray that I had designed and fabricated in my basement. It's an extremely convenient device, but I had found that it wasn't economically feasible to manufacture and sell.

Eight months earlier, I had resigned from an engineering management position at a division of Motorola near Philadelphia, Pennsylvania. At 50 years of age, I had spent the last 30 years working with computers in one form or another; first in the U.S. Air Force, later with Unisys Corporation, and finally with Motorola. I was tired of it, burned out, or maybe it was a mid-life crisis. I don't know.

My wife and I lived alone in a modest ranch home in Collegeville, Pennsylvania – a small town located about 30 miles northwest of Philadelphia. I had saved enough money to pay the bills for a couple of years and start a business of my own. I spent the first several months of my temporary retirement playing golf every day, from morning until night, sometimes even in the snow. Finally, by February 2007, I had begun to work in earnest on the inventions and business ideas I'd had when I left Motorola.

The television was tuned to C-SPAN and its *Washington Journal* program, a broadcast from Washington D.C. that I watched almost every morning. At some point I glanced over my laptop screen and saw a woman on the television talking about how, a month earlier, she and her family had been stranded on an airplane for several hours without food or water. She said the toilets in the restrooms had overflowed and that a woman on the airplane had to make diapers out of men's T-shirts for her baby. The chyron – the graphic at the bottom of the screen – said the woman's name was Kate Hanni and that she was "Lobbying for Airline Standards."[3]

Hanni said she was getting six-hundred e-mails a day from people who were joining her newly formed grassroots organization. She said that it was her first-ever trip to Washington, D.C. She had traveled from California to visit members of Congress to try to get a law passed to stop airlines from holding people on the ground in airplanes for several hours.

Except for a few minor mistakes, she appeared to be a trained media professional. She was poised, articulate and attractive. She said she had no idea how the legislative process worked, but that she was just going to show up in congressional offices and figure it out as she went along.

How cool is that? I thought. Her story reminded me of an unpleasant experience I'd had on an American Airlines flight several years earlier:

"Ladies and gentlemen, it doesn't look like we're going to be able to take off for a while," our pilot announced over the public address system as we backed away from the gate at Dallas/Fort Worth International Airport. "There's some weather in Philadelphia, and as soon as we have more information we'll get back to you. Thanks for flying American Airlines."

We taxied around the airport for so long that I had the impression that the pilot was going to drive the airplane to Philadelphia on the ground. When the plane finally stopped, I could see from my window seat that we were about a half mile from the terminal. That gave me a perfect vantage point to watch scores of airplanes take off and land while we sat in the blazing sun without air conditioning.

Initially, I wasn't all that concerned about the delay. I had plenty of work to do on my laptop and, as long as I kept my mind occupied, I didn't notice the time ticking by. Then my laptop's battery died. A workaholic, all I could think of was the time wasted as I watched black-and-white sitcoms on an overhead television monitor instead of being able to work inside the airport terminal near a power outlet.

I began to notice the acrid smell of other humans. A baby cried somewhere behind me. I wondered how the parents were coping. One hour turned into two, and then another. There were periodic announcements that the captain was still trying to get us airborne, but all I wanted to hear was, "Buckle your seatbelts."

It wasn't the first time this had happened to me. *What gives airlines the right, the arrogance to hold people on airplanes on the ground for hours,* I wondered. I stared at a nearby emergency exit over the left wing. I opened the emergency card and studied the instructions. I wondered how far it was to the ground. It looked dangerously high near the fuselage, and there was nothing to hang onto. I thought if I could get to the end of the wing, I might be able to hang off of something there and drop safely to the ground.

I considered writing a note to the pilot, but no matter what I conjured up in my mind, it seemed as if that could be interpreted as a hostile act. I didn't want to do anything that might frighten anyone, but I thought I might prefer to spend the night in a jail cell rather than on that airplane.

Finally, the captain announced that we were going to take off. Cheers and claps erupted from the cabin. I remained silent and annoyed, but glad to be underway.

An hour after we were airborne, the captain announced that he was sorry for the delay back at the airport. He also said that it was the first officer's first flight in this kind of airplane and flying this route, so the captain was going to let him navigate through the Northeast Corridor. I wondered what that meant. *Just point the plane on a compass heading for Philadelphia,* I thought. *How hard is that?*

We began our descent into Philadelphia a couple of hours later. The captain announced over the PA system, "Ladies and gentlemen, I want to commend the first officer on a great job flying through the Northeast Corridor." *Whoopdeedoo,* I thought.

There was a light drizzle as we descended through the night sky south of the airport, but visibility below was clear. Suddenly, it seemed as though the pilot had lost control of the speed and altitude of the airplane and was feverishly trying to compensate – it felt like a rollercoaster. I saw the beginning of the runway stream past below. The pilot throttled back on the power and we dropped like a stone, but I could see that we were too high and too long to land – most of the runway now far behind. Suddenly the engines roared back to life, full power. The airplane pulled up and turned to the right.

What the hell is going on up there? I wondered.

After the airplane was in a stable turn, the captain came onto the PA system and said, "Sorry folks, there was traffic down there on the runway so we had to go around."

Bullshit, I thought. *He overshot the runway.*

We circled around for another approach. It was like a horrid instant replay. I thought for sure there had to be something wrong with the airplane, that the pilot couldn't land it for some reason. My fingernails gouged into the armrests. There was the runway, and there it went by again. We pulled up and went around again. That time the captain made no announcement, not a word. Then it hit me, *He's letting the rookie try to land the plane – with ME in it – and this after we sat on the ground in Dallas for hours!*

After the captain landed the airplane on the third go-around, as smooth a landing as I had ever experienced, I made a silent vow that if I was ever able to do anything about all of that callous behavior, I would. That vow was silent only because the cockpit door was closed when I got there, otherwise the captain would have gotten an earful. The daily routine of my career prevented me from doing anything about it then, and eventually the event slipped into a distant memory only to be resurrected whenever people were talking about their own airline *horror* stories.

Now, as I watched this Kate Hanni woman on C-SPAN, I thought it was amazing what she was doing. She was taking action on behalf of herself and passengers from other flights that were affected that night. It seemed like a remarkable display of courage and determination. I couldn't have been more impressed if she had been a modern day Susan B. Anthony or Alice Paul.

When asked by the C-SPAN host what people could do to help, Hanni said that viewers should sign an online petition. I used my Web browser to locate the petition, which consisted of a brief letter that urged Hanni's congressman, Mike Thompson, to support an airline passengers' bill of rights.

The petition showed that 1082 people had already signed, so I was the 1083rd. I wondered why there weren't more signatures, considering that Hanni had said she was getting 600 new members per day. I also thought it odd that the petition didn't say anything about joining her organization. Nevertheless, I provided my name, telephone number, e-mail address and a comment: "If I had the time, I would have organized this myself. Also had several similar experiences." Then I thought, *Well, I finally did something!*

Two weeks later, on February 14, Valentine's Day, an ice storm blanketed the northeastern United States. Inaccurate weather forecasts, combined with an airline culture that, rightly or wrongly, focused on getting passengers to their destinations, resulted in one of the most infamous stranding events in U.S. history. JetBlue in particular, had long-since prided itself on having the fewest cancellations of any airline. While other airlines cancelled most of their flights, JetBlue tried to plow forward with all of its operations in and out of JFK International Airport.

JetBlue's operations personnel relied on a weather forecast of a mix of snow and rain. Instead, an eight-hour long ice storm turned the airport into a skating rink and paralyzed ground operations. Airport gates were occupied by airplanes that couldn't move, and there weren't enough gates available to accept all of the arrivals. There were also no gates available to accommodate flights that might have otherwise returned from deicing pads or airport ramps. At least one of those airplanes, and its passengers, sat on the frozen ground for eleven hours.

The story made headlines for days, and many articles would be written in the future that would incorrectly credit this incident as the impetus behind the airline passengers' rights movement. Still, while reporters interviewed some of the passengers from the JetBlue airplanes, at the forefront of the media storm was Kate Hanni. As founder and spokesperson for the newest and perhaps only airline passengers' rights organization in the country, Hanni appeared on several newscasts to urge the American public to join her organization and to call on Congress to support airline passengers' rights.

I hadn't seen those newscasts, but they were cited in newsletters that I began to receive by e-mail from Hanni's organization, presumably because I had signed the petition. The newsletters asked for volunteers to do things such as set up a website and go to Washington to lobby Congress. They also urged recipients to contact their congressmen, and to donate money and frequent flyer miles to the organization. Oddly, the newsletters were poorly written, rife with errors.

I had some free time and it sounded interesting. Despite a 30-year career in the computer industry, my true passion was history and politics. There was little I enjoyed more than a lively debate about political controversies, and I could argue either side of many issues with equal passion.

Twelve years earlier, my wife and I had gotten married during the first week in November so that our anniversary would sometimes fall on Election Day – when we would cancel out one another's votes. Our Christmas tree was adorned with ornaments from historical sites we had visited such as Mount Vernon and Monticello. Others were decorated to mark significant political events such as President Bill Clinton's impeachment and the Bush-Gore hanging-chad election of 2000. I was a C-SPAN addict and had often fantasized about a career in politics. Lobbying on behalf of airline passengers' rights might be as close as I would ever get.

Washington D.C. is about a three-hour drive from the Collegeville area, a trip I had made many times to visit the historical sites there. I replied to the e-mail and wrote that I could go to Washington to lobby if someone would train me. I also offered to create a website for them. Throughout my business career, I had written many technical manuals, training guides and marketing materials, so I wrote to let them know I had writing experience – a skill they obviously needed. No one responded to my e-mail.

A few days later, I received another newsletter that asked for the same things. I wrote back and made the same offers. Again, no one responded. After the third go-around, I gave up. I clicked on a link at the bottom of one of the newsletters to unsubscribe. That didn't work either. The newsletters kept coming. Finally I replied, "You guys are more disorganized than the airlines. Please take me off your list!"

My telephone rang about twenty minutes later. The voice at the other end said, "Hi, this is Kate Hanni."

Indignantly, though politely, Hanni explained that her organization, the Coalition for an Airline Passengers' Bill of Rights (CAPBOR), was very well organized. She said they had regional coordinators throughout the country and their jobs were to manage state coordinators. The state coordinators were responsible for contacting coalition members in their states to mobilize them to take action – to contact Congress. She said that all of her volunteers had been too busy with other things to reply to my e-mails.

She told me that CAPBOR now had over 14,000 members, and that the membership was defined by the number of people that signed the online peti-tion that I had signed on February 1. That meant that the petition had increased by 13,000 since I had signed it, indicating a fair amount of public support for the issue. Much of that growth, I thought, was probably due to media attention surrounding the Valentine's Day strandings. At anywhere near that rate of growth, I estimated that CAPBOR could exceed 140,000 members by the end of the year. Hanni asked me to send her my resume and then she would see where I might fit in.

A few days later, she called again and offered me the role of regional coordinator for Pennsylvania and Washington, D.C. She said that they didn't have coordinators for those areas, so part of my role would be to find volunteers to fill those positions. In the meantime, I was to act as both regional and state coordinator. I wondered how it was possible that she didn't have a coordinator for Washington, D.C., of all places, but it seemed interesting and I was honored that she chose me for that responsibility.

Over those first couple of weeks, Kate and I talked often on the telephone. While she was already involved in real-world politics, it was obvious to me that she was not a student of government. Nevertheless, while she may not have gotten passing grades on a civics test, she seemed to be determined to get a law passed to prevent airlines from holding passengers on "tarmacs" for several hours, and she didn't care about the things she didn't know – those were minor details for others to worry about.

When I asked what she meant by "tarmac," she said she meant anyplace at an airport where an airplane was on the ground.

Despite some gaps in her knowledge, she seemed friendly, driven and determined. Our conversations weren't limited to official activities though. She was unusually forthcoming with all sorts of personal information. After just a couple of telephone conversations, she began to talk as if we had been friends for years.

She told me that she had been the highest selling real estate agent in the Napa Valley for the past several years, and that she had given that up to work for an airline passengers' bill of rights. She said she was a singer in a rock band, that she could play several musical instruments, that her husband was a wine expert, and that they had a 12-year old son. She also had a 22-year old son from a previous marriage. During one of our conversations she told me that, the previous June, she had been assaulted, and nearly raped and killed by a man posing as a home buyer.

I thought it was amazing that she could rebound from something like that and do what she was doing. I'd had a couple of traumatic experiences in my own distant past, and I hadn't dealt with them nearly as well as she apparently had. Here was a woman who had been trapped on an airplane for over nine hours, had fought off what I knew had to have been a terrifying, life-altering assault six months earlier, and she had given up a lucrative real estate career to devote her life to helping airline passengers.

I was hooked. I would do whatever I could to help.

MARCH 2007

The Holy Grail

ON MARCH 1, Congressman Mike Thompson introduced an airline passengers' rights bill in the U.S. House of Representatives. Thompson's bill would give passengers the right to deplane after a three-hour tarmac delay if it could be done safely, and it gave the pilot the option of two half-hour extensions if he or she thought the plane had a reasonable chance of taking off in that timeframe.

On March 11, Senator Barbara Boxer of California, joined by Senator Olympia Snowe of Maine, followed suit with a passengers' rights bill in the U.S. Senate. That bill was similar to Thompson's except that it allowed for only one half-hour extension after a three-hour delay.

But getting a bill introduced in the House or the Senate is only the first step in a long process. A bill can have all sorts of changes, amendments, along the way. Unless the bill has strong bipartisan support, it's a marathon with no guarantee it will ever pass. In early 2007, there wasn't enough support on either side of the political aisle for those bills to go any further than they already had.

On March 18, just over a month after the Valentine's Day strandings, Kate called me and said that there had been another tarmac stranding incident in New York. She said that thousands of people had been stuck on planes for up to ten hours.

"This is great, Mark. The more strandings we get the better! We need to mobilize our members right now to call Congress."

How dumb are these airlines? I wondered. *Two months of bad publicity and they haven't learned a thing.*

She sent me a spreadsheet containing the contact information for all of the CAPBOR members in Pennsylvania and Washington D.C., so I began to e-mail them. I wrote what I hoped would be an inspirational message and provided useful information such as the telephone number for the U.S. Capitol switchboard:

Thank you for signing the petition for the Airline Passenger Bill of Rights. Because this issue is important to all of us who travel by air, I volunteered to help Kate Hanni get this important legislation passed into law. But we can't do this without you! Yesterday, it happened again. Passengers in NY held hostage on airplanes for over nine hours.

It took me several hours to send the e-mails because my Internet service provider had limits on how many e-mails I could send at once. When I told Kate that I finished sending the e-mails, she asked me to call each person. I told her that I really didn't like the idea of calling people that I didn't know. She assured me that all of the people I would be calling were dedicated to the cause and they wanted to hear from us.

Reluctantly, I gave it a try. Most of the calls led to answering machines, and some were wrong numbers. When I got to talk to someone, the reception was mixed. Sometimes they were cooperative and promised to call their congressman's office, but almost as often they scolded me and asked where I got their phone number. Some said they never signed a petition, and "take me off your list" was a common and discouraging refrain. It was so discouraging that after about fifty phone calls I stopped calling people and began to wonder where that list really came from.

When I told Kate about this, she said that they weren't having a problem anywhere else. "Maybe we need to find another coordinator," she said.

I was disappointed and felt I had let her down. Nevertheless, that was the end of me making telephone calls. Curiously, I had a similar problem with the e-mails I sent. Many of them were rejected because of invalid e-mail addresses, and many people replied and demanded that I take them off the mailing list. My Internet provider even shut down my e-mail account for a couple of days because they said I violated their anti-SPAM policies.

Within a week Kate asked me to send another e-mail. She wanted me to send e-mails to some additional states because the volunteers for those states had disappeared – they weren't responding to her attempts to contact them, she said. It was an all-volunteer organization, so it seemed plausible that some people may have dropped out. I found myself sending e-mails to people in Virginia, Massachusetts, North Carolina and Arizona.

Because of the additional states, it took almost a week to send the e-mails. It was tedious and time-consuming work. This time, to avoid any possibility that the recipients might think I was sending them SPAM, I included a thumbnail photograph of Kate that she had sent to me. That didn't change the results. The feedback was roughly the same. A handful of people thanked me for what I was doing. Some complained. Most didn't respond at all.

Again I told Kate about the results. She repeated that they weren't having a problem anywhere else. That was disappointing, especially since she had also told me that the other coordinators were now using the text from my e-mails as templates for their communications with members. The only explanation I could think of was that *I* was the problem.

Meanwhile, I began to take an interest in news articles about airline passengers' rights that Kate sent to me. An Associated Press article said that, according to government statistics, only 38 planes had been stuck on the tarmac for over five hours in 2006. *How can that be true?* I wondered. The article also included a quote from an Air Transport Association spokesman:

> [David] Castelveter said a passenger who needs to get
> somewhere might prefer sitting on the runway for a few hours to
> risk having the flight canceled or further delayed because the
> pilot is required to taxi back to the gate.[4]

I want to get off of the plane. I thought. *An airline shouldn't have the right to keep people sitting on a tarmac in a cramped airplane indefinitely!*

I had spent four years in the U.S. Air Force, but I spent all of that time working with computers. I didn't know much about airplanes, commercial aviation, airline lobbyists, or anything else to do with airlines for that matter. What I did have was an inquisitive mind and a determination to learn as much as possible about whatever it was that I was working on. This would be no different. Like Kate, I would learn as I went along.

On the Web I learned that the Air Transport Association (ATA) was an organization in Washington, D.C. that lobbied Congress on behalf of most of the major airlines. The ATA would be one of our primary opponents, and countering their arguments would be a key objective in trying to influence members of Congress.

Another objective would be to keep the media and the public interested in the subject. The media and the public have short attention spans and without continuous attention to the issue, there would be little chance that Congress would act. By late March, the media and the public were already focused on more important topics such as the Iraq War, and less important ones such as the death of Anna Nicole Smith.

Even in the wake of the Valentine's Day JetBlue tarmac strandings, many of the articles published seemed to side with the airlines in opposing federal legislation, citing the small number of flights that sat on the tarmac for more than five hours. If the comments written for the online versions of articles in *USA Today* and the *New York Times* were any gauge of public sentiment, the majority of the public also thought the problem was too small to require federal intervention. Numbers were the key. I went on a mission. There had to be official airline statistics somewhere.

With the Internet, the World Wide Web and Google being the wondrous things that they are, it didn't take long to find the website for the Bureau of Transportation Statistics, a department within the U.S. Department of Transportation. I found that the BTS keeps fairly detailed statistics about airline flights going as far back as the mid-1990s.

I started by trying to find information about the Valentine's Day tarmac strandings, but there wasn't any data available for February. Then I decided to try to find information about Kate's flight. I downloaded a database from the BTS website that contained all of the flight information recorded for December 2006. There were about 550,000 flight records for the month, one record for each flight.

I examined the first few records in the database and found that they contained information such as the time a flight took off, where it landed and at what time. Each record also showed how long the airplane was on the tarmac before it took off and after it landed. When I found the record for Kate's flight, I was confused. According to the official record for American Airlines Flight 1348 on December 29, 2006, the flight took off from San Francisco, but it never landed – anywhere. It wasn't like the other records.

At first, I considered the possibility that American Airlines intentionally omitted the tarmac data so that no one would know how long the airplane sat on the ground. But I'm not one to believe in conspiracy theories, so I searched for documentation or federal regulations that defined airline data reporting requirements. I found a document called "Directive 14" on the BTS website that explained why there was no tarmac data for her flight:

> When reporting on-time flight statistics for diverted flights ...
> the carrier should report zeros for the wheels-on time and gate-arrival time ...

When a flight lands at an airport other than the one where it was originally scheduled to land, it's called a "diverted" flight. According to the BTS directive, when a flight was diverted, the airline wasn't required to report where the flight landed or how long it sat on the tarmac when it got there. Even if the airline had reported that information, there was nowhere to put it in the database. I looked at the records for other diverted flights. They were all missing the same data.

My heart was pounding. *I'm onto something here*, I thought. Kate's flight wasn't included in the government's tarmac delay statistics. *It's as if it never happened!*

The BTS website showed that there were 16,186 diverted flights in 2006. Since they didn't track the time those flights were on the tarmac at the diverted airport, that meant there were 16,186 flights that had no tarmac data for 2006 alone! It wasn't just Kate's flight that wouldn't show up in the statistics. There were over 16,000 other flights that wouldn't show up either.

I went on to find that if an airplane left a gate, sat on the tarmac and then was canceled, there was no tarmac data reported for that either. I couldn't tell how many flights fell into that category, but 121,934 flights were canceled in 2006, and surely some percentage of those had also not been counted. Many of the JetBlue flights were canceled after sitting on the tarmac for several hours in February, so those wouldn't appear in the statistics either.

Directive 14 also said that only airlines that accounted for at least one percent of passenger revenues had to report any of this data. That meant airlines with under $743 million in revenue during the prior year, including Spirit, USA 3000, and other smaller but popular airlines, were exempt from the reporting requirements in 2006. International flights weren't covered either, including flights made by U.S. carriers. So if someone flew from Europe to New York on any U.S. or international airline and sat on the tarmac for ten hours, that flight wouldn't be counted.

The airline tarmac delay statistics were woefully incomplete and I could prove it using the government's own documentation. Even more amazing was, except possibly for some airline statistics geeks in the bowels of the Department of Transportation, neither the government nor the news media was aware of it.

I couldn't believe my eyes. I double checked everything and then I triple checked. It was real. I jumped out of my chair and paced around the house repeating, "Oh, my god." In the course of three days, I had found a way to defeat one of the main arguments being made against federal airline passengers' rights legislation. Less than three months after Kate's stranding, I had found the Holy Grail! All we had to do was say that tens of thousands of flights were being excluded from the tarmac statistics, and that the government can't rely on the statistics at all!

And then another possibility occurred to me. *What if airlines were forced to report these statistics and that, along with the threat of negative publicity that would come with it, reduced or even eliminated extended tarmac delays?*

I sent an e-mail to Kate, explained what I found and waited for a reply. She sent me an e-mail that asked if I could come to Washington in April for a Senate hearing, and another that said she wanted to make a "stuck on a plane" video. It wasn't the enthusiastic response I expected.

APRIL 2007

A dream come true

FINALLY, ON APRIL 1, Kate asked me to send her the records for thirteen other American Airlines flights that she said were on the tarmac on December 29. She was taking an interest in the statistics discovery, but it seemed to me that she was in the weeds, not grasping the big picture. The issue wasn't about thirteen flights – it was about being able to refute the accuracy of all of the statistics. We discussed the matter a few times on the telephone, but each conversation left me more frustrated than the last. She seemed so absorbed with her own tarmac stranding story, that everything else was just noise.

IN LATE MARCH, the Senate Commerce Committee had announced that it would hold a hearing on April 11 about the recent tarmac stranding events. Senator Boxer arranged for Kate to testify at the hearing.

When someone testifies before a congressional committee, they have to provide the committee with a written version of their testimony a few days in advance. On April 3, Kate asked me to help "finish" her written testimony for the upcoming hearing.

I was a little surprised that I had been given this honor. *Surely, one of the other 14,000 members would be more qualified to write this,* I thought. I asked her to send me what she had written so far, and she sent me a detailed account of her travel ordeal from the time her flight left San Francisco until she landed in Mobile Alabama, 57 hours later. It was barely an outline, let alone almost finished.

After a few days of work and numerous phone calls, we finally had a version of her testimony that seemed acceptable. In it, I had included a few paragraphs about the airline statistics discovery. During the preceding week, I had continued to try to explain why the discovery was so important. Kate was appalled that her flight didn't show any tarmac time, but she didn't seem interested in the broader importance of the statistics issues.

I wished that I could have touched on broader airline-related service issues in the testimony, but I didn't know much about them. When I saw the final version of her testimony a week later, it was different than what I had written. I assumed that the revisions had been made by a public relations firm in Washington that Kate referred to as "Southpaw."

She had told me that Southpaw had been writing press releases and providing other media related services. Whoever had revised the testimony, I had to admit that it was an improvement over what I had written. Someone had addressed the broader subjects that I couldn't.

After I finished with her testimony, Kate asked if I would send e-mails to encourage as many CAPBOR members as possible to attend the Senate hearing. She wanted me to e-mail members in all 50 states. It would have taken me a month to do that.

"That's a lot of work, Kate." I said. Where are the state coordinators?"

She said that she didn't know where they went, that none of them were responding to her e-mails or phone calls. She said that she suspected that the person who was coordinating them had "alienated them."

There's something strange going on, I thought. I was beginning to suspect that she was exaggerating the existence of other volunteers. Whatever the case, I told her that I couldn't possibly do what she was asking.

Soon thereafter, I got an e-mail from a Kathi Browne, the only other volunteer from whom I had seen an e-mail up to that point. At that time, the CAPBOR board of directors was comprised of Kate, her husband and Browne. Since I told her I couldn't do it, Kate had asked Browne to organize people to show up at the hearing. Based on the e-mail that Browne sent, there were about twenty people on the list. But for a few exceptions, they all lived within driving distance of the Washington, D.C. area.

Kate suggested that we should have a way to identify coalition members when they arrived at the hearing – lapel buttons – so I started to create what would become the CAPBOR logo. I had always admired the Presidential Seal, so I used its colors and font style. Kate provided a cartoon-like airplane with a passenger riding on top. A day later I completed the final logo. It would become the most recognized symbol for the coalition except for Kate herself. We used it on buttons, business cards, letterheads, the website and everything else.

On April 11, my wife and I drove to Washington. The hearing was to be held in the Senate Russell Office Building. We entered the main entrance of the building into a three-story rotunda surrounded by Corinthian columns. "Look up there," I said, pointing to television cameras and lights perched on a balcony that encircles the rotunda above. "That must be where the news crews interview senators," I said. This is so cool, I thought.

Outside the hearing room, the CAPBOR button on the lapel of my suit was successful in attracting the attention of other coalition members, and we began to introduce ourselves to one another. In all, about 20 people had promised to attend the hearing. As far as I could tell, a fair number had.

Kate arrived moments before the hearing was scheduled to start. We introduced ourselves to one another, but there was no time to get acquainted – the hearing was starting.

The senators sat behind a large, semi-circular desk, elevated slightly higher than the floor. The first panel of two government witnesses sat facing the senators at a table. Each witness was accompanied by a handful of staff members who sat in reserved seats behind their bosses. The rest of us sat farther back in the gallery.

The first witness to speak was Michael W. Reynolds, Deputy Assistant Secretary of Transportation for Aviation and International Affairs. Reynolds talked about how DOT Secretary Mary Peters and the department were addressing the issue of long tarmac delays. He said that the Secretary had directed the Inspector General's office to conduct an investigation into the December 29 and Valentine's Day tarmac strandings.

Then he seemed to downplay the incidence of tarmac strandings. He said, "… it is important to keep the issue of tarmac delays in context … DOT statistics show that, in 2006, less than 1/200ths of one percent of all flights by the largest airlines were delayed by more than three hours … your chances of being on the tarmac for greater than five hours were about one in two hundred thousand."

He has no idea what he's talking about, I thought. Not even senior officials for the Department of Transportation were aware that the airline statistics were woefully incomplete.

When the senators finished questioning the first panel, the second panel took their seats at the witness table. In addition to Kate, the panel included Ed Mierzwinski, Paul Hudson, Kevin Mitchell and James May, whom I recognized as the president of the Air Transport Association.

Ed Mierzwinski was the director of consumer programs at the U.S. Public Interest Research Group (US-PIRG), a non-profit organization head-quartered a few blocks from the Capitol. He spoke in support of Senator Boxer's bill, and he would become an extremely important ally and advisor in the future. I came to learn that he had already been advising Kate on the basics of running a grassroots organization, including the structure of region-al and state coordinators, which had already evaporated if it ever existed.

Paul Hudson was a lawyer for the Aviation Consumer Action Project (ACAP) which had its roots in Ralph Nader's network of organizations. Tragically, Hudson's only daughter had been killed in the Pan Am 103 bombing over Lockerbie, Scotland in 1988, and he subsequently lobbied for sanctions against Libya, the bombers' homeland. In his testimony, Hudson attributed declining levels of airline customer service to deregulation, airport congestion, and airlines' focus on their bottom line at the expense of customers' needs. Hudson would later join the CAPBOR board of directors.

Kevin Mitchell was the chairman of something called the Business Travel Coalition, an organization that advocates on behalf of corporate travel managers and business travelers. He would at first be an adversary and then an ally in the cause for airline passengers' rights. During his testimony at this hearing, he argued against passengers' rights legislation.

Since Kate would be fourth to speak, I decided to follow the DOT staff members out into the hall. I introduced myself to one of them and explained that the airline statistics that Reynolds had just talked about were fundamentally flawed. He was very interested, gave me his card and asked me to send him a detailed e-mail on the subject.

I returned to my seat to hear Kate speak. I listened intently, anxious to hear my words about the airline statistics reach the ears of the senators. Finally she reached that part of the testimony:

> Airline and government agencies intentionally fail to maintain statistics for flights that never reach their destinations. So if an airline leaves the gate but never takes off, neither the airlines nor the government keep statistics about those flights. They're just a single flight cancellation in the government's book.

Her delivery was perfect. If I hadn't known better, I would have thought she was an expert in the subject. The testimony listed examples of diverted and canceled flights that sat on the tarmac, and then it continued:

> To the Secretary of Transportation, it's as if they never happened. … Except for the people trapped on those runways like us and other members of our coalition, no one knows exactly how long all of those flights were held because there are no statistics kept. The reality is that airlines conveniently aren't required to report the amount of time those planes sit on those runways.

> Why is the failure to maintain these statistics so important? The problem may be orders of magnitude greater than delay statistics currently maintained by the government, but without valid statistics, nobody knows the full extent of the problem – including our lawmakers.

I was so moved by the moment that I found myself fighting back tears. Never in my wildest dreams would I have thought that words I had written would be heard within the walls of a U.S. Senate hearing.

When it was his turn to speak, ATA president, James May, argued that a three-hour rule would result in increased inconvenience for airline passengers. He said that if planes had to return to gates to deplane passengers at three hours, it was likely that those flights would be canceled and passengers would end up spending nights in hotels or in airports rather than reaching their destinations.

May said that the increase in cancelled flights would cause problems for unaccompanied minors and more bags would be lost. There would be more missed meetings, missed vacations, missed funerals, and he said that a canceled flight at one location had a cascade effect down the line where other airline passengers were waiting for that airplane.

All of that sounded like scare tactics to me. *But what if he's right?* I wondered.

After May completed his testimony, Senator Boxer laid into him. "You're living in a dream world," she scolded. She asked how he could possibly oppose her airline passengers' bill of rights. She told him that her own daughter had been stuck on a plane for over four hours.

Boxer then asked an open-ended question that gave Kate the opportunity to talk for almost five minutes. She was compelling as she ad-libbed about the horrors that she and others experienced that night in Austin. She said that ambulances had to be called to one of the planes to assist a paraplegic with a colostomy bag. Mothers ran out of formula and diapers for their babies. There was no food, no water and the restrooms were inoperable, she said.

She was so persuasive that I wished the senators would call for a vote on airline passengers' rights right then and there.

After the hearing, I met Burt Rubin. Rubin was a lawyer in private practice in the Washington area, and he said he had been involved with an airline passengers' rights movement that had sprung up after a high-profile stranding incident in 1999 in Detroit, during which passengers had been stuck on the tarmac for several hours.

In that incident, Northwest Airlines had been unprepared for a blizzard that struck the Detroit airport in January of that year, and passengers sat on planes for as long as 8.5 hours. An airline passengers' rights initiative was started at that time, but was later quashed when the airlines issued a set of voluntary commitments and promised Congress that they would do better in the future.

Rubin told me that the real problem with the airlines was something called "pre-emption."

Prior to 1978, the government controlled airline ticket prices, routes, and also the ability for new entrants to compete with the other airlines. In 1978, the Airline Deregulation Act (ADA) was passed to enable free-market, open competition forces to act on the airline industry. The ADA also prohibited – pre-empted – states from enacting any laws that would regulate the airlines in regard to price, route, or service. It also meant that airline passengers had little or no legal remedy when it came to suing the airlines for anything that was deemed to be service-related, like tarmac strandings.

Rubin said that unless that law was changed, airlines had no incentive to stop holding passengers on tarmacs for hours. He thought that the airline passengers' bill of rights should do that. Between Burt Rubin and James May, I began to realize that there was far more that I didn't know about commercial aviation than what I did know.

The next day, Kate received an invitation to testify before the House Aviation Subcommittee on April 20. Despite how well she performed at the Senate hearing, I was concerned that she still didn't seem to appreciate the significance of the statistics issue. It was one thing to read testimony, quite another if Congress or the media were to ask questions about it. I could envision a reporter or congressman asking her a question about the airline statistics, only to have her stumble awkwardly through an answer. I wanted her to look good.

Kate sent the hearing invitation to me and asked if I had seen any of the news articles that had been published after her Senate testimony. Concerned that she seemed more interested in getting her name in the newspapers than anything else, I replied:

> Have not seen articles. But here's the thing. Either you need to
> get up to speed on this statistics thing, or we need to get
> someone to testify about the statistics. This is a critical issue. It
> is possibly as least as important as your own story. We have to
> demonstrate that the airline's and the government's stories are
> totally flawed and baseless.

Unsurprisingly, that touched off a series of contentious e-mails and telephone calls. During one of those telephone calls, I quizzed her on why virtually everyone had already abandoned the cause. She was remarkably candid with her answer. She said that some of the volunteers complained that she seemed to be making herself the center of attention – instead of the tarmac stranding issue. One complained that Kate's name was printed in larger letters than CAPBOR on an item of stationary. Many of the volunteers, all women, had gotten frustrated and abandoned the cause.

As a spokeswoman, Kate was perfect. She had a personality and look that was made for television, an incredible gift and advantage to the cause. Having watched her work the room after the Senate hearing, I noticed that she was a master at making a positive first impression. She was cheerful, confident and charming. But having now worked with her for two months, I also found her to be self-absorbed and manipulative, personality traits that could wear thin, especially among members of the same sex.

She seemed to be great at attracting people and forming relationships, but not so great at keeping them. It seemed to me that something needed to change. I thought we needed to let someone else deal with however many volunteers remained. That person, I hoped, would be Kathi Browne. It also seemed to me that Browne was better qualified to make most of the other day-to-day decisions for CAPBOR. I kept this to myself for the moment.

As for finding someone else to testify about the airline statistics, I said we should locate an expert from the Bureau of Transportation Statistics. She wouldn't consider that and she was offended that I brought it up. Still, she didn't seem to be interested in learning anything more about the subject.

Two days later, Kate wrote to me that CNBC and Bloomberg wanted to interview her about the airline statistics. She also wrote that Senator Boxer's office was "blown away [by the statistics discovery] ... They were amazed by us, our investigation and what we were revealing."

Now she was interested. The statistics discovery would start a tidal wave of media coverage that would last for months. And forever after, whenever there was something interesting to report about the government's monthly release of airline statistics, reporters would call Kate for a comment.

More importantly, the discovery elevated Kate and CAPBOR to a new stratosphere of credibility with the media and the government. She was instantly transformed from a tarmac stranding victim into a consumer advocate for any airline issue. That credibility and status would give her a pass with even the most experienced and respected journalists – to publish and broadcast almost anything she said.

IN EARLY APRIL, someone had contacted Kate and told her about a flight that had been bound for Denver, but was diverted to Cheyenne, Wyoming because of a snowstorm. He and the other passengers spent the night in Cheyenne, some in the airport and some in nearby hotels. The next morning, the passengers watched in bewilderment as their airplane departed without them, empty but for the crew. The passenger said it cost him $3,000 to get home. He sent Kate a video of the airplane taxiing away from the gate.

In hearings that I had watched on television in the past, I noticed that there were large television screens on the walls of some of the rooms. I wondered if there was a way to connect to those screens and play that video during Kate's testimony. I contacted the committee's staff and they confirmed that I could connect to their audio/visual system with a laptop computer. I spent the next several days revising Kate's testimony to incorporate the Cheyenne video, and I added more emphasis to the statistics. I also created several slides about the statistics to project onto the screens.

On the day of the hearing, I arrived early to test my computer with the hearing room's audio/visual system. I sat next to Kate at the witness table and waited for her turn to testify. The witness panel for the hearing was composed of David Neeleman (CEO JetBlue), James May, Kevin Mitchell (chairman of the Business Travel Coalition), Paul Ruden (a lawyer for the American Society of Travel Agents) and Kate Hanni.

Except for Kate, each of them testified in opposition to legislation that would require airlines to let passengers deplane after three hours on a tarmac. Most members of the committee agreed with them. Chairman Costello chided James May for the behavior of the airlines, but he gave them an out, "If the airlines won't fix the problem, I will," he said. Even well-known consumer allies such as Peter DeFazio (D-OR) were opposed to a "one size fits all" solution, meaning a three-hour limit was unworkable.

In addition to the claim that the problem was too small to require federal intervention, the argument against a three-hour limit was that passengers would prefer to sit on the tarmac for several hours rather than have their flights canceled, which would result in missed vacations, business meetings, or other timely appointments.

Opponents also argued that airports were not configured in such a way that would allow airplanes to get out of line and return to the terminal, nor would it be possible to send buses or stairs out to airplanes to deplane passengers. The general consensus among opponents was simply that airline operations were too complicated to be saddled with a three-hour rule, that airlines and pilots needed more flexibility.

At the time, I didn't know enough about airport configurations or airline operations to know whether any of those arguments were plausible. I did know that airlines should not be allowed to keep men, women, children, babies and people with medical problems sitting on airport tarmacs for nine hours and sixteen minutes.

When it was Kate's turn to testify, I started my laptop and waited for the right moments to transmit the statistics slides and the Cheyenne video to the television screens on the walls.

It was almost one year to the day since I had resigned from Motorola, not entirely sure what I wanted to do with the rest of my life. Now, there I was sitting at the witness table in a congressional committee hearing with somebody reading testimony I had largely written. It was like a dream that I never could have dreamed had come true. My interest in participating in the political process had always been in vague, ethereal terms. I never had a specific image of what form it might take. As I sat there at that table, I thought my life couldn't possibly get any more interesting.

After the hearing, I met Kathi Browne in person for the first time. She hadn't been able to attend the Senate hearing, but we had talked often on the telephone and shared many e-mails. Burt Rubin was there too. He reiterated his concern that Congressman Thompson's passengers' rights language didn't address what Rubin thought was the more important issue – to make it easier for airline passengers to sue the airlines.

Rubin's emphasis on the inadequacies of Thompson's bill made Kate suspicious of his motives, and Kate later told me that she was worried that Rubin was trying to "take over." For the next few months, except when she really needed him for something, she froze him out of most conversations about strategy or policy.

I didn't understand how he could "take over." Except for Browne and me, it was becoming more and more evident that there weren't any other volunteers that were involved on a day-to-day basis. While several people had shown up at the Senate hearing, it was clear that most of them were civics tourists who had little if anything to do with the ongoing effort. Few of them had shown up for the House hearing and sadly, Browne wouldn't be around for much longer either.

Two days after the House hearing, Kate asked me to write a press release about her House testimony and the airline statistics discovery. For reasons unknown to me, Southpaw, the public relations firm that had been writing press releases up to this point, had withdrawn their support.

Press releases were issued to generate media interest – so that reporters would contact Kate for interviews on whatever the subject of the press release happened to be. The releases needed to be short and to the point, usually no more than 400 words and, as Kate explained, they needed to be "juicy" to catch the media's interest. Once written, we would send them to a wire service where they were published. Reporters monitor those wire services for stories of public interest.

While Browne, Kate and I circulated the draft of my first press release, I received a CAPBOR newsletter in a unique writing style that I now recognized as Kate's. Because of the difficulty of sending newsletters from our individual e-mail accounts, Kate had purchased a service that enabled her to e-mail newsletters to thousands of people with little more than a few button clicks. She had written:

> Kate, with the Help of Mark Mogel a supertalented researcher,
> finds evidence that the government intentionally releases
> statistics that they know are incomplete ... it wasn't brain
> surgery to figure out that something was missing. ... Mark
> Mogel, one of our super smart and super dedicated people ...
> thanks to Mark Mogel for his extended e-mailing and Research
> and Development help ...

It didn't surprise or even bother me that she took credit for the statistics discovery, but the "it wasn't brain surgery" remark stung. I also felt that the gist of the newsletter was manipulative. With Southpaw gone, she needed me more than ever and she probably thought the back-handed compliments and effusive praise were motivational. The newsletter was also filled with grammatical and spelling errors. This incident sparked a series of heated e-mails and phone calls among the three of us. Browne was upset that Kate would send something so amateurish to the members. How could she send something like that to 14,000 people?

I soon learned that this wasn't the first conflict between Kate and Browne in the short history of CAPBOR. In the e-mail conflict that followed, Kate wrote that she never had as many issues with two people as she had with Browne and me. Whatever their history, it was obvious that Browne had had enough.

I tried to persuade Browne to stay because I valued her organizational skills and dedication to the cause. I wrote an e-mail in which I recommended that we divide up responsibilities so that Kate would have responsibility for dealing with the news media and Browne would be responsible for everything else. It was to no avail. Browne resigned from the board anyway.

A couple of days later, now four months since her tarmac stranding in Austin, Kate called me and said that Paul Hudson, whom she had met at the Senate hearing, was going to assume Browne's position on the board. She asked if I would also consider joining. Browne had warned me that the request was coming and I was ready with an answer.

"No," I said.

"Why not?" she asked.

I reminded her that, at times, we hadn't gotten along very well. I also said that I would be in a better position to help if I didn't have to worry about day-to-day legal, financial and business issues.

Perhaps referring to the e-mail in which I had written that Browne might be better suited to run CAPBOR, Kate asked, "Mark, you don't get what I bring to this coalition do you?"

"That's where you're wrong, Kate. I get you completely. You're fantastic at forming connections and relationships. I've never seen anyone better at speaking confidently about subjects you don't understand, and you can take over a room like no other. You have charm and charisma galore. You are the perfect spokeswoman," I said.

"Well," she said, "I guess you get me after all."

MAY 2007

Damien

IN EARLY MAY, Kate sent me an e-mail that contained new airline passengers' rights language that Senator Boxer planned to try to have included in the FAA reauthorization bill.

The FAA reauthorization bill is an appropriations bill – a bill that funds a government agency for some period of time. This bill would fund the Federal Aviation Administration for three or four years. Long term funding was necessary because the bill would fund multi-year projects such as large-scale airport improvements and something called "Next-Gen."

By now I had learned that flying a commercial airliner from Dallas to Philadelphia was not as simple as setting a compass heading for Philadelphia. Pilots have to navigate through a series of ground-based radar stations, and their altitudes, routes and speeds are directed by air traffic controllers on the ground during the entire trip.

Because our air traffic control system still uses 1950's-style ground-based radar, commercial and private jets have to navigate from smaller air-highways to super-highways such as the one that runs through the Northeast Corridor. Just like highways on the ground, air highways have limited capacity, so there is a limit to how many airplanes can be using them at the same time. All of this contributes to excess fuel consumption, pollution, longer than necessary flight durations and even ground delays.

Next-Gen is intended to alleviate these problems by using the Global Positioning Satellite System (GPS) for navigation. Theoretically, a GPS-based system would allow airplanes to be spaced more efficiently because computers could maintain separation better than humans, and airplanes can fly more direct routes to their destinations thus allowing more airplanes in the sky, less fuel consumption and pollution, and fewer ground delays.

The FAA reauthorization bill would fund the development and implementation of Next-Gen, and getting passengers' rights language into the FAA reauthorization bills in the House and Senate would be a major coup. Stand-alone bills, such as the airline passengers' rights bills introduced by Boxer and Thompson, are much more difficult to get passed.

I noticed loopholes in the language that Kate sent to me. The loopholes would have allowed each airline to set its own time limit for tarmac delays. So if an airline said it would let passengers off of an airplane after ten hours, Boxer's language would make that legal. Also, the language also only mentioned departures, so diverted flights like Kate's wouldn't be covered.

I wrote to Kate and told her about the loopholes and omissions in Boxer's language. She replied, "We don't want to throw out the baby with the bath water," meaning that Boxer's language was better than nothing.

In my opinion, Boxer's language was worse than nothing. Referring to the Antichrist character in *The Omen* movie series, I replied, "The baby's name is Damien." I also pulled Paul Hudson and Ed Mierzwinski into the e-mail discussion.

Mierzwinski said that we should encourage Boxer to make changes, but that we should support her publicly. "Boxer is your champion," he wrote. He pointed out that we didn't have any passengers' rights language in the House version of the FAA reauthorization bill, and that it was better to have something in the Senate version of the bill, even if it wasn't what we wanted.

Unlike the House, where the majority can pretty much do whatever it wants, the rules of the Senate give the minority party, the Republicans in 2007, much more power. The ranking member of the Commerce Committee, Senator Ted Stevens (R-AK), opposed a three-hour rule, so the language that Boxer proposed was the best she was able to get added to the bill at the time.

It's common to look to campaign contributions to explain the positions that politicians take, but it's difficult to establish direct links. The senior members on both sides of the Senate Commerce Committee had received roughly the same amount of campaign funds from airline-related contributions in the preceding years. A more revealing statistic was that in 2006, before CAPBOR, the ATA spent just over $3 million in lobbying expenses. By the end of 2007, they would spend over $7 million – much of that dedicated to lobbying against airline passengers' rights.

Mierzwinski advised that our best hope was to take small steps with the bill and keep the tarmac stranding issues relevant through media pressure. He also said that we needed to be patient; that it usually takes years to get consumer legislation passed. Disregarding his advice to publicly support Boxer, Kate and Hudson skewered the bill in a story that appeared in *USA Today*:

> Paul Hudson, who heads the Aviation Consumer Action Project,
> said the bill would do more harm than good and he now opposes
> the legislation unless it can be changed. 'This would seem to
> give a green light legalizing very long airline confinements,'
> Hudson said.

Kate Hanni, a California Realtor-turned-advocate after her flight
was delayed for eight hours in December, said she is pressing
senators to change the legislation. Hanni stopped short of
condemning the entire bill, saying it has enough new passenger
protections to make it a partial victory.[5]

After catching hell from Boxer's office, Kate claimed that the reporter
had misquoted her, a claim that she would often make in the future whenever
she spoke out of turn. Senator Boxer's language, with the loopholes, was
added to the FAA reauthorization bill in the Senate. Those loopholes would
remain in the bill for the next two years.

ON MAY 10, Kate called to tell me that she had uploaded a video to You-
Tube. It was a music video that she said she had made "a few years ago," and
it featured Kate singing a song that she had written. The refrain was, "If you
want to be with a girl like me ...," and the video showed her flirting with a
man at a pool party. The main theme was interlaced with scenes of Kate and
two other women engaged in a sultry bump-and-grind.

The video was interesting and professionally done, but I worried that it
might undermine the image I thought she was trying to project – that she was
the altruistic leader of a consumer's rights movement. I also worried that the
video might cause people to question both her motives and her judgment. It
had been uploaded to YouTube under her own name, and the search tags,
visible to anyone, were "sexy, bikini, mile high club, hot hot hot."

There was no bikini or mile-high club activity in the video, but those
were the least of my concerns. My immediate reaction was to write to her,
"You can't submit a video saying you're hot and sexy under your own name,
blonde-head." Then I called and asked if she thought that the video was the
right image for a consumer advocate. I also expressed concern that the video
might attract the wrong kind of attention from potentially dangerous people.
All in all, it seemed like a very bad idea. Kate wasn't worried. She said it
would draw more attention to the cause. *It'll certainly do that*, I thought.

The next day, she sent me an e-mail and asked if I could meet her in
Washington the following Monday:

2:30pm. I hope you can make it. Let's talk strategy. I'm really
feeling a bit alone. ... I could use some support going to
members offices to see if we can throw Damien out of the bath
water!

It would be my first time visiting members' offices to lobby, so I went
to Washington to listen and learn. Our first meeting was in Senator Boxer's
office. Kate made it a point to meet with someone in Boxer's office when-

ever she was in town. During that meeting, Kate explained the issues we had with Boxer's language. Paul Hudson had already written to them and they already knew about our concerns, but they listened patiently and finally said that they recognized the issues with the language. They said they couldn't change it without Senator Stevens' approval.

The routine I observed during other office visits was that Kate would start out by telling the story of her tarmac stranding. She also emphasized that her flight, and others like it, weren't included in the tarmac statistics. Then she would ask the staff person if his or her senator would co-sponsor Boxer's stand-alone bill. Mierzwinski had advised that the more co-sponsors we could get in the Senate and in the House, the more likely the individual bills might be passed, or at least voted on. At that time, there were only five co-sponsors for Boxer's bill.

At the end of each meeting, Kate would leave behind a packet of articles that had been published about CAPBOR and tarmac strandings. All of that was good, but the middle parts of these meetings had me a bit perplexed.

She spent, I thought, an inordinate amount of time complaining about everything she didn't like about the airlines, government loan guarantees, seat pitch, and a host of other things that didn't have anything to do with our primary goal; a tarmac time limit. As a former project and engineering manager, I knew it was critical to keep meetings focused on specific issues. Otherwise, people would leave meetings wondering what the meeting was about. Nevertheless, I held my tongue in my first meetings with Kate.

I also wondered how she had been getting from one office to another in the past. She had told me that she had been to the Senate office complex four or five times since the founding of CAPBOR, yet she seemed to be continuously lost and disoriented. Curiously, I found myself leading her from one office to another despite the fact that I had only been there once in April for the hearing.

Between two of our meetings, we stopped for a snack in a cafeteria in the basement of the Hart Senate office building. She reached into her large tote bag in which she carried her laptop and a hodgepodge of other things. I had picked it up once for her earlier. It weighed at least twenty pounds.

"Hey, here's one of my CDs," she said.

There were a dozen or more of the compact discs in her bag. In addition to the news articles, she had also been handing copies of the CD to staffers before we left their offices. I hadn't yet seen it up close. It said "Kate Moon" on the cover – her "stage name," she said. She also said that it contained her music video and several other songs she had written. I unfolded the cover and found a photograph of Kate wearing a paper-thin, white, midriff halter top – a photograph that a centerfold would be proud of. She said the photo-

graph had been taken under the Golden Gate Bridge a few years earlier. I
shot her a puzzled look.

"It was cold under that bridge," she giggled.

"Apparently," I said. "You're handing these out to staffers?" I asked.

"Sure! I gave them to the guys at the hotel too."

Who would hand something like this out to strangers, and why? I
wondered. I was about as confused as I could possibly be. I had known many
women in my life, never understood any of them, and the woman sitting
before me was more of an enigma than all of them combined. But Kate knew
something that I only understood in an abstract sense – *sex sells*.

At the end of the day, we walked outside to hail a taxi for her. We
paused on the sidewalk. "Mark, I can't do this alone. Please help me," she
said.

Except for Mierzwinski and Hudson, both of whom had other daily
priorities, she was for all intents and purposes alone and, as far as I could tell,
Hudson lived in Florida most of the time. Despite the progress already made,
this was going to be a long haul and would require a variety of skills and
talents that CAPBOR obviously didn't have. Unless she got some help, there
was no way a passengers' rights law would be passed.

I still had plans for other business ventures, and despite the sympathy I
felt for her at that moment, it had sometimes been difficult to work with her
for the last two months. On the other hand, it had also been some of the most
satisfying, interesting work I had ever done. I was conflicted.

As I pondered how to answer, Kate noted that we both had blue eyes
and blonde hair. "People will think we're brother and sister," she said.

Having completely derailed my thoughts with that comment, I could
only say, "I don't know, Kate. I'll have to think about it."

I had parked my car about 25 miles north of Washington and taken a
train to Union Station. Kate offered to give me a ride to the station in her cab.
I thanked her, but I told her I would walk.

I had witnessed many momentous political events in this country's history. As a teenager in 1973, I had been glued to the television for the entire
summer watching the Watergate hearings. I had later been mesmerized by
the Iran-Contra, Keating Five and Whitewater hearings. All of these events
had exposed corruption of some government officials and had exonerated
others. But the most important thing to me was that it seemed as if our
democracy had worked, that the media and the government had been doing
precisely what they should be doing. While not always perfectly, the interests
of the people had been served; something that gave me faith in our system of
democracy.

It wasn't just the high-profile events that interested me though – I could
also be found watching hearings on C-SPAN on mundane subjects like tele-

communications reform. When C-SPAN2 and C-SPAN3 were added to the cable lineup, I thought I had died and gone to heaven.

By the time I reached the Christopher Columbus memorial in front of Union Station, it occurred to me that I wasn't watching history in Washington unfold on television. I was *in* Washington with the possibility of *making* history. I turned and looked back at the Capitol dome. *Maybe I have died and gone to heaven,* I thought. I decided that I would help Kate on a part time basis until she could find someone else.

The next day, an article appeared in the *New York Times* that described a ten-hour tarmac stranding on April 24. In that incident, an American Airlines flight had been diverted from Dallas to Midland, Texas, and the small regional airport had no gates or stairs able to accommodate a Boeing 757. Passengers said that they ran out of food and water. Mothers shared formula for hungry babies. Toilets were filled to the rims. After five hours, the airline had five pizzas delivered to the plane to be divided among the 70 passengers. The reporter, Joe Sharkey, also wrote:

> Kate Hanni, whose plane was one of several that sat on the
> tarmac for hours in Texas on Dec. 29, has been organizing
> fellow passengers to lobby Congress to demand a bill of
> passenger rights. Ms. Hanni says the group now has 15,000
> members ...[6]

Everyone who was anyone in Washington read the *New York Times*, and articles like this kept the tarmac stranding situation relevant. But the irony of that particular paragraph was not lost on me considering the conversation that Kate and I had the day before. *Where are the fellow passengers?* I wondered. *Where are the 15,000 members?*

On the 17th, Kate wrote from Napa and asked if Paul Hudson or I would be willing to go to New York City to testify at a hearing on behalf of a New York airline passengers' bill of rights law. It was the first any of us had heard there was an effort to enact such a law, and the state's senate had already approved the bill.

I had no desire to go to New York to testify about anything. Throughout my business career, I had been routinely called upon to speak in front of groups of people. I could do it, but I would have preferred to jump off of a tall building. I also didn't understand how a state could enforce a passengers' rights law. It seemed to me that only the federal government could enact and enforce such a law. I wrote back to Paul Hudson and Kate:

> I would say that the order of preferred speakers would probably
> be Kate, Paul and then [me] ... Seems to me that the NY law

would be redundant in the wake of a federal law, and a law that only can only require snacks be served at that.

Thankfully, Kate decided she would fly back to New York for the hearing, but the subject of state-sponsored airline passengers' rights laws would evolve into a contentious issue between Kate and me in the future.

By mid-May, less than five months after her tarmac stranding in Austin, Kate had asked me to assume responsibility for managing the e-mail lists, the petition and the e-mail accounts. She also asked me to maintain the website, to start writing newsletters, and to contact reporters to try to develop interest in passengers' rights stories – something she called "pitching media." I was already writing press releases.

Basically, I was now the de facto communications and information technology director with a staff of one – me. Despite the fact that I had told her that I could only work on airline passengers' rights on a part time basis, one-by-one, she had convinced me to assume all of these responsibilities "temporarily." I would later explain this to a reporter for the *New York Times* for an article that would be published in September 2007:

> 'She ropes you in,' said Mr. Mogel, 51, and a semi-retired
> software engineer. 'I wanted to scale back. But little by little –
> can you do this? – I'm back at it full time.'[7]

The FlyersRights.org website was a curiosity in and of itself. It was composed of cartoon-like figures that had obviously been created by talented professionals, but it wasn't finished and it looked more like a comic book than the website for a passengers' rights organization. All Kate would tell me was that she couldn't get the original development company to complete the work, so I began working on a redesign of the website in my spare time.

On the 18th, I wrote and sent my first CAPBOR newsletter using the e-mail service that Kate purchased in April. I configured the newsletter so that recipients could unsubscribe by clicking on a link at the bottom. For some reason, many of them e-mailed us directly and asked us to unsubscribe them, and many of them weren't happy. One of the respondents complained to Kate that he never signed the petition. She forwarded his e-mail to me and wrote:

> I've e-mailed this guy back and told him he is removed and also
> explained to him, several times, that aside from someone
> manually entering his name it couldn't have gotten there. He
> seemed to think we purchased his name and info somewhere.

I had received the same kind of responses for this newsletter and for the e-mails I sent months earlier. Some of the recipients accused us of stealing their e-mail addresses. Some threatened to file lawsuits or report us to the Federal Communications Commission (FCC) for violating anti-SPAM laws.

I suggested that we set up a membership process called "confirmed opt-in" or "COI" that would eliminate the problem. COI is a process used by most websites that require registration. The *USA Today* website, for example, requires readers to register before they can comment on articles. The reader fills out a form with his or her name, e-mail address and other contact information. *USA Today* then sends an e-mail to the registrant with a link. The registrant clicks on the link to activate the membership. This ensures that there is a match between the registrant and the e-mail address.

The way the airline passengers' rights petition was configured, anyone could add names, signatures, from a phone book or an e-mail list. Judging from many of the responses we received, there was evidence to support that theory. There was no way to be sure that the signatures were valid. In addition, it was probable that some people signed the petition to support airline passengers' rights as a general concept, but had no idea they were joining CAPBOR. The petition didn't mention CAPBOR and wouldn't until four years later when it was acquired by another online petition service.

Meanwhile, Kate disagreed with my suggestion to implement an opt-in process. She replied:

> Well, where we agree is that the folks are crazy and think they
> didn't sign the darn thing. It's important that we be able to
> include as many members in our midst as possible. There are
> members of Congress who have signed our petition who aren't
> victims, they just want to see what our message is. So everyone
> is a member until they specifically request not to be, even if
> they opt out of the e-mails.

I didn't understand why people who didn't know they were *members* of CAPBOR would request to not be *members*. I did understand one thing; the more signatures there were in the petition, the more formidable we would look to the news media and the government.

Four days later, I wrote and sent a second newsletter:

> Speaking to Kate Hanni on May 14 in Washington D.C.,
> Senator Barbara Boxer said, 'I want the coalition to know that
> Senator Olympia Snowe and I will continue to fight for the
> strongest possible Passenger Bill of Rights language.'
>
> The larger we get and the more progress we make, the more
> people we need to volunteer and help organize. We're looking
> for volunteers throughout the country to help with coalition

activities. It's a great way to make a difference, and do things
you never dreamed you could do.

Barbara Boxer hadn't spoken to Kate on May 14, but her office gave me
permission to attribute the quote to the senator. In fact, we would rarely meet
with a senator or representative when visiting Senate or House offices. However, we always make it look like we had in the newsletters. It was so rare to
meet with a member of Congress that, in June, we would sit through an entire
meeting with Senator Mark Pryor of Arkansas without knowing it was him.
We assumed he was a staff person. Both Kate and I phrased questions as;
"What would the senator think about ... this or that?" Hours after the
meeting we learned that it was Pryor. That was a little embarrassing.

As for volunteers, we genuinely needed and wanted more people to get
involved and help. The problem was that we rarely got any responses. And
even when we did, we were too busy with day-to-day activities to deal with
them. When someone did offer to volunteer for something, the help was
usually inadequate or short-lived.

ON MAY 24, Kate asked me to use the names and addresses from the petition to generate thousands of letters to fax to members of the Transportation
and Infrastructure Committee, particularly chairmen Oberstar and Costello.

The generation of so many letters required knowledge of a computer
program known as a "mail merge," knowledge that Kate didn't have. She
knew what was possible, but she needed someone else to generate the letters
for her. When I sought outside guidance as to whether or not this was
"ethical," although my real concern was if it was legal, Kate shut me down
by telling the person not to respond to me. She then sent me a hastily written,
error filled, angry e-mail in which she said she had permission from each of
the signatories of the petition to use their names:

> It's imperitive that the absolute accurate representation should
> be made here. The other text that would have been included in
> the letter, as expiAINED EARLIER WAS THE PETITION
> PREAMBLE TEXT WHICH CLEARLY SPELLS OUT THAT
> THEY WERE SENDING THEIR THOUGHTS ON TO Mike
> Thompson and other members of Congress in an effort to get
> this done.

> Also, we have asked our memers permission and have receied
> overwhelming support for us to take these and he[p them get
> presented to their members.

I wasn't trying to make her angry. I was genuinely concerned that she might get herself, and me, into a lot of trouble. I knew it was impossible that she had permission from all of those people to use their names considering the fact that large numbers of them had reported the newsletters as SPAM and some had threatened us with lawsuits.

Furthermore, the petition preamble read, "To: U.S. Congress - Mike Thompson." What was *clear* to me was that the petition was addressed to Congressman Mike Thompson. It had been created before Thompson introduced his airline passengers' rights bill in the House and, fortunately or unfortunately, the preamble and text of the petition couldn't be changed. The petition was hosted by a third party website.

I renewed my concern about the legality of this endeavor, and she replied with another e-mail in which she told me that one of the attorneys told her that all of this was perfectly legal. Knowing that none of the attorneys knew what I knew, and suspecting that she hadn't given the attorney the full story, I told her I wouldn't help with the project. Instead, I found something else to do that I hoped would turn her attention in another direction.

A week earlier, Ed Mierzwinski suggested that we find some way to get Representative Peter DeFazio (D-OR) onto the passengers' rights bandwagon. DeFazio was clear during the House hearing that he didn't agree with a three-hour tarmac rule, but as a long-time consumer advocate, Mierzwinski thought that DeFazio might be willing to support something. We still didn't have any passengers' rights language in the House FAA reauthorization bill, and perhaps DeFazio could break the ice by introducing something – anything at all.

Mierzwinski explained that when the Senate and the House pass different versions of the same bill, senior leaders in the House and the Senate come together in what is called a conference. Then the horse-trading begins, with each side having to give up something in return for something else.

If there were passengers' rights provisions in the Senate bill, but none in the House bill, there was a greater risk that all of the passengers' rights language would be dropped during conference. If we had any kind of passengers' rights language in both bills, even if it was different, there was a greater chance that some of it would be kept. We needed something in the bill that could be labeled as airline passengers' rights. Mierzwinski suggested that we send a letter to DeFazio to ask him to support – something.

The Library of Congress maintains a website that contains the history of all bills that have been submitted since 1989, so I spent the next few days researching any commercial aviation bills that DeFazio had written or co-sponsored. I also watched a few committee hearings and documented anything DeFazio said about commercial aviation. I synthesized all of that into a short list of possible amendments to the FAA reauthorization bill:

disclosure of flight delay information at time of purchase; accurate disclosure of the reason for delays in progress, and; publicizing the DOT's complaint hotline number on tickets or boarding passes.

I drafted a letter to DeFazio with the list of possible amendments. Kate asked one of our attorneys to write some sample legislative language to complement the recommendations. Then she sent the letter to a member of DeFazio's staff. It was a lot of work, and this is a process that I would repeat many times in the future with other members of Congress. Sometimes it worked, most of the time it didn't, but it only took one success to get the ball rolling.

Meanwhile, Kate had not been distracted from her goal. She found someone else to generate the letters and she faxed them, unapologetically, to members of the House Transportation and Infrastructure Committee. On the 29th, she wrote to me:

> I have NAME REDACTED helping me fax out the remainder
> of the letters and I have sent/faxed a thousand or so myself. We
> need help in a big way!!! So many different things to do and so
> few hands!

I could only hope that my concerns about the legality of all of that were unfounded and that she had gotten sound, well-informed legal advice.

NEAR THE END of May, someone with a blood clot contacted Kate and told her that he got the clot as a result of sitting on an airplane on the tarmac for 3.5 hours. Notwithstanding the fact that millions of airline passengers spend far longer than 3.5 hours flying across the country and internationally every day, this gentleman's story would be pluralized and repeated in count-less television interviews and articles. Kate had a remarkable talent for making one incident or story sound like thousands.

She sent a letter to DOT Secretary Mary Peters that said, "There are reports of passengers being deprived of needed medications, incidents of deep vein thrombosis as passengers are forced to remain in their seats for hours on end ...."

I was learning that, if she couldn't dazzle them with the facts, Kate would not shy away from exaggeration.

On May 31, I sent Kate an update on the petition. Oddly, the petition had swelled to nearly 14,000 signatures by the end of February, the first full month of the coalition. However, in April and May, we had averaged only about 200 new signatures per month. It seemed as if public interest in airline passengers' rights had already waned.

Kate didn't seem surprised or concerned about the dramatic decrease in signatures. She didn't even address my concern. Instead, she sent me a screenshot, a picture of her computer screen that featured a pornographic e-mail titled "MILFs do things so dirty it will make you blush." It didn't make me blush, but it made me wonder what the hell she was thinking.

JUNE 2007

Happy Birthday

IN LATE MAY, Kate, Paul Hudson and I had begun to work on a report card that would grade each major airline against the number of tarmac delays they had during the previous six months. The report card would also discuss how airline contracts of carriage measured up in regard to addressing tarmac delays and other customer service issues. Mainly, the report card would give us a great reason to hold our first press conference.

Hudson researched and compared airline contracts of carriage and customer service plans. Kate put together a handful of pages with reports of tarmac strandings from the petition, and from e-mails and news reports. I created several pages of airline tarmac delay statistics, presented in a way that wasn't available from the BTS. I also wrote an executive summary and developed a grading system to rank each airline's performance against each of the categories. We added a couple of pages to demagogue the DOT's oversight of airline statistics and other commercial airline subjects. I then compiled everything into a 40-page document – the report card.

On the morning of June 13, we met in a conference room at the US-PIRG (U.S. Public Interest Research Group) offices in Washington, D.C. In addition to Kate, Hudson and me, three other passengers' rights advocates had traveled to Washington for the press conference; Jennifer Shirkani, Cindy Bouchard and Cathy Ray. So by now at least a few other volunteers materialized, although they hadn't worked on the report card.

Cindy Bouchard was a former customer service representative for a major airline. Cathy Ray had been stranded on one of the airplanes in Austin. Jennifer Shirkani was a frequent business traveler who had kept track of her own extensive delays in airports and on airplanes.

This was the first time I'd met US-PIRG director, Ed Mierzwinski, in person. I had seen him at the Senate hearing in April, but I didn't know he was advising Kate at the time. Mierzwinski was a gracious and patient host. He walked us through a rehearsal of the report card presentation. He coached us to be brief when we spoke – stick to sound bites.

Afterward, we all walked a few blocks to the Cannon House Office Building. That was where Kate's congressman's office had reserved a room for the press conference. When we got there, the room was crammed with cameras, lights and news reporters. I'd never seen anything like it.

Hudson spoke about airline contracts of carriage. When a passenger purchases an airline ticket, it forms a contract. The contract of carriage describes the legal obligations between the passenger and the airline. When things go wrong, such as when bags are lost or a flight is canceled, then the passengers' rights and the airline's legal responsibilities are spelled out in those contracts.

Hudson also talked about customer service plans in which airlines document things that they aren't contractually required to do, but will *try* to do in the event of an irregular event such as a tarmac stranding.

When it was my turn to speak, I gave an overview of the airline statistics pages, and I described how and why the statistics in those pages were flawed and incomplete. As I looked at the sea of reporters before me, it struck me that many were probably the same reporters that had been using airline and government statistics in their articles without knowing the truth. When I read the Associated Press article in March, I knew immediately that the statistics for tarmac strandings had to be wrong, and it only took me another three days to prove it. *Where are the investigative reporters?* I wondered.

Finally, it was Kate's turn to speak. In the weeks preceding the press conference, when the report card was in its earliest development stages, I had cautioned her to be accurate with the data she included in her pages, to have factual backup for the numbers she used. She was using news articles and other empirical data to construct her pages. It was obvious early on that American Airlines, the carrier that stranded her on the tarmac for over nine hours in December, would bear the brunt of the negative publicity from the report card.

On one page of the draft report card she indicated that American had 87 airplanes stranded for over four hours on December 29. The articles and spreadsheets she sent to me did not support that number, and an ongoing investigation into the incident by the DOT's Inspector General would later put the number at 44. I warned her that if she couldn't back up her data she could put our credibility at risk, and it was possible that she could face a lawsuit. American might then subpoena the sources for the data she claimed to have, but didn't. She wasn't worried. She replied:

> If American Airlines questions me or comes after me we will
> simply make a public plea for them to 'come clean' show us we
> are wrong.

Her logic escaped me.

Because the airline tarmac statistics were woefully incomplete, there was really no way to know which airline might have been the worst tarmac stranding culprit during the past six months – there were no valid statistics from which to draw a conclusion. In a sense, that was the real point, and I had written as much – buried in the fine print of the report card – for reporters who could read between the lines. At least one news organization had *gotten it*. ABC News reported on our press conference later that evening:

> While it's not hard to see why some airline passengers are fed
> up, the [report card] data is challenging to sort out, and even
> Hanni's group admits its report is incomplete and does not
> contain complete statistics.[8]

And yet, even ABC News included an unsubstantiated claim in their report. In the context of lengthy, mass tarmac stranding events such as the JetBlue incident in February, they quoted Kate, "The DOT and the airlines are lying to the general public about the possibility of being stranded, *and it is happening every day.*"

Kate concluded the report card press conference with a set of dubious, yet imaginative awards. American, whether deserved or because we simply had more negative information about that airline than any other, was the recipient of the worst: "When you're on the ground, they treat you like dirt."

Kate also announced a new, toll-free, 24/7 hotline for airline passengers to call when they were stuck on the tarmac or had any other airline related complaints. The hotline was a Web-based, virtual PBX. People could call and leave messages. An audio file of the message was then sent automatically by e-mail to Kate or whoever else was on the distribution list. The e-mail also showed the telephone number of the caller. Kate wanted to find people to return those calls.

She tried to enlist me, but I said no. I agreed to research and document all reports of tarmac strandings that were received, but I had no intention of returning telephone calls to strangers at 3 p.m. let alone possibly 3 a.m.

Nevertheless, it wouldn't take long for the hotline to prove to be one of the most ingenious public relations moves of all. It gave Kate a platform to provide the news media with exaggerated statistics about tarmac strandings.

In the hours and days immediately after the press conference, all of the major news programs ran stories about the report card and the hotline. Three weeks later, appearing on Fox News, I watched as Kate told the two hosts, "Within three hours we had 900 phone calls from people that had been stuck on planes." Both of the hosts spontaneously responded, "Wow."

I said "Wow" too. Heretofore, Kate had sent me only five tarmac stranding calls to research and document. *Where are the other 895?* I wondered.

A few days after the report card press conference, Kate called me and apologized for an article in the *Washington Post*, an article I hadn't yet seen. Kate swore that she told the reporter that I had made the statistics discovery but, "They wanted to attribute it to me for some reason," she said.

"I'll call you back," I said.

I found the article on the *Post's* website. Kate had been credited for the quirk in the statistics that I uncovered:

> Kate Hanni of Napa, Calif., who formed the coalition after sitting in an American Airlines plane for more than eight hours after her flight was diverted last December, said that many more long waits are omitted than are included by the DOT. She discovered the quirk in the stats after looking for info about her long wait and finding that her flight hadn't been included in DOT tallies.[9]

I sighed. I had been a long-time admirer of *Washington Post* reporters Bob Woodward and Carl Bernstein of Watergate fame. I didn't have a desire for publicity, but it would have been nice to see my name in that particular newspaper. Still, I found it highly unlikely that a reporter for a newspaper like the *Post* would jeopardize her or her newspaper's credibility over something so petty.

Like some of the female volunteers who had come and gone before me, I too had observed that Kate seemed to need to be the center of attention, and this episode was just the latest confirmation of that. But I also knew, if we were going to get anywhere with airline passengers' rights, we needed a focal point for the media. That focal point was Kate. And she was right about one thing; it was all about the media, and the media seemed to love what she was feeding them.

I called her back and told her that I wasn't doing this for publicity or recognition. "If the opportunity comes up, feel free to throw me a bone, but I see my role as making you look as good as possible. You're the star," I said.

"Thanks Mark. You rock!" she said.

I WROTE ANOTHER newsletter on June 18. In it, we asked our members to contact committee chairmen Jim Oberstar and Jerry Costello to encourage them to add passengers' rights language to the FAA reauthorization bill. Despite the publicity we had generated up to this point, we had just learned that the bill was going to be introduced without passengers' rights language.

By now, I had discovered that our newsletter e-mail system produced interesting statistics about each of the newsletters we sent. I checked the statistics for all of the newsletters Kate or I had sent since April. They showed that people had been unsubscribing by the hundreds, and half of them had registered SPAM complaints with their Internet service providers. *Why would our members complain that we were sending them SPAM?* I wondered again. Even worse, the statistics indicated that less than one percent, or approximately 150 of the recipients, had clicked on links in the newsletters to contact their congressmen.

Since the newsletters seemed to be ineffective, I decided that we should try something different to try to get passengers' rights language added to the House FAA reauthorization bill. I suggested that we run radio commercials in Jim Oberstar's and Jerry Costello's congressional districts. I thought if Oberstar and Costello saw that CAPBOR had the time and resources to arrange for radio advertising, surely that would get their attention. Kate agreed and asked me to find out how to do that and what it would cost.

I was unable to find a radio station that I was comfortable with in Chairman Oberstar's district in Minnesota. His district was some 200 miles from Minneapolis, and I wanted to run the ads in a major city. Fortunately, Jerry Costello's district in Illinois was directly across the Mississippi River from St. Louis where there were plenty of radio stations from which to choose. Costello was a liberal, and I thought he might be especially sensitive to any local publicity that would portray him as anti-consumer.

I contacted several radio stations in St. Louis, and finally settled on a news radio station, KMOX. They were the top-rated talk radio station in the region and they told me that Jerry Costello even called in from time-to-time, depending upon the topic being aired. "Costello's local office listens to us," they said. When I had all of the pricing and other details worked out, I wrote a script for the commercial and sent it to Kate to record the audio:

> In the past year, thousands of airline passengers have been
> trapped on airport tarmacs for up to twelve hours with no food,
> no water and overflowing toilets. Congressman Jerry Costello
> said 'if the airlines won't fix the problem I will.' But he hasn't
> fixed the problem. Tell Chairman Costello to stand up against
> the airlines so your family can fly without being held hostage.
> Paid for by the Coalition for an Airline Passenger's Bill of
> Rights - Flyersrights.org or 1-877-Flyers6.

The radio station's producers were so impressed with the commercial that they invited Kate to appear as a guest on the *Paul Harris* show on Friday, June 22.[10] I took that afternoon off to play golf. My cell phone started to ring when I reached the fourth hole, and it didn't stop until I rounded the turn. There were about ten voicemails from Kate. When I called her back, she was breathless.

She said that Chairman Costello called in halfway through the radio show and he said that passengers' rights language would be added to the FAA reauthorization bill. She also said she had just gotten off the phone with reporter Joe Sharkey of the New York Times. She had called him to tell him the news. She said that Sharkey mentioned that he might want to write a book with her, and she said that he also thought her story would make a great movie. "Like a Kate Brockovich kind of thing!" she said excitedly.

I had reminded Kate numerous times that I couldn't keep working with her full-time – I needed to do something to make money. I still had plenty of savings set aside for my other business ideas, but I didn't plan on exhausting those savings to pay the monthly bills while working on airline passengers' rights. Now, Kate offered a solution to that problem.

"I need you, Mark. If you stay with me I'll give you 25 percent of the book and the movie." She said that she wasn't sure how she would work that out with her husband, but she would figure it out. "I promise you, my word is golden," she said.

The concept of a book and a movie certainly seemed plausible. Even if we failed to get airline passengers' rights enacted, her story already seemed tailor-made for the silver screen, and what a story it would make if we were successful. I could envision the final scene; Kate standing behind President George Bush as he handed her one of the pens he used to sign the bill.

Despite frequent disagreements about tactics, strategy and maintaining credibility, Kate and I were becoming friends. Because of that, I took her at her word. The FAA reauthorization bill was scheduled to be voted on by the end of September, so I agreed that I would stay with her at least until then. That bill, as I understood at the time, was a "must pass" bill, meaning that it had to pass to keep the FAA running. What I didn't know, and wouldn't find out until September, was that Congress' has a different definition of "must pass" than mine.

Two days later, Kate threw me a bone, but it wasn't exactly the *Washington Post*. It was a piece in an aviation industry news service. She sent me a link to the article and wrote:

> Listen, you are gonna be in the press, the movie, the book, hell,
> I wouldn't have placed that ad in Costello's backyard had you
> not pushed it, found the radio station and made the connection.
> We need to find an actor that looks like you? Got any ideas? I
> think Gwyneth could play me.

In jest, I replied that Brad Pitt should play me. I bear no resemblance to the actor, and I also thought it would be highly unlikely that anyone would be playing me in any movie. I felt I had made a significant contribution to the cause, but this was the *Kate Hanni* show and I had no illusion or desire that it would ever be anything else. I found the statistics article on the Aero-News Network (ANN) website:

> CAPBOR tells ANN the group's Chief Research Director, Mark Mogel, discovered the DOT was not counting flight diversions and cancellations as 'time on the tarmac' in its computations of airline delays.[11]

"Chief research director," I chuckled aloud. Kate had given me a title that made it sound as if I had other people working for me. As for her promises of me being in the press and a movie, I didn't understand why she thought those things would be important to me – apart from the possibility of profiting from them. By now she had told me that she had always wanted to be a rock star, to be famous. I could only assume she was projecting her own desire for fame upon me, as if she thought that everyone must want to be famous. *It will be a lot easier to maintain her energy and focus if she's obsessed with something selfish rather than something selfless,* I thought.

But I also began to wonder if any of this was really about airline passengers' rights and tarmac strandings. We were both motivated by life-long dreams – hers was apparently fame, and mine was to participate in the political process. I wondered if we were deceiving ourselves, and others, that our motivations were altruistic. *Heaven help us both if we're not doing this for the right reasons,* I thought. With decades of first-hand experience, I knew that karma could be a bitch.

A FEW DAYS later, Kate wrote to tell me that a law firm in Washington, the LawMedia Group (LMG), could help us *again*. "I already know the devil we are playing with there," she wrote. "Do you see any inherent dangers?" she asked.

I didn't know who LMG was, what devil she was talking about, or how they could help us *again* since I didn't know they had been helping in the first place. I called her to get clarification. She said that the people who worked for Southpaw, the public relations firm that had been writing press releases and performing other media related activities until April, were all the same people as LMG.

"What do you mean they're all the same people?" I asked.

"They're all the same people," she repeated.

I was totally confused – didn't even know what questions to ask about LMG or Southpaw. I asked what she meant by the "devil."

She said that LMG was behind some kind of "small plane alliance" that was lobbying against "user fees." She said she wasn't exactly sure what that meant, but she had a feeling that it was something we shouldn't be involved with. She asked me to look into it further. I told her that I'd get back to her as soon as I figured out what the hell was going on.

Within a day, I pieced together a puzzle that answered her questions and others that had been dogging me for months.

Since our earliest telephone conversations, it was obvious to me that Kate had very limited knowledge of the federal government. Even in her C-SPAN appearance, she had admitted that she didn't understand how the legislative process worked. Visiting Senate offices with her in May, I noticed that she seemed lost in the Senate office complex that she said she had visited several times before.

All of this had left me wondering how she could have shown up in Washington, D.C. in late January and started a lobbying campaign by herself – the image she had portrayed to both me and the media ever since. The more I got to know her, the less plausible this and many other things seemed. I would now learn what really happened. I started my search for answers at the beginning – the very beginning.

After the December 29, 2006 tarmac stranding incident in Austin, a brief article was published by the Associated Press that described the event in general terms – no passengers were mentioned. Other journalists from around the country then scrambled to find passengers from those airplanes. A series of coincidences led NBC News' producers to Kate. Articulate, sympathetic and photogenic, NBC had found the perfect tarmac stranding victim.

On January 10, 2007, Kate appeared on NBC's *Nightly News* in an interview taped at her home in Napa.[12] The interview focused entirely on the tarmac stranding – there was no mention of airline passengers' rights. The segment was replayed on NBC's *Today* show the next day, and it was rerun several times on MSNBC. Unfortunately, I had already reached a roadblock. I called Kate and asked how she got connected to Southpaw.

She said that soon after the NBC story aired, someone called her and told her that he worked for a Washington, D.C. public relations firm called "Southpaw." He pitched an idea; if she would be interested in spearheading a grassroots movement for airline passengers' rights, they would get her started, arrange for media interviews, write press releases and coach her on how to lobby Congress. They would support her any way they could. Kate agreed.

I was able to pick up the rest of the history from a series of e-mails that Kate forwarded to me. By January 22, Southpaw had written letters for Kate to send to Congress, and they had also developed a list of airline passengers' rights. On January 23, they hosted a teleconference between the news media and Kate. At the time, Kate was corresponding with approximately 13 other passengers and a few of them also participated in that conference call.

Southpaw provided Kate and those passengers with a set of talking points for the teleconference, and Kate thus announced to the media that she had formed a coalition that would be lobbying Congress to pass a comprehensive bill of rights for airline passengers. She also announced that she had written to the chairman of the Senate Commerce Committee to demand that he hold hearings on the subject of tarmac strandings.

Scores of newspaper articles were published during the week that followed, and Kate appeared on several television shows from a studio in San Francisco. A few days later, she flew to New York City to appear on ABC's *Good Morning America* on January 27. Five days after that, she appeared on the C-SPAN program where I had first seen her.

Contrary to her statement on the C-SPAN broadcast that she had just shown up in Washington to lobby and would figure it out as she went along, it was actually Southpaw who assisted her in making congressional appointments, coached her on what to say during those meetings, and physically led her from one office to the next. And that's why, I now understood, she seemed disoriented when I was with her in the Senate office buildings in May. Prior to that, she'd always had a guide. In one of the e-mails I traded with Kate, she wrote about Southpaw:

> They had a whole staff of people doing things. It was so helpful, they had NAME REDACTED walking me around DC, making all of the leave behind kits, creating the press releases, and selling them through to the press. ... They could guarantee us coverage on any issue.

After the Senate hearing in April, Kate learned from a reporter that the members of Southpaw's staff were actually members of another Washington, D.C. public relations firm, the LawMedia Group (LMG). Until then, she thought she was working with Southpaw, a public relations firm whose only agenda, as far as she knew, was altruistic.

For reasons unknown to both Kate and me, Southpaw had stopped helping her immediately after she learned that they all actually worked for LMG. That was when Kate asked me to start doing all of the media related tasks that Southpaw had been doing. That's also why she wrote to me in early May that she felt alone – because she was alone.

Curiously, I found no evidence of a Washington-based public relations firm named Southpaw anywhere on Web. The only evidence I found that Southpaw existed at all was on the Federal Election Commission's website. Southpaw had submitted lobbying disclosure documents that contained little useful information except for one thing; the street address and telephone number on those disclosure forms were exactly the same as LMG's.

LMG had a website that described the company and its mission. It seemed that LMG was also a public relations firm, one that catered primarily to Fortune 100 companies. Its primary expertise, according to the website, was in mounting 360-degree media campaigns to achieve their client's goals.

> Our goal is to dominate the media environment on behalf of the client. We work on a 24-hour clock and place rapidity and quality of response above all else. By design, our team is led by experts who have had decades of experience managing the highest profile campaigns – for presidential candidates, U.S. senators, governors, members of Congress and leading corporate clients.

According to a bio attached to an opinion piece he wrote for the *Nation* in 2002, LMG's founder, Julian Epstein was, "chief minority counsel to the House Judiciary Committee and, before that, the majority staff director of the House Government Operations Committee."

Other members of LMG, I found, had been employed by CBS, CNN, the Democratic National Committee and the White House. If someone had a public relations problem or need, LMG had the experience and government and media connections to get things done.

According to an article that had been published by Bloomberg News in May, LMG had been retained by members of the general aviation community to create and run an organization to lobby against a tax that was pending before Congress. The tax, called a "user fee," was intended to shift part of the tax burden for funding the FAA from the commercial airlines to members of the general aviation community, particularly corporate and private jets.

Senator Jay Rockefeller (D-WV) had added the user fee language to the Senate's version of the FAA reauthorization bill. He thought, as did others, that corporate and private jets were not paying their fair share of the cost of running the nation's air traffic control system. He argued that corporate and private jets consume the same FAA resources as a commercial airliner, and thus they should pay more for that privilege.

Furthermore, because the taxes collected from the commercial airlines were actually paid for by their passengers, it was actually airline passengers who were subsidizing the FAA resources used by corporate jets, private jets and the millionaires flying in them.

Thus, the battle lines had been drawn long before CAPBOR came onto the scene, with commercial airlines in favor of user fees, and the general aviation community, led in part by LMG, opposing them.

LMG had mounted a full-scale campaign against user fees. That campaign included the creation of an organization called the "Alliance for

Aviation across America," which was funded by trade associations that represented private pilots and corporate and private jet owners.

The Bloomberg News article published in May exposed LMG's role in both the alliance and airline passengers' rights, although neither Kate nor CAPBOR were mentioned by name:

> The alliance is run by the Law Media Group, a Washington lobbying firm. Gil Meneses, who works out of Law Media's office, helped push an effort by consumers to enact an airline-passenger bill of rights. He says his work on the consumer legislation was voluntary and unconnected to Law Media's lobbying for small-plane groups.[13]

If LMG's airline passengers' rights effort was "unconnected to lobbying for small-plane groups," I wondered why they hadn't communicated openly with Kate as LMG from the beginning. Was CAPBOR just another part of their campaign to defeat the commercial airline's agenda? I also wondered why they were now willing to help us again.

Whatever their reasons may have been, I now understood who had gotten her started, who had been supporting her, and how she had made it as far as she had before my involvement. It didn't change how I felt about continuing with the cause. It may have even stiffened my resolve. It seemed to me that Kate had been used and, by extension, so had I. There would come a time when I would learn that the role of public relations firms in Washington politics can be far more nefarious than what I understood at the time, but for now I remained naïve, still believing that the will of the people and our democracy, with the aid of a scrupulous press, would prevail at the end of the day.

Meanwhile, as for LMG's offer to help us *again*, we could have used the help, but I told Kate that I was concerned that any appearance that we were being assisted by the public relations firm behind the small-plane alliance could hurt us politically. The user fee issue cut across party lines. Democrats disagreed strongly with other Democrats, and the same discord existed within the Republican Party. Also, since the adoption of user fees could have resulted in lower ticket prices for airline passengers, it was something we should have been supporting, not opposing.

Sometime later Kate would tell me that a member of LMG told her that they had gotten her started to "create another thorn of the side of the airlines," part of LMG's strategy to create a comprehensive media campaign on behalf of their clients. None of this would preclude her from maintaining a relationship with LMG in the future, but she was now on a more level playing field. She knew who was who, and what was what. As they say, politics makes strange bedfellows.

THE DAY AFTER I completed my research into Southpaw and LMG, Kate wrote and asked me to come to Washington. "I'm all alone in DC and it's my birthday. I would love some support! Ain't too proud to beg."

The House Transportation and Infrastructure Committee was scheduled vote on the FAA reauthorization bill by the end of the week. The committee majority had been tight-lipped about what was going to be in the bill. As far as we knew, despite what Chairman Costello told her on the radio, there was still no airline passengers' rights language in the bill. There was little we could do to influence the outcome at that late stage, but the next day I drove to Washington to lend whatever support I could give.

When I was somewhere north of Baltimore on Interstate 95, Kate called and said that she had just gotten word that language addressing the airline tarmac statistics issue was going to be in the FAA reauthorization bill.

"You got your statistics in the bill, Mark," she said. "We still don't know if there will be passengers' rights in the bill, but your statistics are in there. Isn't that exciting?"

Tears involuntarily welled in my eyes. "Thanks, Kate," I managed to say. "I'll be there in about two hours. I can't talk now." I hung up.

I couldn't remember a time in my life when I felt a wave of conflicting emotions like I did at that moment. On one hand I felt a great feeling of pride and satisfaction. On the other, I wondered if I had spent my entire adult life working with computers when I could have been doing something like this, perhaps was born to it. *How can I possibly top this?* I wondered.

In Washington, Kate and I looked on from the gallery as the House Transportation and Infrastructure Committee passed the FAA reauthorization bill with language that addressed many of the airline tarmac statistics deficiencies – and they included passengers' rights language in the bill. That language didn't require airlines to allow passengers to get off the plane during a long tarmac delay, but it did require them to provide essential needs like food, water, proper ventilation and working lavatories. The bill had to be approved by other committees before it went to the House floor for a vote, but it was a great start.

"Happy birthday, Kate," I said.

"Happy birthday my ass," she said. "I want deplanement language."

"You are something else," I said. Do you know that?"

"You have no idea," she said.

JULY 2007

Saving money

AS REPORTERS BEGAN to ask Kate for technical details about the airline tarmac statistics, it became necessary to pull me into the conversations. Because there were already two publicly available, but divergent versions of the story, one that Kate had made the discovery and one that I had, we devised another story to try to reconcile the discrepancy. We began to tell reporters that Kate had suspected that there were problems with the statistics and that she had directed her research department to look into it.

The Bureau of Transportation Statistics had held a public meeting about the airline statistics in Washington on June 20, a meeting that I attended. That meeting, and the fact that the government was taking the issue of tarmac statistics seriously, had reinvigorated the media's interest in the subject. In the two weeks since, Kate had been involved in dozens of press interviews, and I was pulled into several of them. One of those interviews resulted in an article that was published in *Time* magazine on July 5:

> But according to the BTS records, flight 1348 was simply
> 'diverted.' 'It's like our flight didn't even exist,' says Kate
> Hanni, a passenger onboard flight 1348. ... When Mark Mogel,
> a member of Hanni's coalition, logged onto the BTS website to
> find data on Hanni's flight delay, he turned up empty-handed.[14]

The tarmac statistics issue had reached a climax. NBC's *Nightly News* led its broadcast that evening with a story about the airline statistics and they showed a video clip of Kate from our report card press conference in June. ABC News covered the story during their evening news broadcast, and the story appeared in the *New York Times* and every other major news outlet the following week.

This two-week period of media coverage was the single most defining moment for Kate, CAPBOR and the future of airline passengers' rights up to that point. We had succeeded in getting airline passengers' rights language added to the House FAA reauthorization bill, and the government was taking the statistics issue seriously. If there had ever been any doubt within the news media about Kate's rightful claim as the premier consumer advocate in the country for airline passengers' rights, these two weeks put an end to that question, and we were just getting warmed up.

On July 6, now feeling invincible, Kate wrote to Chairman Costello's legislative director and asked if Costello was going to include deplanement language in the FAA reauthorization bill. She threatened she would go back on the radio in St. Louis if he didn't. The legislative director replied that Costello had no intention of changing the bill.

She then sent an e-mail to Paul Harris at KMOX and asked to reappear on his radio show to provide an update on passengers' rights issues. Harris invited her to appear on the radio with him on Monday afternoon.

On Monday morning, July 9, Kate arrived in Washington on a red-eye flight, and I drove from Collegeville to meet her at her hotel. We took the subway to Capitol Hill and Senator Boxer's office, a mode of transportation that Kate hadn't used before. Kate had been telling me that our expenses were outpacing donations, so I had suggested that we start using the subway to save money over using taxi cabs.

Senator Boxer had written to each of the major the airlines and asked them to provide her with their customer service and contingency plans for dealing with long tarmac delays. Boxer's office gave us copies of the letters and plans that the airlines sent to them. However, because some of the documents contained internal airline operational procedures, Boxer's staff emphasized that we shouldn't tell anyone that we had them or where we got them. They handed me a stack of paper about four inches thick, and then they let us use a nearby conference room to start reading them. Kate used the telephone in the conference room to call KMOX.

I started to read the airline plans while Kate was being interviewed. During the interview, she kept her word and chastised Chairman Costello for not including deplanement language in the House bill. Then, ten minutes into the interview, I heard her say, "We're actually here, I'm in Barbara Boxer's office right now and we're reading through the airline's plans …"

I spontaneously waved my arms, exclaimed, "No, don't tell them that!"

Startled, she mouthed back, "What?"

When the interview was over I said, "[Boxer's staff] just told you not to tell anyone you have these or where you got them, and you probably just told about a hundred thousand people!"

The next day, she sent me a link to Paul Harris' website where the radio host had posted an audio file of his interview with Kate. I could barely tell where I had startled her. After I listened to the interview, I congratulated her on keeping her composure. "It's the mark of a true star," I wrote.

She replied that she had missed out on a music record deal when she was in her twenties, "I always wanted to be a star. I was born to perform! Now it appears there may be another way with advocacy, which is actually just as rewarding if not more so."

A week later, I sent Kate a three-page summary of the airline customer service and contingency plans. Kate forwarded the summary to Senator Boxer's office and told them that the analysis was done by CAPBOR's research department.

The most surprising thing I had found in the airline plans was in a letter from Delta's CEO in which he described what Delta did when things like bad weather caused irregular flight operations to occur; "it's just easier to load the planes and get them out [onto the tarmac]."

That statement was indicative of the arrogance of many in the airline industry. While some airlines had gone to great lengths in the past few months to develop plans to address the tarmac delay problem, others thumbed their noses at it. There was a prevailing attitude among the airlines that we had no chance of getting a law passed – that we would eventually give up and disappear. They would be proven to be wrong about that.

Continental, Northwest and United each had definitive deplanement timeframes in their customer service plans that ranged from three to four hours. Still, the plans contained wiggle words like *endeavor* and *reasonable effort* which gave them the option to do nothing. Only one carrier, Southwest, mentioned their customer service plan as an integral extension to their contract of carriage.

American Airlines had a deplanement policy in its contract of carriage, but it was followed by a disclaimer that blunted its enforceability; "We are not responsible for any special, incidental or consequential damages if we do not meet this commitment."

JetBlue had established a written passenger bill of rights soon after the Valentine's Day incident, and they had the most definitive policy, but they promised to deplane passengers only after a five hour delay.

Regardless of the effort or lack thereof by the airlines, whatever they promised was voluntary and they could rescind or modify those policies at their whim. Federal legislation was necessary to provide passengers with permanent protections, no matter what the airlines promised they would or wouldn't do.

My problem was that I didn't know what that legislation should say. For Kate, the answer was simple – a three or four hour time limit. Because of my engineering background, I knew that nothing is ever simple. Whenever a change is made to a complex system, there is the potential for negative, unintended consequences.

I had made a genuine effort to try to understand airline operations, but the more I learned, the more I found that I was only scratching the surface –

that our national aviation system is part art, part science and part magic. It comprises far more than airplanes, airports and radar systems. The day-to-day dynamics of the system are affected by pilot and flight attendant contracts, airline schedules, a variety of ground personnel, a cornucopia of FAA regulations, the weather, airport capacity and configurations, airport security, hardware maintenance and reliability and, above all, people making decisions about how to orchestrate all of this every day.

Still, in the face of airline arrogance and their apparent lack of common sense and compassion, federal legislation, whatever its unintended consequences, was the only viable option. And the airlines had made one serious miscalculation – they could never have imagined two more determined partners than Kate Hanni and me.

BY MID-JULY, a new character had emerged on the scene. Jack Corbett was a partner at a Washington law firm, and he had been corresponding with Kate in the background for a month or so. He would gradually take a more active role in advising us and preparing legislative language.

Ed Mierzwinski provided valuable advice on general lobbying strategy and grassroots organization, but he wasn't an expert when it came to the challenges we faced in making arguments against those set forth by airline lobbyists. Kate still didn't fully trust Burt Rubin, although he would take a more active role in the future when she felt more secure in his loyalty to her. Paul Hudson had experience in government affairs and commercial aviation subjects, but he wasn't as responsive as Kate wanted. Kate's patience was measured in seconds, not hours or days.

Kate and I lacked the legal skills, lobbying experience and commercial aviation knowledge that was necessary to formulate strategy and write effective letters to Congress and DOT officials on these subjects. Corbett would fill that void. He had been lobbying Congress and the Department of Transportation on behalf of airport clients for years, and with him on board, there would be little we couldn't do.

For the next two weeks, media outlets gave Kate more opportunities to deride Chairman Costello for not including deplanement language in the House FAA reauthorization bill. On July 20, Costello personally called Kate and asked her to provide his office with specific amendments to the bill. I spent the next few days working with Corbett and Hudson to put together a letter for Costello's office. I also created a side-by-side comparison of the House and Senate bills that highlighted the differences between the two bills. I sent the documents to Costello's legislative director and signed the e-mail, "Research Director, CAPBOR."

KATE AND I met again in Washington on the morning of July 25. That day, a producer for CBS News and a reporter for NPR accompanied us as we visited congressional offices.

We started in Senator Frank Lautenberg's (D-NJ) office where we met with the senator and his lead transportation aid. Kate was as charming and personable as I'd seen her. Even though it was her first time meeting him, she called the senator by his first name and told him that he was far too handsome to be 83. She thanked him profusely for an amendment that he had gotten into a bill to provide the DOT with $2.5 million to investigate airline consumer issues. Much of those taxpayer dollars would be wasted on regional consumer forums that had little if any value, but Lautenberg would be a staunch ally going forward.

Later, before we met with one of Senator Olympia Snowe's aides, the CBS television producer asked Kate and me to walk around the corner of a hallway and then to walk back toward him while he filmed us. "What's going on?" I asked Kate.

"It's called a B-roll," she said. "They do it for when they piece the story together. Just act like you're talking to me about something important."

This is not a good idea, I thought. Kate and I had recently been spending a lot of time on the telephone. It wasn't unusual for her to call me ten or more times on any given day. She always had an official purpose, but then the subject would often change to unofficial, personal things. The amount of time we spent on the telephone was raising eyebrows in my house and in hers. Furthermore, our newsletters, which both of our spouses received, suggested that there was a small army of lobbyists with Kate when she was in Washington. It wasn't true, and I worried that if either of our spouses saw this news story or others, they might start asking uncomfortable questions such as, "Where's the rest of the army?"

"What if your husband sees this and it's just you and me walking down this hall?" I asked.

"I hadn't thought of that," she said as the producer filmed us walking into Senator Snowe's office.

Later, we went to the other side of Capitol Hill to the House office buildings where we met with Kate's congressman, Mike Thompson. Kate was less than charming during that meeting. There was tension in the air. A couple of weeks earlier, Kate had told a reporter that she didn't think Thompson was working hard enough to get co-sponsors for his passengers' rights bill in the House. When the reporter told Thompson what Kate had said, Thompson responded, "anyone with an ounce of common sense [would know better]." That quote appeared in the article, and Kate took it personally. She was so furious that for months she tried to work "common sense" into every sound bite she gave a reporter.

Next we met with members of Jerry Costello's staff. I had the distinct impression that they weren't all that impressed with Kate, although they weren't outwardly disrespectful. They may have not been happy with our radio commercials and Kate's appearances on the St. Louis radio station. Their body language betrayed their attitudes – arms folded, short answers. They didn't seem interested in having a conversation.

From there we met with the transportation aid for my congressman, Jim Gerlach (R-PA). The upshot of that meeting was that they didn't think we would get deplanement language added to the House FAA reauthorization bill. It would have sounded arrogant, but I was tempted to respond, "You have no idea who you're dealing with." I was beginning to think that with Kate in the foreground and Jack Corbett and me in the background, anything was possible.

We didn't have any meetings scheduled the next day, so we spent most of it walking from one congressional office to another. We dropped off news media articles about airline passengers' rights and tarmac strandings, and we collected business cards for legislative aides. The intense meeting schedule the day before was mostly for the benefit of the media people that followed us around. Most of the time we only had a couple of meetings scheduled per day, and often there were no meetings at all.

It's difficult to get appointments with most congressional offices unless you are a constituent. One of our strategies was to send out newsletters that asked our members to make appointments with their congressmen, and then we would attend the appointment on their behalf. One problem with that was we didn't get much participation – no more than five or six appointments in a week, often fewer. Even when we did get an appointment, we sometimes got thrown out. We went to a breakfast one morning to meet Senator Sherrod Brown (D-OH). When he learned that neither of us was from Ohio, he politely asked us to leave.

What really mattered was that we were in Washington doing something. By now the Washington press corps was completely enamored of Kate, and we always notified them by e-mail and telephone when she was in town. Then we would just wait in one of the cafeterias for an interview. Even if we didn't have any congressional meetings, Kate would do an interview in one of the rotundas in the Senate or House office buildings, and she would tell the interviewer that her feet hurt because of all the meetings we had.

On Friday morning, we met with Bill Richard, Jim Oberstar's chief of staff. Kate was nauseous during that meeting and she spent most of the time in a nearby restroom. By now, I was more than capable of having meetings on my own, and had even developed an agenda that I asked Kate to stick to. I had also asked her to spend less time talking and more time listening. She didn't always follow my suggestions, but the meetings had improved since I had first started. Meanwhile, in Oberstar's office, I came away with quite a gem while Kate was in the restroom.

It seemed that Oberstar, the chairman of the committee that oversees the airlines and all other forms of transportation, had been bumped from a Northwest Airlines flight to Washington a few weeks earlier. He had to charter a plane to get back in time for an important meeting. That news wasn't going to change the world, but it was a nice little tidbit that nobody else knew, and it provided us with a wedge to have conversations with reporters about airline bumping compensation and policies – another airline passengers' rights issue that we would take on.

On Friday afternoon, Kate and I left Washington in my car – bound for Collegeville. We planned to play golf on Saturday, work for the rest of the weekend, and then return to Washington on Sunday night. As we headed out of the city in my eight-year old, four-door sedan, I made a wrong turn and found myself going the wrong way on a one-way street. That prompted Kate to tell me what a great driver she was – implying, perhaps correctly, that I wasn't. She said she owned a Lotus Elise that she raced on a track in California where all of the other drivers admired how good she was.

"I've never had a spin-out," she said.

"Me either," I said.

It's usually about a three-hour drive from Washington to Collegeville, but in the heavy outbound Washington traffic of that Friday afternoon, compounded by thunderstorms, it would take five hours. Kate, who seemed to always be on her cell phone, was having a strange and inappropriate conversation with someone.

"Who are you talking to?" I finally asked.

"I'll call you back," she said into the phone, and then she hung up. She told me that she had been talking to a guy from California who had seen a photograph of her, and he was fascinated with her hands. Apparently, he had told her that she had the most beautiful hands he had ever seen and he wanted to meet her to photograph them.

A day earlier, I had listened to her go into excruciating detail about her June 2006 assault with a reporter from the *San Francisco Chronicle.* Among other things, she told the reporter that, since her assault, she worried continuously about her personal safety and people stalking her.

"You're worried about stalkers and you've been talking for over an hour to some creep with a hand fetish?" I asked.

"Yeah, I guess you're right," she said.

She looked at her tote bag on the floor of the car, saw the *Kate Moon* CDs inside and said, "I'll just send him one of my CDs and then I won't talk to him anymore, okay? But I have to call him back and get his address."

"Kate!"

Later that evening, I dropped Kate off at a local Collegeville hotel. The next morning, we went to my club for a round of golf. When I introduced Kate to an exceptionally attractive female employee there, the two of them seemed to take an immediate, fascinating dislike to one another. Kate spent the next half-hour telling me that the other woman was jealous of her – resented the fact that another "queen bee" had invaded her territory.

"Women are intimidated by me," she said.

She added that, when she was selling real estate, she had to dress conservatively and devote most of her attention to wives because otherwise they would have seen her as a threat.

"It's the woman who chooses the house. That's how I made the sale."

With single male buyers it was a different story. She said she once sold a property to a man who told her at the closing that he had no idea why he was buying it.

"I don't doubt that for a second," I said.

Despite some of Kate's idiosyncrasies, I had already concluded that she may well have been the best salesperson I had ever seen. Realizing that the "one woman crusade" image wasn't politically effective, she had morphed her public persona into one that had the media believing that she was leading an army of volunteers and lobbyists, a thriving coalition of active and dedicated members.

Thanks in large part to Ed Mierzwinski and Paul Hudson and their connections, she had also garnered support for airline passengers' rights from U.S. PIRG, the National Association of Flight Attendants, Consumer's Union, the Consumer Federation of America and Public Citizen.

Ironically, the flight attendants' union later withdrew its support. Kate thought it was a personal vendetta against her by the union's female president. The AFA had issued a press release in June 2007 announcing support for passengers' rights, but soon thereafter Kate couldn't get anyone from the AFA to return an e-mail or telephone call. That would send Kate on a mission to discredit flight attendants. She would not forget the slight. A year later, reporter Joe Sharkey would write in his personal blog:

> Kate Hanni, of the passenger rights coalition, is prominently
> urging passengers to make video recordings of misbehavior by
> flight attendants and other untoward incidents on airplanes.

Kate and I spent the rest of the weekend working on a variety of issues. I wrote letters to each of the congressional offices we visited the prior week to thank them for their time. I also prepared and sent another newsletter:

> Kate and other coalition members called on several senators and
> representatives this week to fight for deplanement and other

language. We've made a great deal of progress on some
language, but we've hit a brick wall in getting definitive
deplanement language.

For those of you who can, please plan to be in DC this week to
meet with your Representative. Even if you can't make it to DC,
you might be able to set up a conference call with your
representative and Kate Hanni. If interested, please call Kate at
the number at the bottom of this email and we'll help set this up.

The *other coalition members* had been just me, of course. And except
for Lautenberg and Thompson, we hadn't met with any other senators or
representatives. Not surprisingly, we didn't get any volunteers to set up meetings or to help us lobby in Washington, although one gentleman from
Arizona responded that his congressman was useless.

We headed back to Washington on Sunday afternoon. When we reached
the Windsor Park hotel, Kate got out of the car and offered to help with the
bags. I told her I would get them while she checked in.

The Windsor Park had been Kate's base practically from the time she
first started coming to Washington, perhaps now a dozen times since. It was
a quaint, seven story hotel on Embassy Row. There were suites on each floor,
each with a dinette, an outer room with a sleeper, and a separate bedroom
with two double beds. Kate always got a suite.

The hotel lobby wasn't much larger than the living room in a middle-
class home, and having been there so many times, the desk clerks knew Kate
on sight. By the time I had the luggage transferred from my car to the lobby,
she had disappeared.

"Where did she go?" I asked the desk clerk.

He pointed toward the ceiling.

"Key?" I asked.

He eyed me suspiciously and handed me a room key, one of those old-
style keys with a room number tag and steel key attached.

I managed to squeeze myself and a luggage dolly into the one and only
tiny elevator, and pressed the floor button. A few moments later I knocked on
the door. A voice from inside asked, "Who is it?"

"Serial killer," I answered.

I heard a laugh. The door opened.

"Are you sure about this?" I asked.

"We'll save money," she said.

"What about the desk clerk?"

"I told him you were gay."

During our drive to Washington, I had asked Kate to call ahead and see
if she could reserve a room for me at her hotel. Up to this point, whenever I

had stayed overnight, I stayed at a Red Roof Inn about 25 miles north of Washington and commuted back and forth into the city by train. It didn't make sense for me to double-back 25 miles after I dropped her off. Kate had started to dial the number for her hotel, but then said she could barely afford to pay her own expenses, let alone mine. She suggested that we could share her hotel suite to save money. Her suite had a separate bedroom and it was "silly" for us to stay in separate hotel rooms when she had an entire bedroom that wasn't being used. She usually slept on the sleeper in the outer room, she said.

I thought that it was enough that I was putting so much time and effort into this endeavor. If I had to use my own money for expenses, I would have put a stop to this already. As I stood in the doorway of Kate's hotel room, a doorway that suddenly felt like a precipice, I thought, *we're both responsible adults, what can happen?*

That night, after a couple of glasses of wine, she let me know in no uncertain terms that she wanted to do more than save money in that hotel room. Later, as I watched her sleeping, I was more confused than ever. *I don't understand this woman at all,* I thought. I looked at her, wondered who she really was. She was intelligent, but in some ways she seemed to have the personality and judgment of a teenager which, ironically, was also part of her charm. She knew me well enough by then to know that she was safe with me, but seducing me, I thought, was an extraordinary risk, especially for someone who had been nearly raped and killed just 13 months earlier.

We had only one congressional meeting the next morning, so we spent the rest of the day working in a tiny office at US-PIRG, a few blocks from the Capitol. They had, by now, granted us use of the space when we were in town. Kate spent most of the afternoon talking to reporters on the telephone. I contacted about twenty congressional offices to see if we could get some appointments. I managed to secure only one meeting – with Congresswoman Zoe Lofgren (D-CA). Nevertheless, Kate wrote to one of our lawyers, "We visited 20 offices on Friday and will do at least another 20 today."

Propaganda, I learned, was not intended just for the media, the government and our members, but also for the other members of our inner circle – Corbett, Rubin, Mierzwinski and Hudson. There was now a circle within the inner circle, one that consisted of only two – Kate Hanni and me.

Meanwhile, I felt incredibly guilty about having slept with her. Kate noticed my pensive mood and spent the entire day saying, "You only live once, Mark." While she seemed completely at peace, even happy, I spent the entire day wondering who *I* was. The morning light brought with it both sobriety and the realization that there was no turning back. I couldn't undo it, but I still had the ability to stop it and leave. I didn't. I was living in a political adventure that I thought couldn't possibly get more interesting, and yet it had.

Later that afternoon, I took Kate to a medical clinic on Pennsylvania Avenue to deal with a possible health problem. While I was in the waiting room, a television tuned to CNN showed FBI agents swarming a house. The chyron said that the house belonged to Alaska Senator Ted Stevens. Stevens was the ranking member on the Senate Commerce Committee, and he had been a major obstacle in getting effective airline passengers' rights language added to the Senate's FAA reauthorization bill. The FBI's search warrant was based upon allegations that Stevens had lied on his Senate financial disclosure forms and that he had accepted undisclosed gifts and services from third parties.

When Kate emerged from her medical examination, I pointed to the screen and told her what was happening.

"Good, fry the son of a bitch," she said.

Six months later, Kate would participate in a joint press release with Mark Begich, the Democratic candidate running against Stevens for his seat. Begich had promised to support changes to the loopholes in Boxer's language which Stevens had blocked. Begich won the seat by less than a thousand votes. After he was elected, Begich withdrew support for changing the loopholes. Kate later sent me her theory on his change of heart.

"It's about the airlines threatening to remove air service to remote and not so remote areas that are vital to their economy. It's what happened to Begich."

Her point was that airlines were blackmailing some members of Congress – that they would stop servicing remote communities in their districts if they supported airline passengers' rights. This was just one of many conspiracy theories Kate had related to me about why Congress and the airlines behaved the way they did. She was also convinced that airline pilots intentionally stranded passengers on tarmacs because their contracts specified that they didn't get paid at all or as much when they were sitting at a gate. There was always some factual basis combined with a peculiar view of human nature behind these theories. She seemed to think that the airlines, and just about everyone who worked for them, were evil.

Leaving the clinic, we decided to have dinner at a nearby outdoor café. Over a couple of drinks, Kate leaned toward me with a wide smile and said, "Mark, make me famous. Make me a star."

"What do you think I've been doing for the last five months?" I asked.

She said that she wanted a television show or to be elected to some kind of political office. "We'll work together. It'll be fun!" she said.

"I'm the wrong person to get you all of that, Kate. I don't know how to do any of that. But I am going to help you to get this law passed. Maybe that will lead to those other things," I said.

Ironically, the *San Francisco Chronicle* published an article the next day about Kate's airline passengers' rights crusade and how her 2006 assault had inspired her to get involved in the cause. For some reason, the reporter included many of the excruciating details about the attack that I had listened to Kate tell him a week earlier:

> He forced her down again, pulled her shorts partly down and pushed up her shirt. She may have persuaded the man not to rape her by telling him that her first husband had died and that 'if you kill me, my son will have no parents and will kill himself.' In fact, her son had told her that. She kept repeating it, and in the Napa police report on the crime, she called it her 'mantra.'[15]

Her first husband had died years earlier, *but why was it necessary to tell the reporter all of that?* I wondered. Her life, apparently, was an open book.

Meanwhile, there at the outdoor café, I suggested that perhaps I should get another hotel room. Kate said she didn't want me to do that.

"What about your husband," I asked.

"I'm not worried," she replied.

I didn't know what that meant and it wasn't my place to ask. All I knew was that my wife would castrate, kill and then divorce me – in that order.

Months later, after I conceded that I found Kate attractive before our first night together, she wrote, "But it's so flattering to know that you thought I was that attractive before anything happened, because you never let on. You played it totally cool."

I wasn't blind – I had *played it cool* because I was married and so was she. Heretofore, it had been easy to preserve the vows I made when I had gotten married 12 years earlier. But those vows had never been tested like this – a test I had now failed. Kate and I weren't just working together on some business project – our personal fates had become intertwined. We were going to succeed together or we were going to fail together, and we were going to do it on a national scale. There was something uniquely irresistible and exciting about all of that. Whatever our respective reasons, Kate and I would save a lot of money on hotel rooms in the future.

AUGUST 2007

Wiggle words

WE SPENT THE rest of that week working on airline passengers' rights in our tiny office at PIRG. On August 3, Governor Eliot Spitzer signed the New York airline passengers' bill of rights into law. Kate was upset that they didn't include any quotes from her in the press release his office put on the wire, so we issued our own:

> We commend Assemblyman Michael Gianaris, State Senator
> Charles Fuschillo and Governor Eliot Spitzer for their
> leadership in granting passengers on flights operating out of
> New York food, water, fresh air, power, and working restrooms
> on any flight that has left the gate and been on the tarmac for
> more than three hours.

On Friday afternoon, Kate and I went to the U.S. Department of Transportation for our first meetings with officials from that department. One of our meetings was with Inspector General (IG) Calvin Scovel and members of his staff.

The primary focus of that meeting was the IG's investigation into Kate's tarmac stranding and the Valentine's Day strandings. DOT Secretary Mary Peters had directed the IG's office to conduct that investigation prior to the Senate hearing in April. The results were to be published in a report that was expected to drive future rulemakings and actions by the DOT on the subject of tarmac delays and other airline consumer issues.

The only thing the IG would tell us was that the report was scheduled for release in late August, although they had already provided a summary of the results of their investigation into Kate's tarmac stranding. Kate didn't like their summary, and she complained that their investigation into her stranding incident was flawed.

When two investigators from the IG's office interviewed Kate three months earlier on May 4, she told them that they had no food, potable water, and the restrooms weren't functional while they were on the tarmac in

Austin. When one of those investigators telephoned her husband to ask for his recollection, he apparently contradicted Kate. According to the IG's report, he told them that flight attendants had distributed pretzels and crackers, and there was also a "by request service" during which the flight attendants asked passengers in each row what they wanted to drink. "There were various beverages such as sodas, juices, Bloody Mary mix available towards the front of the plane."

There at our meeting, Kate told the IG that her husband didn't understand the question and that they should interview him again.

Apparently, representatives from American Airlines had distributed a paper to the press and the IG's office during the House Aviation Subcommittee hearing in April. The paper essentially said that Kate had not been truthful about the details of her stranding and that news reports about other victims on other airplanes had been exaggerated as well. American said it had sent buses to the airplanes and given passengers an opportunity to deplane, in some cases twice.

Some passengers took the opportunity to get off the planes while others didn't. Some thought they might still make it to Dallas on their flights, and five of the eleven planes diverted to Austin did complete that journey. American also said they had serviced the restrooms and provided snacks and water to the planes while they were on the tarmac. During our meeting with the IG, Kate emphasized that she had not lied about any of these things.

I sat quietly through all of this, but I wondered why this was the first I had heard about American's paper.

Later that afternoon, we also had our first meeting with the operational side of the DOT and several of its high level officials. The main subject of that meeting was airline customer service plans. We came armed with copies of the analysis of the seven customer service plans that I had done for Senator Boxer's office in July. In those plans were interesting airline wiggle phrases such as "we will endeavor" to give passengers the opportunity to deplane after a certain number of hours. We wanted to know if those plans were enforceable.

Because of the ambiguity of those phrases, the DOT officials said they were powerless to penalize carriers for not adhering to them. There were other subjects discussed, but the main reason for these meetings was to get face time with the officials, and to demonstrate that we were knowledgeable, professional, organized and credible. To that end, I would later send them a thank you letter and include minutes of the meetings from my notes.

I took Kate to the airport later that evening for her flight back to San Francisco. I'd spent the last ten days with her, the past five sharing her room. I told her that it had been great fun, but that if I found out that American Airlines had given her an opportunity to get off that airplane in Austin, I was "outta here." Such a revelation would have likely negated everything we had done or would ever do in the future.

"They're lying, Mark," she said.

A FEW DAYS later, Kate wrote to me and others that she'd had enough of her latest stalker – sort of:

> I have a problem with one of our hotline callers who is now leaving me 'stalker' like messages. ... He calls several times a day and wants to talk, now he's angry that I won't take his calls and is getting somewhat threatening saying I'm just like his 'rich' ex-wife. ... I'm going to write him a firmly written letter explaining that I don't have time to chat idly ...

IN EARLY AUGUST, Burt Rubin had floated an idea: Build some kind of airplane somewhere in or near Washington, and challenge members of Congress to come and sit in the plane to experience the conditions that passengers endure when they're stuck on an airplane for several hours. We could call it a "Strand-In," a contemporary version of the sit-in student protests of the 1960s.

It sounded crazy to me at first, but sometimes doing something off-beat is an effective way to draw attention to a cause. We weren't making any progress in getting deplanement language in the House or Senate FAA reauthorization bills, and more publicity could help make that happen.

Ed Mierzwinski visited the National Park Service office in Washington to get a permit to hold the event on the National Mall, and then asked me to take over from there.

I searched the Internet for something that we might be able to use for an airplane. I found a portable carport made of steel tubing and a large tarpaulin cover. The carport arrived in my driveway on August 16. I stood for a long time looking at the six large cardboard boxes. What we were planning was a make or break moment. If we failed to pull this off, it would be a major embarrassment. If we succeeded, we might be able to attract enough public interest and pressure to get the amendments we needed into the FAA reauthorization bills in the House and Senate. Those bills were scheduled to be voted on by the end of September. The Strand-In, I thought, would be our grand finale, less than two weeks before those votes.

The *jet*, as we began to refer to it, would be the centerpiece of the event, but all it was now was a 780-square-foot Polypropylene tarp and 400 nuts, bolts and steel tubes that would have to be assembled by 11 a.m. on the day of the Strand-In. There were a thousand things that needed to be done – an effort that would rival any project I had ever managed in my previous life. I prepared a list of action items and sent it to Kate. She replied with what she probably thought was an inspirational response:

> This will prove to be a book and a movie and we will all be
> included. One commitment you have from me is no matter what
> I'm loyal to a fault and you can count on that I will never
> forsake you for any glory that may come my way. ... I will
> endeavor to include you in all the glory and have you
> experience the kudos you so justly deserve ...

I replied to her, "I see an airline wiggle word in there – 'endeavor' ... I think Continental uses that word [in their customer service plan] when they talk about deplanement. Not enforceable."

It took me two days to assemble the tubular infrastructure of the carport in my yard. Over the next four weeks, I would tear it down and rebuild it several times, looking for ways to reduce the time. The best I could do was six hours. We were going to need help. I sent several newsletters asking for volunteers, but I got no responses.

I thought perhaps one of the local high schools might view the Strand-In as a useful civics project for students interested in government or politics. I contacted principals from two local schools. The superintendent for one of the school districts nixed the idea on the basis that the Strand-In was going to occur on a school day. The principal for the other school district said it didn't fit into their curriculum.

I visited a local college to see if there were any politically motivated groups there, and I placed an ad in the college's student newspaper. A friend of mine had a son at Georgetown and I started corresponding with him to see if he could get some of his fellow students motivated to show up to help. That didn't work out either. I ran into dead ends at every turn.

The funny thing was, while everyone had heard about the JetBlue strandings, nobody I talked to had ever heard of CAPBOR or Kate, and they had no idea what we were doing. Despite the fact that Kate and I worked on the issue all day, every day, and Kate had done many interviews over the past eight months, we hadn't penetrated the public consciousness as much as we thought. It was disheartening, but it just meant we needed to work harder.

By late August I was working from dawn until midnight every day. I spent the daylight hours working on the jet and communicating with the U.S. National Park Service in Washington to coordinate the event on the National Mall. At night there were legislative issues to review, newsletters and press releases to write, media requests to respond to, and many other things.

Kate spent every day pitching stories to the press and, despite the lack of public interest, she was always able to find some media outlet to run something to increase the volume. In one of many stories of its kind, on August 19 she appeared in a lengthy segment on Fox News' *Hannity's America*. The segment was based on Kate's pitch to the show's producers: "Our hotline has gotten over 4000 calls from passengers stranded on airplanes just since June 13." She repeated that statement during the interview.

She had provided the producers with the names of two people that had been stuck on tarmacs in the two months since the hotline was announced. Fox News produced a segment that echoed the CAPBOR mantra, that airline passengers were being held on airport tarmacs for hours on end with no food, no water, and overflowing lavatories – almost every day.

She was also pitching the Strand-In to the media. She told reporters that we were going to have "two-hundred high school and college students, and fifty pissed-off airline passengers." She even started to tell reporters that we had celebrities coming to the event to give speeches. In an interview with Frommer's Travel, Kate said;

> Angelina Jolie and David Beckham evidently have had some
> problems with the airlines, and so we don't know if they will be
> there or not, but right now, we're in the process of hoping that
> that happens – possibly Dana Carvey. [16]

I asked her what would happen when reporters showed up at the Strand-In and none of these students or other people were there.

"Don't worry about it," she said. "They won't remember."

There was something fascinating about all of this at the time; perhaps it was being the only other person who was in on the gag. It seemed harmless enough. Except for Beckham, Carvey and Jolie, who would know that she was making it up?

Meanwhile, I spent several days designing the exterior of the jet, which we had by now christened the "Mock-I." The *fuselage* would feature our website address, "FlyersRights.org," in bright orange letters across the top on both sides. There would be 14 airplane-style windows on each side. Doors, wings and pin-stripes would be simulated with the use of black duct tape. I would place an American flag on each side in the rear, and I would affix CAPBOR logos to the doors – all inspired by Air Force One.

I created the letters and windows on my computer, printed them on sheets of decal paper, cut them out with scissors and fastened them to the tarp. It was a disaster.

SEPTEMBER 2007

On a roll

BY SEPTEMBER 10, between exposure to the sun, and spraying them with water to simulate possible rain conditions, the decals were covered with ugly, dark spots. The edges curled, and most of the decals had peeled off and fallen to the ground. None of the glues I tried would hold anything in place, and it was only nine days until the Strand-In in Washington.

Despite the fact that everything I had read indicated that paint wouldn't adhere to the Polypropylene tarp, I began to experiment with different types of paints and colors. Black and white rust inhibitor paints – that I would need for the windows – held up well to both sun and moisture. The orange paint I would need for the website letters didn't fare as well, but I reasoned that I could use a brush to touch up any letters that might flake off. I didn't want to have to paint all of that by hand though. There were 30 letters and 28 windows, and everything would require at least two coats of paint. Now I had no choice. I prayed for fair weather.

That night, despite my growing doubts that the Mock-I would be ready in time, I created formal Strand-In invitations for Congress, including a map that showed the location for the event on the mall. We had them faxed to all 535 members of the House and Senate.

Also, despite multiple requests in recent newsletters, we still couldn't find a single CAPBOR volunteer to help me build the Mock-I on the mall. Fortunately, Ed Mierzwinski came to the rescue with a PIRG intern who was willing to help for $10 per hour.

On September 11, Joe Sharkey interviewed me by telephone about the Strand-In. His story appeared in Conde Nast's *Portfolio* magazine a week later. The article was titled "The Ralph Nader of the Skies." The article said, "Kate Hanni's persistence, paired with public outrage over air-travel horror stories, got a Passengers' Bill of Rights to Congress."[17] He wrote about me; "Mogel was one of hundreds of volunteers who casually signed up and soon found themselves putting in long days for Hanni."

After I stopped laughing about the "hundreds of volunteers," I wondered what public outrage he was talking about. Sharkey would have no way of knowing that I was unable to find even one volunteer to help set up the Mock-I on the mall. He also couldn't have known that we had raised a grand total of about $20,000 from a pool of now, according to Kate, 18,000 out-raged members. But I wondered where he got the notion that there was "public outrage." There had been a sense of public outrage seven months earlier after the JetBlue tarmac strandings, but that outrage had since waned.

Even 18 months later, NPR would release ratings figures stating it had a cumulative audience of 20.9 million listeners per week. One month after that, NPR would run a week-long series about airline passengers' woes on its highly rated *Morning Edition* program. They invited listeners to participate in an online poll about airline passengers' rights. The survey garnered less than 4,000 votes – 80 percent in favor – 3,200 people.[18] According to government statistics, over 700 million passengers step onto an airplane in the United States every year.

WORKING FROM DAWN until dusk for three days, I finished painting the windows and the website address. I had also painted things such as "Help" and "SOS" in red paint on some of the windows to make it appear as though a stranded passenger had frantically written those pleas using a tube of lipstick from the inside.

Finally, I pulled the tarp over the tubular infrastructure and took a photograph. Just two days before the dress rehearsal, the Mock-I was ready for takeoff – and it was magnificent.

The Mock-I, September 15, 2007 – Copyright © 2007-2012 Mark S. Mogel

On Saturday, I loaded a rented panel truck with the Mock-I, a stereo system, a portable camping toilet, a generator, extension cords, trash cans, tools and other equipment. Kate had flown to Washington earlier that day, and I drove down to meet her at the Windsor Park.

We hadn't discussed much about the personal nature of our previous trip since I dropped her off at the airport in August. Then, a few days prior to this trip, she sent me an e-mail that described in graphic detail what she wanted to do when we met again in Washington. She included a risqué photograph of herself and wrote, "Now that's worth thinking about while doing all this other stuff yes?"

"Uh, yeah," I replied.

When I arrived in the lobby of the Windsor Park, the desk clerk recognized me and handed me a key to Kate's room – without a word.

The next morning, I left Kate at the hotel and drove the panel truck to Lincoln Park, about ten blocks east of the Capitol. I had arranged to meet the PIRG intern there to rehearse building the Mock-I. He brought a friend to help, also for $10 per hour. Unfortunately, after we only had about a third of the infrastructure built, the U.S. Park Police appeared and told us to tear it down because we didn't have a permit.

That was okay. We had erected enough of the tubular sections that the PIRG intern and his friend got the general idea of how to build it. It was mostly repetition after that. We would have less than four hours to build it on the National Mall – where we did have a permit for the 19th – and I was now confident that it could be done with their help.

Kate had previously notified members of the Washington news media about the dress rehearsal, and some of them arrived while we were building the Mock-I. Since Kate wasn't yet there, Del Quentin Wilber from the *Washington Post* interviewed me. Most of his questions about my history and motivation were easy to answer, but then he asked how many people actively volunteered to work for the coalition.

I had been asked this question before by other reporters and I had a stock answer; "I don't know. You'll have to ask Kate." As if on cue, Kate's taxi arrived at that moment. I walked over to help her out and told her what Wilber was asking.

"No problem!" she said.

OK, I thought. *This should be interesting.* Wilber wasn't like most of the other reporters I had talked to up to this point. He didn't want sound bites. He wanted details, job descriptions and phone numbers for other people he could contact. When he asked Kate the same question, she gave him Ed Mierzwinski and Paul Hudson.

Shit, I could have done that, I thought.

"Any others?" he asked.

"Well we have 18,000 members, I don't have them all memorized. I'll have to get back to you with the others," she said.

During the interview, Kate told Wilber that coalition members had donated about $20,000 so far, but that wasn't enough to pay for all of her expenses, so she and her husband had taken out a line of credit on their home. Wilber, with an apparent interest in the psychology behind everything she was doing, seemed particularly interested in why Kate would take out a second mortgage, essentially mortgaging the future of her children, to lobby for airline passengers' rights.

Fortunately, he didn't ask the questions that crossed my mind. *If you have 18,000 members, why do you need a second mortgage to pay expenses, and why are we paying these interns to help build the Mock-I?*

Instead he asked her why she didn't organize people to protest something important like the Iraq War. Kate said that she was dedicated to airline passengers' rights because it was a subject that she understood having been the victim of a tarmac stranding.

She handled most of the interview very well, but knowing what I knew about her dream of fame, I had the distinct impression that Wilber could see right through her. He had asked probing psychological questions, and I worried that his article might not be favorable, that he would burst our bubble and the party would be over.

Meanwhile, the interns and I spread the tarp on the ground so the other reporters could get an idea what the Mock-I looked like. Then I paid the interns and let them go. Kate took the reporters on a tour, walking around the tarp and explaining the inscriptions on the windows. Then she did a couple of television interviews.

After the television crews left, Kate and I folded up the tarp and packed it in the van. Because some of the equipment blocked access to the passenger's seat, Kate had to ride in the back of the van.

"Remind me to put something in the book about this," she said, "Barbie sitting in the back of a panel truck with all these tubes, generators and trash cans. How do you think those interviews went?"

"You were great on the television interviews, but if Wilber writes a story that sounds anything like the questions he was asking, we could be finished. You're going to look like some kind of a nut," I said.

She called Wilber. When she got off the phone, she said there was no reason to worry. "His story isn't about any of that," she said.

I drove home later that night, but I would return in a couple of days. Wilber's story appeared in the *Washington Post* the next day and my concerns had been unfounded – the article was entirely positive:

> Mogel, who remains angry about lengthy tarmac delays he has
> suffered as a business traveler, joined Hanni's group after seeing
> her interviewed on C-Span in February … He said he has come
> to admire her energy and tenacity. 'The airlines picked a fight
> with the wrong woman,' he said.[19]

I drove back to Washington on Tuesday afternoon, the day before the Strand-In. I had been on the road for about an hour when I started to get calls from several reporters and television producers because they couldn't reach Kate. They wanted more details and background for the event. Even someone from the FAA called to ask if we would mind if they sent their public relations crew to cover the Strand-In.

I didn't feel safe driving at 65 miles-per-hour while talking on the phone and writing down telephone numbers, so I called Kate. Annette Hagan answered Kate's phone. Hagan was Kate's best friend from Napa. She had flown in from California to attend the Strand-In, and she was staying in Kate's suite for a few days, which was why I had left.

"Where is Kate?" I asked.

Hagan said that the Air Transport Association was having an outdoor event somewhere, and that Kate had hired someone to wear a Pinocchio suit to go with her to crash the ATA's party and steal the attention of any members of the news media that were there. The point was to demonstrate that the airlines were lying about tarmac statistics, and that American

Airlines was lying when they claimed that Kate exaggerated the circumstances of her stranding.

Great idea, I thought, *but focus please!*

"Annette, somebody has to take these media calls. Kate's voicemail is full, so reporters are calling me. I'm driving on I-95 and I can't handle all of this now."

I no sooner got off the phone with Hagan, when I got a call from an officer at the National Park Service.

"Mr. Mogel, we're seeing reports in the press that you are planning to build a jet on the mall tomorrow. We can't let you do that. You didn't say anything about building a jet in your application, and you can understand that ever since 9/11 there's a great sensitivity to doing something like that, especially on the National Mall."

"It isn't a jet. It just looks like a jet. It's a carport, a portable garage that's painted to look like a jet fuselage," I explained.

"Fuselage – Mr. Mogel ..."

"I sent you guys a photograph in the application!" I exclaimed.

Unfortunately, the photograph I sent to them weeks earlier was of the unpainted carport from the vendor's website, not the finished Mock-I. I spent several minutes explaining that we had four congressmen and dozens of reporters coming to the event, and that the Mock-I was central to the event. Finally, the officer said I could show up and start to build it, but if it looked anything like a jet, I was going to have to tear it down.

When I got to Kate's suite at the Windsor Park, I met Kate's friend, Annette Hagan, and a woman named Anjum Malik. Continental Airlines had lost a precious heirloom that had been in Malik's family for generations. She had brought the heirloom onto an airplane in her carry-on bag. A flight attendant later checked the bag into the cargo hold without Malik's knowledge. When Malik reached her destination, the bag and the heirloom were nowhere to be found. According to Malik, Continental refused to help her recover her bag or compensate her for the lost valuables, so she had joined CAPBOR in the hope of bringing attention to these types of issues.

Kate was lying on the floor with a bag of ice under her head.

"Is everything, okay?" she asked. "I'm really worried about tomorrow."

"Everything is fine," I lied. "Where's the alcohol?"

Later, I retired to a room that Kate had rented for me elsewhere in the hotel. The next morning, I got up at five and drove the panel truck to the National Mall.

Washington was eerily quiet at that hour, the streets nearly deserted. It was still dark when I turned onto one of the gravel paths usually restricted to pedestrian traffic. I was about four blocks east of the Washington Monument. The park service had given me a permit to drive onto the mall, but I still I expected someone to challenge me and ask what I was doing. No one did.

I could see the Capitol bathed in light in the rearview mirror, and the Washington Monument through the windshield – heard only the sound of gravel crunching beneath the tires. I was driving a panel truck down the middle of the National Mall at 5:30 in the morning, and there wasn't anyone in sight. It was surreal.

The park service had granted us a parcel of land between 12th and 13th Streets, one block from the Washington Monument. When I reached the site, I stopped the truck and got out. I pictured the layout of the Mock-I. I decided to set it up so that when Kate stood at the podium, the Mock-I would be visible over her left shoulder and the Capitol would be visible over her right. It would make for historic television images and photographs.

The location was flanked by the Smithsonian Museum of American History on one side and a Metro station on the other. We would get a fair amount of tourist traffic. There was no rain in the forecast. Everything was perfect.

I started to unload the truck. I still had to carry everything about 30 yards across the grass to a spot I judged to be the exact center of the mall. The park service had also been very specific that no vehicles were permitted on the grass, and their paperwork said that if any of their rules were violated they would shut down the event immediately – no questions asked.

I had the truck half unloaded when the PIRG intern and his friend showed up at seven. Dawn broke over the mall as we started to erect the tubular infrastructure. Soon, television satellite trucks started to line up on the side streets. A female CNN producer approached and asked me how long it was going to take to build the jet. She said they were doing a live shot at nine and they wanted the Mock-I in the background.

"But we won't be ready until eleven," I said. "Who told you we would be ready by nine?" I asked.

"Kate," she said.

"I'll do the best I can," I said. "I can't promise anything though."

"Anything I can do to make it go faster?" she asked.

"Grab a wrench," I said.

By 9 a.m., with the help of the CNN producer, we had enough of the infrastructure built so that we could pull the tarp over it. There was still a lot to do, but CNN got their shot.

I noticed a park police vehicle parked nearby. One of the officers walked over to take a look.

"Is this okay?" I asked.

"Yes," he said. "Just don't close up the ends. We need to be able to see what's going on inside."

"No problem," I said with a sigh of relief.

As I had previously arranged, a rental company delivered folding tables, 50 chairs, a podium, a backup generator and other equipment. I had left no stone unturned. Nothing could go wrong. I had backups for backups. That delivery was followed by the delivery of a 40-inch television on which we were going to run a montage of Kate's television interviews.

Inside the Mock-I, we arranged the chairs in rows like the inside of an airplane. We played the sounds of crying babies through the stereo system. The portable toilet was filled with faux feces to simulate overflowing commodes. A humidifier sprayed a foul odor from a liquid Kate had found on the Internet called "Smell of Ass." Everything went like clockwork – we finished just before 11 a.m. I paid the interns, thanked them, and let them go.

More than a dozen television cameras were lined up in front of the podium. There were reporters everywhere. I saw Wilber in the crowd and walked over to thank him for his story in the *Washington Post.* As I approached, I overheard two reporters talking.

One asked, "Where are all the students and passengers they said would be here? All I see are reporters."

The other replied, "It doesn't really matter does it? They got *us* here."

Kate was milling around, talking to other reporters. She had never seen the fully assembled Mock-I in person.

"What do you think?" I asked.

"It looks great! Can you write up some notes for me? I didn't bring any," she said.

"Way ahead of you," I said.

I handed her the introductions I had already written.

"Thank you for all of this," she said, "I'll see you later tonight."

"What about Annette?" I asked.

"I'll tell her I have to go out for an interview," she said.

Four Congressmen had accepted our invitations to speak at the event, including Lloyd Doggett, a Democrat representing a district in Austin, Texas – Anjum Malik's home town and the site of Kate's tarmac stranding in 2006.

John Hall (D-NY), a former lead guitarist for the band Orleans, wore a "When You Gotta Go, You Gotta Go" T-shirt and sat in the Mock-I for photographs. Annette Hagan and Cindy Bouchard snagged several passers-by, tourists, to sit in the plane to make it look full.

Ron Klien (D-FL) announced that he had gotten an amendment in the FAA reauthorization bill that would require the Transportation Department to investigate more consumer complaints, including flight cancellations, overbooking, baggage concerns, and other issues.

But the most important news was delivered in the speech given by Kate's congressman, Mike Thompson. After one committee approves a bill, it typically goes to other committees for their approval. In the case of the FAA reauthorization bill in the House, the bill had to go to through the Ways and Means Committee for approval of whatever funding was necessary to implement the bill. The chairman of the Ways and Means Committee was Charles Rangel (D-NY).

Apparently, Rangel had told Oberstar and Costello that he wouldn't approve the bill unless they included deplanement language. At the Strand-In, Thompson announced that Oberstar and Costello had relented to the pressure, and they added language that would require airlines to define a timeframe for deplanement during long tarmac delays. It wasn't perfect because it didn't specify a time limit, but it was a huge step forward. We hadn't been able to get Oberstar or Costello to budge on this issue for months.

Although Thompson had worked behind the scenes to encourage Rangel to get the deplanement language added, there had also been external pressure that I learned about from an article published later that day:

> Charles B. Rangel, D-N.Y., chairman of the House Ways and Means Committee, which contributed the tax title to the reauthorization till, said he expected a debate focused on money. Instead, his committee was inundated with complaints from airline passengers.

> 'I was a little surprised that when this issue actually came before the full committee, rather than dealing with the question of revenue, I had to deal with the issue of outrage,' Rangel said.[20]

At the time I thought that it was an amazing accomplishment because it meant that the coalition had exerted that pressure on Chairman Rangel and his Ways and Means Committee. The public at large wouldn't have had any idea that any of this was going on, so it had to have been the coalition.

It was also a surprise to me because by then I was convinced that the coalition was mostly an illusion. Kate had convinced a few faces to show up at an event or to lobby now and then, but for the past five months, she and I were doing 99 percent of the work and lobbying ourselves.

Earlier in the month, I had written and sent two newsletters. Both newsletters urged the coalition to call, fax and e-mail members of the Ways and Means Committee and ask them to amend the FAA reauthorization bill to include deplanement language. Remarkably, the coalition had responded in a big way, and for the next two years this was a complete mystery to me.

We had run campaigns like that in the past, always asked for people to e-mail us back to let us know they had contacted someone. The response rate had been dismal at best – probably around one percent – less than two hundred people, not nearly enough to constitute a wave of public outrage for one congressman let alone an entire committee.

Two years later, I would wonder how it was possible that the Ways and Means Committee had been "inundated with complaints from airline passengers" – presumably our members. I went back through my e-mails for September 2007. I had been so busy with other matters at the time that there were dozens that I hadn't read. And there, buried in an e-mail thread, I found that Kate had once again enlisted the help of a third party to generate thousands of letters using the petition. Rangel and his Ways and Means Committee hadn't been inundated by complaints sent from airline passengers. They had been inundated by thousands of letters sent from Kate's fax machine.

When congressional offices receive comments about any particular issue from their constituents, whether by phone, fax, or e-mail, they keep a tally on a spreadsheet or something similar. While most congressional offices have processes in place to account for the calling and letter-writing campaigns sponsored by many organizations every day, they don't have the ability to tell if someone would use the names of their constituents to generate letters on their behalf.

ONE DAY AFTER the Strand-In, Jerry Costello and Jim Oberstar amended the FAA reauthorization bill to include the deplanement language, and then the House of Representatives voted on the first piece of federal airline passengers' rights legislation ever to come before the legislative branch of the federal government.

We watched the vote unfold on C-SPAN from the conference room at PIRG. When the ayes reached the one-vote majority of 218, we celebrated with cheers and hugs. In less than eight months, we had achieved what many had told us would be nearly impossible.

The next day, Kate and I drove the panel truck and the Mock-I back to Collegeville. I had arranged for Kate to stay in a neighbor's guest house. We spent the weekend working on her testimony for a hearing the following week, and then we returned to Washington on Monday. Three days later, Kate again testified before the House Aviation Subcommittee. At the end of the hearing, Chairman Costello offered these closing remarks:

> Let me say to Ms. Hanni, as Chairman Oberstar said, we not
> only thank you but your members for your active involvement,
> and I would tell you that we are only halfway through the
> process, and I would encourage you to spend time over on the
> other side of the Capitol, in the other body, to inspire them and
> to make certain that they take a look at H.R. 2881. If they do,
> we think that if those provisions are contained in a final

legislation signed by the President that it will go a long way to helping passengers in the future.

It's impossible to quantify the amount of publicity we got from the Strand-In. It was covered by every broadcast, cable network and print medium. It led on Internet news teasers like America Online, and the story continued to appear in the media for weeks afterward. But the Strand-In was more than just a grand publicity achievement. Because of the obvious effort and complexity of putting on such an event, it added to the illusion that there was a large, vibrant organization behind Kate. Nobody could have dreamed that it was put together by just two people, and it elevated Kate's and CAPBOR's status even higher.

Combined with Chairman Rangel's pressure on Chairmen Oberstar and Costello to include deplanement language in the bill, ostensibly based on overwhelming public pressure on his committee, people came out of the woodwork with offers to befriend and assist Kate.

There was a vice president from Flightstats.com, a former Inspector General for the Department of Transportation, a high level official for the National Air Traffic Controllers Association, and the president of the trade group that represents all of the major airports in the country, just to name a few. And on September 27, President George W. Bush ordered Secretary Mary Peters and FAA Administrator Robert Sturgell to "present him with a plan to do two things: reduce air congestion, which has brought gridlock to the skies; and improve the flying experience of passengers."[21]

We were on a roll. More importantly, no two people could have been working harder and yet having as much fun.

AT THE END of September, I learned something I didn't know about appropriations bills. If Congress can't agree on a new one, they extend the old one. Disagreement over the user fee issue had prevented the FAA reauthorization bill from being voted out of the Senate Commerce Committee, and this extension would supposedly give senators time to resolve their differences. And so my involvement with Kate and airline passengers' rights was also extended.

OCTOBER 2007

The Ralph Nader of the Skies

ON OCTOBER 1, in what had become one of my customs, I wrote and sent thank-you letters, in Kate's name, to the congressmen who attended the Strand-In. I also sent letters to Jerry Costello, Jim Oberstar, other key congressmen, including Charlie Rangel, to thank them for adding deplanement language to the FAA reauthorization bill.

Back in Napa, Kate sent Joe Sharkey and me a draft of a couple of chapters that she thought might be included in their book. One of the chapters was, by turns, a comedic and profoundly harrowing account of her assault, and the humor was intentional. She wrote to Sharkey, "I'm not a great writer but hopefully you can see the tragedy and humor and see if it's redeemable in any way, shape or form!"

One of the things that immediately struck me upon reading the account of her assault was that she had written that the masked assailant had made the appointment to see the vacant house by calling her cell phone.

That's one stupid criminal, I thought. I called Kate.

"Kate, did the police look at your cell phone?" I asked.

"No, why?" she asked.

I told her that all they had to do was look at her incoming calls and trace the number, that they could subpoena the phone records from her cell phone provider. "They still can," I said.

She said that the Napa police were incompetent and that they also lost hair and blood DNA evidence. She said that she was also 99 percent sure who the assailant was, that she gave the police his name, but they never interviewed him. She also told me name of the person she suspected.

"I'm so sorry," I said. "That had to make the whole situation even worse."

"It was horrible," she said. She explained that, shortly after her assault she had spent a month in treatment, recovering from the trauma at a health spa in Antigua. Soon after she returned, she felt like she had made a lot of progress. Then the tarmac stranding in December had brought back all of the feelings of being trapped and helpless. She said she didn't want to talk about the assault and the past anymore – she just wanted to move forward to get a tarmac law passed.

I told her that she might very well be the most courageous person I had ever met. "That whole story scares the shit out of me," I said. And it did.

When I was a youngster, I experienced a rape incident that scarred me for life, although I was not the victim. A friend and I had been hiking along a river, following a set of railroad tracks through a heavily wooded area. A man approached us from behind, said that he worked for the railroad and that we were trespassing.

We apologized, but the man said that wasn't good enough. He said he was going to take my friend down to the river bank to "teach him a lesson." The man told me to stay where I was, that he would be back for me. In what was perhaps the most pivotal moment of my life, he had chosen my friend to take first, to rape – a concept that, at that young age, I wasn't even aware of. But I knew that whatever was happening, it wasn't good.

When they disappeared through some trees and down the bank toward the river, I climbed an embankment on the other side of the tracks and ran to a factory beyond. I found an open door and stumbled in, dazed and confused. The men working inside looked at me as if to ask, "What are you doing here, kid?" I was so terrified that I couldn't speak. I opened my mouth, but no words would come out. I had no idea what was happening or what to say.

I left the factory and back-tracked the route my friend and I had come. I stopped on the other side of a bridge over the river that I knew he had to cross to get home. Sometime later, I can't remember how long, my friend made it back across the bridge. We sat and talked for a long while. He told me things that the man had done to him that were unimaginable; so abhorrent, so painful, that I thought I would throw up. We cried for hours.

I was so disappointed in myself that I hadn't been brave, hadn't done something to try to stop it – hadn't told someone in the factory that my friend was in trouble. I was so terrified by whatever unknown horror was occurring that I had been paralyzed, although there had been nothing wrong with my feet. I felt like a coward, and would carry the guilt and shame of that day for the rest of my life.

I empathized with Kate more than she could have known. I understood the feelings of helplessness, the horror, the terror of an assault or rape. Those demons had been tormenting me for the past forty years. I could have been the victim that day, and in lesser ways I was. Yet, in stark contrast with Kate's account of her incident, there was nothing remotely humorous about mine. Even forty years later, the memory of that incident, and the devastating effect it had on my friend, could still reduce me to tears and despair.

When I read Kate's account of her assault and saw the humor interspersed with the drama, it seemed inappropriate to me, almost impossible. *I guess we all deal with trauma in our own ways,* I thought.

IN RESPONSE TO President Bush's commercial aviation improvement edict in September, DOT Secretary Mary Peters and FAA Administrator Robert Sturgell had announced that they would convene a task force of industry experts and consumer representatives to look into gridlock in and around the New York City area airports. According to the DOT, the JFK, LaGuardia and Newark airports were responsible for one-third of the country's flight delays, and each delay at one of those airports had a ripple effect that caused delays at other airports around the country.

One of the causes for the delays at these airports was that the airlines scheduled more flights than the airports could handle even in ideal weather conditions. Flight delays worsened further when weather conditions and visibility deteriorated because, for safety reasons, air traffic controllers imposed greater spacing between aircraft. Another cause for the delays was congestion in the skies around these busy airports. Over 3,500 flights operate every day in an airspace that is only about 100-square-miles. The task force was charged with finding solutions to these problems.

David Stempler (president of the Air Traveler's Association) and Kevin Mitchell (chairman of the Business Travel Coalition) were chosen to represent consumers' interests on the task force. Each of them had been representing consumer interests for years, and despite the fact that she had only been on the scene for about nine months, Kate was furious that she wasn't selected. She decided to mount a public character assassination crusade against both of them.

Stempler and Mitchell, then well-known consumer advocates to one degree or another, were each on the record with their opposition to passengers' rights legislation. Mitchell had testified in that regard during same hearings in which Kate appeared. He had said that legislation wasn't necessary; that it would result in higher airfares and more flight cancellations. He believed that the marketplace would take care of the tarmac stranding problem, although he conceded some level of federal oversight was probably necessary to enforce existing airline customer service plans. Stempler had publicly espoused similar views.

At first, I didn't think Kate was serious about the character assassination plan, but when she learned that Kevin Mitchell lived about ten miles from me, she asked me to go to his house on a trash day to steal his garbage. She wanted me to look for any papers that might reveal connections with airlines, other organizations, or anything else that could undermine his credibility as a consumer advocate.

"Kate, you can't be serious," I said. I told her I wouldn't do it.

She actually got angry at me and said that she would hire a private investigator to do it. I told her to imagine the headlines if somebody got caught stealing trash for her, and that tactic was abandoned, although she persisted with her overall crusade.

Ever since Joe Sharkey's *Ralph Nader of the Skies* article was published, Kate was determined to someday wear that crown. She wasn't as worried about Stempler's and Mitchell's positions on airline passengers' rights as she was intent on trying to eliminate what she perceived as two obstacles to achieving her dream.

I wanted to help her to achieve that dream, but I thought this character assassination business was absurd and politically dangerous. I told her that she had already eclipsed Stempler in name recognition and popularity with the media. Whatever his views happened to be, we would eventually silence him without ever firing a shot. Engaging in a public smear campaign would only draw attention to him when he was barely getting any attention from the news media as it was.

As for Mitchell, he represented a specific segment of consumers, business travelers, and since we were appealing to a broader base of consumers, we had already differentiated ourselves from him. Besides, he seemed to have garnered a fair amount of respect in the aviation industry and in the government, and it seemed particularly dangerous to attack someone with his credentials.

I also thought that Kate was simply not qualified to be on this particular task force, so unqualified that I was relieved that she hadn't been selected – it could have been a terrible embarrassment. I urged that, rather than a crusade against Mitchell and Stempler, we should try to work within the system to get her on another task force or committee. If we appeared petty now, it wouldn't look good for the next opportunity. These arguments fell on deaf ears.

Since I wouldn't help with this project, Kate enlisted someone at LMG to do some Mitchell-Stempler research for her. She asked someone else to write letters that she planned to send to Stempler and Mitchell. The letters would ask Mitchell and Stempler to reveal things about their finances and other proprietary matters that they probably wouldn't or couldn't answer, but that inability to respond would be used against them. She then drafted a press release titled "Coalition for Airline Passengers Speaks Out against False Champions!" The release challenged Stempler and Mitchell to answer the questions posed by the letters.

By October 2007, Kate and I had begun to use instant messages to communicate more efficiently. With instant messaging, we would now often be in continuous contact from early morning until late at night. My instant message name was "Flyersrights."

We spent a half-hour discussing what she had learned so far about Stempler and Mitchell. Although I was opposed to the project, I stayed in the loop to ensure she didn't turn it into a wholesale disaster. While I thought we were discussing the character assassination letters, she told me that she was trying to enlist the help of Senators Lautenberg and Boxer to get Mitchell and Stempler pulled off the task force.

10:19 P.M.	Flyersrights: I thought these letters were going to Mitchell and Stempler
10:20 P.M.	Kate: No, did you read the e-mail from Lautenberg's guy NAME REDACTED. I love the guy. He said for me to get him any information I felt I should about Mitchell and Stempler and he will get it in front of Lautenberg.
10:20 P.M.	Flyersrights: no I didn't read that
10:22 P.M.	Kate: I forwarded you an e-mail, the last one. Well that's what I've been referring to for the last, say, 20 minutes sweetems.

I found the e-mail from Lautenberg's staff member. Kate had written to him and implied that Stempler and Mitchell were poor choices for the task force. She had also e-mailed Senator Boxer's office with the same purpose. Lautenberg's staff member had responded, "Send me some background on these appointees, on why they are terrible choices for a panel, and I'll get it in front of the Senator."

That was a different situation than the assassination by insinuation letters. If she was going to send something to a Senate office, I wanted to ensure it was accurate and true. I asked her to send me what she planned to send to Lautenberg's office, but it was late so I went to bed. Impatient as she was, Kate sent her e-mail to Lautenberg's office before I had a chance to review it. Except for alleging that Mitchell's website was funded by the airlines, the e-mail appeared to contain publicly available, inconsequential information.

Fortunately, the imprudence of the press release and letters was finally impressed upon Kate, and the matter was temporarily dropped. In the midst of all of this, Kenneth Mead, a former inspector general for the DOT, had also contacted Kate and offered to provide advice and assistance. According to the Bloomberg article that had been published about LMG and the user fee issue in May, Mead had also been retained by members of the general aviation community to lobby against user fees. According to Kate, she had been introduced to Mead through a member of LMG.

As had others, Mead advised Kate that a frontal attack against Mitchell and Stempler was a bad idea. He suggested that she should try to get a newspaper to run an op-ed.

Two weeks later, Kate wrote, "I got Joe Sharkey to agree to write an article about Stempler for Tuesday's column. Should be juicy."

On December 11, 2007, on the heels of the release of the New York airspace task force report, Joe Sharkey took shots at both Stempler and Mitchell in the *New York Times*:

> Mr. Mitchell and Mr. Stempler are knowledgeable about air travel. Both are routinely mentioned in news reports as consumer advocates for airline travelers. But are they, really?[22]

Sharkey would later take issue with the notion that Kate had anything to do with the article. "Nobody 'gets' me to write a column, including my (wonderful) editors," he would write in an email to *Travel Weekly* in July 2010. "That column came about because I'd long been curious about the way the media (including me on occasion) quoted David Stempler and Kevin Mitchell as go-to authorities on consumer travel and passenger advocates."

Kate's penchant for character assassinations wasn't limited to people in the airline industry. Earlier in October, Kate had been given the impression by an editor at *Glamour* magazine that they wanted to do a photo-spread and story about her. The project fell through. While she still turned heads, she thought *Glamour* had snubbed her because of her age. She wrote to me:

> Hey, not enough attention from you today. Where you been? I'm updating my treo and no Mogel. Now I've got NAME REDACTED and Glamour Magazine to assassinate (metaphorically).

Any perceived slight, no matter how small, real or imagined, could send Kate into orbit. She asked me to find anything damaging I could about the magazine and the editor, but like the Stempler-Mitchell matter, I wouldn't help. I also made a mental note to try to avoid ever doing anything that might make her turn her gun sights in my direction.

I drove to Washington on Sunday the 28th and met Kate at the Windsor Park. We were scheduled to have our first in-person meeting with Ken Mead the next day. We took my car to Mead's office the next morning and met Jack Corbett in the lobby. Kate wanted to spend an hour or so alone with Mead, so Corbett and I waited at a coffee shop across the street until she called for us to join them. At the coffee shop, Corbett told me that the Air Transport Association's headquarters were upstairs. We were only a couple of blocks from the White House – prime real estate.

Once the four of us were together in his office, Mead provided useful insight into the workings of the DOT, staff members of various key members of Congress, the Bush administration, and a variety of other issues. Kate's main take-away from the meeting was that Mead suggested that CAPBOR broaden its scope to include airline health and safety issues, and she was determined to do that despite the fact that we had no idea what any of it meant. This would be the source of much conflict and angst in the future.

After the meeting, I retrieved my car from a nearby parking garage. When I pulled up to the curb outside Mead's office, Kate got into the front seat, and Corbett asked if he could ride with us to the DOT meeting that we were scheduled to attend next. Corbett had never appeared in public with Kate and me before that, and I hadn't expected him to go with us to the DOT meeting that day. Up to that point, he had been cautious about publicly associating himself with us, worked in the background, providing valuable strategic advice and pro-bono legal work.

I looked at the floor in the back of my car – empty water bottles and newspapers strewn about. I didn't mind if Kate saw the mess. I often marveled at how fast she could transform spotless hotel rooms and bathrooms into national disaster areas, but I was embarrassed that Corbett would see my car in that condition. I reached into the back of the car, made room for his feet, and sheepishly invited him to join us.

Our main purpose for this, our second DOT meeting, was to find out how we could get Kate onto the list of names for any future DOT sponsored committees or task forces. At the DOT that morning, we learned that the process was remarkably arbitrary and informal, and the DOT officials agreed that Kate would be considered for any future committees. They also told us that the administration was considering a rulemaking proposal that they thought we would be very happy with, but they couldn't tell us what it was until it was officially announced. Afterward, Corbett speculated that they were going to initiate a rulemaking process that would address the issue of tarmac strandings, though he doubted that we would be happy with it. He would be correct, as he usually was.

On Wednesday, Kate and I went to Union Station for a meeting I had arranged with an expert in growing non-profits through better organization and fundraising – two things that we needed desperately. I had met him at my golf club a few weeks earlier. He was eminently qualified – had accomplished things on an international scale that made what we were doing look like child's play. Kate would eventually reject working with him, not because of his ability or experience, but because the literature he subsequently sent to us mentioned a Christian book, *The Purpose Driven Life*.

On our way to that meeting, as we stood on the stairs of a long escalator leading down to the subway, she told me that the book deal that she had promised to share with me *probably* wasn't going to work out. "You might have to write your own book," she said. She said hadn't been able to figure how to tell her husband about our deal – 25 percent of the proceeds. She said she would make up for that by bringing me in as a paid consultant if there was a movie.

At the time, I thought it would have been impractical for me to write a book – there would have been little for me to write about. I was disappointed, but only mildly so. I hadn't expected money from a book when I started working with Kate. I could now envision some kind of paid, public relations or other politically-related role for myself in the future. Kate had made that dream possible for me, just as I was making her dream possible for her.

However, regardless of any book or movie deals, I had already decided that I wasn't going to continue to work on all of this without having a greater sense of control. I was concerned that some of her antics could undermine the cause. I wasn't willing to continue to exert considerable effort into something that could be ruined by a single lapse in judgment.

I told her, gently, that if I was going to continue to work on airline passengers' rights, that she and I had to be full partners – that I would have an equal say in policy decisions and whatever we did in the future. She agreed, said that we were already partners. "We're in this together, Mark."

On Friday night, Kate planned to have dinner with a union official for the National Air Traffic Controllers Association (NATCA). Like other first time meetings, she wanted this one to be private – she was more persuasive that way. I packed up and drove home. Kate flew back to California on Saturday.

NOVEMBER 2007

Hanni, Branson and Gore

KATE WENT ON a cruise with her husband in early November and left me to run the coalition in her absence, which simply meant responding to media inquiries. While she was gone, I finished my redesign of the FlyersRights.org website. I had been working on it for the past couple of months, and it made CAPBOR appear to be much more legitimate and organized than the cartoon style of the previous version.

By the time she returned from the cruise, her fertile imagination had spawned another idea to generate publicity – this one would precede the busy Thanksgiving travel season. She called it "The Holiday Program." She described it in an e-mail to Senator Lautenberg's office:

> Every Hub in the Country, especially the eastern Corridor will
> have at least 3 Coalition members handing out brochures,
> hotline numbers and we will be able to tell them what to do if
> they are stuck or even about to board a chronically delayed or
> canceled flight.

Joe Sharkey wrote about it in his blog on November 15:

> Kate Hanni tells me that she and her 20,000 or so volunteers in
> her Coalition for Airline Passengers Bill of Rights are loaded
> for bear during the new travel-torture season, which starts
> tomorrow.

And on U.S. PIRG's website:

> Flying this holiday? Watch for passenger rights volunteers in
> the airports. Members of the PIRG-backed Coalition for an
> Airline Passengers Bill of Rights or flyersrights.org are
> leafleting in airports around the country today.

She created a brochure to hand out to passengers in airports. It included a blank page for passengers to use to create a petition to send to the pilot if they were stuck on the tarmac. "We, the passengers, want to be returned to the terminal immediately where we may advocate for ourselves." If the pilot wouldn't return to a gate, the brochure instructed passengers to sing the lyrics to a song that Kate had written called "We Gotta Get Outta this Plane," a parody of the 1965 *Animals'* hit, "We Gotta Get Out of this Place."

On November 15, she arrived in New York City and kicked off the holiday program in an interview on a local National Public Radio station, WNYC. She told the host that she was "committed to spending every holiday, the day before and day of return travel, in an airport handing out our Stranded Passengers Survival Guides."[23]

She appeared on several other national programs over the next few days, including CNN, Fox News and the CBS *Early* show. In addition to using sound bites that I had prepared for her after I watched a recent House Aviation Subcommittee hearing, she told each of the hosts that she had volunteers stationed at airports all over the country to hand out the survival brochures.

A few days later, just before Thanksgiving, I drove from Collegeville to JFK International Airport to scout a location for a press conference to announce the start of the holiday program. The New York/New Jersey Port Authority, which ran the LaGuardia, JFK and Newark airports, had refused to give us a permit for the press conference, so we planned to just show up and let them throw us out in front of the media if they wanted. I found a spot in a parking lot with the American Airlines terminal visible in the background.

Kate arrived with a producer from *Dateline NBC* who was working on a feature about her. During the press conference, Kate talked about the callous behavior of the airlines, and how we were the only consumer group that really cared about airline passengers. She announced that we had volunteers at airports all over the country handing out survival guides with information that airline passengers needed to survive the impending disaster that would accompany the most traveled period of the year, the period between Thanksgiving and New Year's. She also announced that we had people manning the hotline, live, twenty-four hours a day, seven days per week. The story appeared on several New York City television stations that evening, and the Associated Press gave the holiday program national coverage.

There was just one problem – it wasn't true. We had one permit for the Dallas/Fort Worth International Airport, and there was one volunteer there handing out brochures, but he was the only one anywhere in the country. There weren't any other permits or volunteers anywhere else, and Kate had no intention of handing out brochures in airports during the holiday season – she was scheduled to fly back to California the next day.

As a result of multiple newsletter requests, we did have a handful of people who said they were willing to answer the hotline, but most turned out to be less than reliable in that regard. All but one had jobs that precluded them from answering the hotline during the day, and nobody was going to answer the hotline in the middle of the night. All of these volunteers would disappear by the end of January.

I was supposed to go to the airport with Kate the next day to put on a show of handing out leaflets for the benefit of the *Dateline* producer, but Kate and I had an argument at the hotel the night before. She wanted to promote a particular airline in the next report card in the hope that they might give her free airfare. I was opposed to using the report card for that purpose. The airline was exempt from reporting tarmac statistics, so it was impossible to know if they were any better or worse at stranding passengers on the tarmac than any of the others.

She was insistent, wouldn't budge. Neither would I. There couldn't possibly have been two more stubborn people in that hotel room. To ensure that she understood that policy decisions and the pact we made in October were more important than our personal relationship, I packed up and left.

She returned to JFK with the *Dateline* producer the next day and wanted to give him a demonstration of how our network of volunteers would handle a live hotline call or stranding situation. She called and asked me to give her the weather forecast and flight delay status for JFK.

"I can't," I said.

"Why not?" she asked.

"I'm on the golf course," I said.

She flew back to California that afternoon. Angry that I was playing golf when she needed me, she wrote, "I will find a backup for these situations so that I can get information I need when it's urgent to get it."

"Good luck with that," I replied. "We've been trying to find backups for months!"

As far as I know, *Dateline* never ran their story. However, on the same day as the press conference, *Travel Weekly* published an article that listed Kate, along with Sir Richard Branson and Al Gore, as one of the top 33 most influential people in travel.[24]

WHEN KATE DID in-person interviews with reporters, she wanted them to be her new best friends forever, and she was often successful at doing just that. A few days before I joined her in New York, she wrote about one of the reporters she met; "He said I had beautiful eyes and asked if I wanted to go out tonight. ... I said I'd have a drink with him tomorrow night. ... I'm sort of stunned. He's like 15 years younger than me. He knows I'm married."

Our personal relationship at this time would be best described as a "friends with benefits" affair. Still, I found it odd and somewhat disturbing that Kate would tell me things like this. I wondered if her purpose was to make me jealous. There was also a "hot pilot" that she met in an airport once, and she flirted with him for months by e-mail. At some point, I asked her why she felt the need to tell me these things. She said it was because we were friends. "I should be able to tell you these things."

Whether or not that particular reporter initiated the *date*, it was common for Kate to invite reporters, airport executives and even government officials for private dinners or drinks when she was in Washington or New York. She did background checks and Google searches to find any personal history that was available, and then used that information to ingratiate herself with them.

There was information on the Internet about one government official's extensive religious background. In every conversation with him, Kate would find ways to work in a religious phrase, even if it was as simple as "God bless you," a phrase definitely not part of her normal lexicon.

The bottom line with Kate was, as she often said, "I always get what I want." That was certainly true from what I had seen so far, and in an article published seven months earlier, she had told a reporter something similar when she was interviewed about her then fledgling cause:

> 'It's given my life new meaning,' said Hanni, 46, an
> acknowledged Type A personality who doesn't take 'no' for an
> answer. 'Just ask my mom,' she said.[25]

And some of the things she got people to do, especially men, were simply amazing. Two weeks after she had dinner with the air traffic controllers' union official in October, she wrote to him, "Have you made any headway with regards to that idea we talked about? … Please help, really need a miracle."

The fact was, as I would later learn, that the hotline wasn't getting anywhere near the tarmac stranding calls that she told the media it was getting. She did need a miracle. She had asked the union official if he could get air traffic controllers to contact us when they observed tarmac strandings of over three hours.

The union official replied, "Hey, I think we have something … we are working on a very informal system that is being coordinated with targeted airport reps. … We hope this to be operational next week."

This "informal system" would yield only one tarmac stranding in early 2008, but the possibility that air traffic controllers might now have another task in addition to their primary mission, "the safe, orderly, and expeditious flow of all military and civilian air traffic," was simply astounding to me.

She did always seem to get what she wanted and, when she didn't, I had learned that she could behave like a spiteful, spoiled child.

When I refused to steal Kevin Mitchell's trash in October, she accused me of not caring enough about the cause. In the days after I left New York, when I refused to let her promote an airline in the next report card, she said there must be something wrong with me, that I was unstable ... "poisonous."

"Maybe we should go our separate ways," I said.

She said she didn't want that. She just wanted me to be more open minded, and then she renewed her argument about promoting the airline in our next report card in the hope of getting free airfare – an argument that I would eventually let her win.

LATE IN NOVEMBER, as Corbett had predicted, the Department of Transportation announced a series of rulemaking proposals to address tarmac delays and bumping compensation. This was an aspect of government that was unfamiliar to me. I knew that rules and regulations adopted by administrative agencies had the force of law, but their ability to issue those regulations was limited to previous statutes or powers granted to them by Congress. I had thought that something as wide-ranging and complex as tarmac strandings would have to be enacted by Congress.

The power to change bumping compensation rules and airline statistics reporting were well within the DOT's jurisdiction. However, requiring airlines to have contingency plans for tarmac delays was a bit of a stretch. The DOT determined that it had that authority under a section of the U.S. Code that prohibited airlines from engaging in unfair or deceptive practices:

> ... the Secretary may investigate and decide whether an air
> carrier, foreign air carrier, or ticket agent has been or is engaged
> in an unfair or deceptive practice or an unfair method of
> competition in air transportation or the sale of air transportation.

The DOT rulemaking process starts with an announcement that they are considering solutions for a particular problem, like tarmac delays. Along with the announcement, they release a proposal for how they plan to do that. In the case of tarmac delays, Corbett was also correct about the fact that we wouldn't like the DOT proposals. The DOT proposed to require airlines to develop contingency plans to provide essential needs like food, water and operable lavatories, but they didn't propose any tarmac time limits. Airlines would be able to set their own.

After they announce a proposal, they open up the issue for public comment for some period of time. Written comments for passengers' rights and airline statistics proposals were due in late January.

After the first round of public comments are assimilated, the next step in the process is to issue a new rulemaking proposal, using the comments they agree with and discarding the ones they don't. Then they repeat the process at least once more before they announce the final rule. All of this can take anywhere from a few months to several years depending upon the complexity of the rule and other factors.

Kate was anxious that we get our input submitted to the DOT as soon as possible, so I wrote a lengthy document with our comments – it would be months before Corbett, Rubin and Hudson would weigh in. She wanted me to fax 20,000 copies of the document to the DOT, one for each signature then in the petition. This was similar to the request she made in May when she wanted me to generate letters from the petition and I had refused.

I was willing to use people's names if they gave us explicit permission, so I wrote and sent a newsletter that asked our members for one thing – to let us know if we could submit our DOT rulemaking comments in their names. I sent the newsletter from Kate's FlyersRights.org e-mail address, so there was no ambiguity about from whom the newsletter came. This was the first time we ever sent a newsletter that polled the members on a specific question. All they had to do was answer "yes" or "no." We received a total of 175 responses from our 20,000 active and dedicated members.

I thought we should fax one document with 175 names attached to it. Kate wanted to bury the DOT in documents, so I faxed 175 separate documents to them for inclusion in the docket. Days later, when I checked the online docket, I saw that the DOT had gone to the trouble of posting each document with the names of the individuals at the bottom of each, even though all of them came from the same fax number – mine.

On November 18, another article by Joe Sharkey appeared in the *New York Times*:

> Kate Hanni, a Napa. Calif., real estate agent who was among thousands of passengers stranded on airplanes at airports near Dallas last Dec. 29, has rallied 20,000 supporters in a coalition pressing for a so-called passengers' bill of rights that would, among other things, require the airlines to allow passengers to get out of a parked plane after more than three hours.[26]

If there was anyone else as deserving of credit for the progress we had made up to that point, it had to be Joe Sharkey and the *New York Times*.

DECEMBER 2007

Secret agents

IN OCTOBER, THE Air Transport Association filed a lawsuit against the State of New York with regard to its new airline passengers' rights law. That law was scheduled to go into effect on January 1, 2008. Paul Hudson and Burt Rubin filed a petition with the court, an amicus brief on behalf of CAPBOR that would let them intercede on the side of the state in the lawsuit.

This seemed highly unusual to me. I didn't understand why we would waste time and money on a state-based airline passengers' rights effort, but I was willing to go along with it for the time being. Even the state recognized they had no authority to force airlines to allow passengers off of airplanes during extended tarmac delays, and their law only provided for adequate food, water, ventilation and working lavatories.

The amicus petition for CAPBOR to join the lawsuit was granted by the judge, and a hearing was scheduled in Albany for December 18. On December 16, I met Kate at JFK as she arrived from San Francisco. I was going to drive us both to Albany, but a major snowstorm crossing through New York and into New England put an end to that plan. Instead, I left my car in a parking lot at JFK, and we took a train to Pennsylvania Station in Manhattan, then another train to Albany.

Two days later, we met Paul Hudson at the United States District Court for the Northern District of the State of New York. Assemblyman Michael Gianaris (D-Queens), one of the two legislators who had sponsored the New York law, was already in the courtroom when we arrived.

Hudson, along with an assistant attorney general for the state, argued before Judge Lawrence Kahn that not all state laws were pre-empted by the Airline Deregulation Act. They said that there should be exceptions made when it came to a state's obligation to protect the health and safety of airline passengers. They argued that New York should be able to require that an airline provide food and water to passengers when an airplane was parked on the tarmac.

As we did wherever we went, we had notified the local media that Kate would be in Albany. They were waiting for us outside the courthouse when the hearing ended. I had also sent several newsletters to the membership to encourage New Yorkers to attend the hearing. Kate thought that the more people we had at the hearing wearing CAPBOR buttons, the more likely it was that the judge would rule in favor of the law. There were some things that weren't worth arguing about.

No one had shown up inside the courtroom, but I was soon to learn that one coalition member was waiting for us on the sidewalk outside. Throughout the press conference, I noticed a young man, perhaps thirty, standing off to the side. He seemed strangely out of place and had a unique appearance – one that stood out in the crowd. After the press conference, I struck up a conversation with him.

"Hi, did you come for the hearing?" I asked.

"I came to see Kate," he said.

"So you got the newsletter?" I asked. He nodded.

"I didn't see you inside," I said.

"She looks just like in her music video," he said.

This guy is a little creepy, I thought.

When Kate finished talking to a reporter, I decided to introduce the young man to her. I was slightly concerned, but I was so surprised to see someone show up for something that it seemed only fair. Besides, we were on a crowded sidewalk outside of a courthouse. There wasn't any immediate danger.

Kate said hello to him, but he didn't seem able to talk anymore. He just stared at her for several awkward moments. Kate said she was cold and went back into the courthouse. With Kate out of sight, he seemed to lose interest and disappeared down the street. Later, as we chatted in his car, Hudson told me that I needed to be more careful.

"OK," I said.

About an hour later, Hudson dropped Kate and me off at the Crowne Plaza hotel. On our way to the elevator, Kate grabbed my arm and pointed toward the gift shop. The young man from the press conference was standing in the doorway.

"Stay calm," I said as we stepped into an elevator. He exited the gift shop, stared directly at Kate as the elevator doors closed.

"Oh my God, Mark!" she exclaimed. "What are we going to do?" She was frantic all the way to our room.

Once she was safely inside the room, I went back downstairs to try to find him. This may not have been the smartest thing to do, but since the rape incident with my friend forty years earlier, I sometimes overcompensated, possibly trying to prove to myself that I'm not a coward.

I looked in the gift shop, lobby, restaurant, bar, and outside the hotel entrance. Not finding him, I went to the front desk and asked to talk to someone from hotel security. I explained the situation and gave them a detailed description. None of the people behind the desk had seen him. They also didn't believe he was a guest. They hadn't seen anyone that matched the description I provided – they would have remembered him. The woman who ran the gift shop remembered him, but she hadn't seen him since. They promised to watch for him.

When I got back to the room, Kate was still frantic. She wanted to know how he found her. She thought that somebody must have told him where she was staying. "Well, it could only have been you or me, or deductive reasoning on his part," I said. "It wasn't me, so that leaves you, or maybe he just took a guess. This is the probably the best hotel in the city and it's only a few blocks from the courthouse."

"I didn't tell anyone where we are," she said.

I only half believed her. She had a bad habit of telling virtual strangers things she shouldn't tell them. The day before I met her for the first time at the Senate hearing in April, she wrote to tell me she was staying at the Windsor Park, but that she didn't want anyone else to know. *Why are you telling me then?* I wondered at the time.

I told her that the young man had mentioned her YouTube music video. It wasn't the first time that subject had come up either. Months earlier, Kate sent me one of apparently several hotline recordings in which a guy was apparently *drooling* over her video. I called him and told him to stop harassing her. He was defiant, said that I had no right to call him, but he never called the hotline again.

"Kate, I warned you months ago that putting that video on YouTube was a bad idea. Please take it down," I said.

She promised that she would take it down, but she never did. Months later, she would send me another video that she wanted to post on YouTube. In that video, she talked about a hotline call she received about a tarmac stranding, but her low-cut blouse exposed so much cleavage that I thought it would only invite more trouble. She complained that I was too conservative, but she would re-record that video from a better camera angle. Sometimes I wondered if she intentionally invited drama and trouble. I also wondered if she might get *me* killed one of these days.

We had planned to leave Albany the next morning to return to JFK, and then California and Pennsylvania respectively, but that afternoon we got word that DOT Secretary Mary Peters was going to make an important announcement in Washington the next morning.

The task force that was formed in October to study the causes of airport congestion in the New York City area had by now issued a series of recommendations for reducing that congestion. Peters was going to announce which of those recommendations the DOT was going to approve. We didn't know which ones, but it was a publicity opportunity we didn't want to miss.

I booked a room for the following afternoon at the National Press Club in Washington for $570. That was a lot of precious coalition money to spend, but it was too late to get a free room on Capitol Hill. We took a train from Albany to Pennsylvania Station in Manhattan, where I put Kate on another train to Washington. I took another train to JFK to retrieve my car.

We were off to Washington for a press conference the next day, and we had no idea what we were going to say. When the task force report was issued two weeks earlier, Kate asked me if we should issue a press release with our position. I had written back, "Do we have a position?"

When I read the report I thought, *I would have to have thirty years of aviation experience to understand all of this. Thank heavens she wasn't appointed to this task force.* The first three recommendations were:

Reduce Excessive Spacing on Final Approach - adhere to standards, continue to look at ways of improving safety and increasing throughput with final compression studies.

Eliminate pass back restrictions to NY area airports for Destinations 500 miles or more.

Airspace Flow Program (AFP) Utilization in High volume/Delay triggers.

They might as well have been written in Greek, and there were 74 other recommendations just like those. I asked Kate to try to find out what the DOT planned to do so that I could narrow my focus to those subjects. The DOT never revealed what they were going to do in advance, but Kate had developed a relationship with one of the DOT's high-level political officials.

Kate talked to the DOT official often on the telephone. She characterized her conversations with him as "top secret," and when I was present, she asked me to remain quiet so he wouldn't know I was listening. I don't remember any secretive substance ever being discussed. What amused me was the secret agent approach that Kate took with some of her contacts. She referred to them as "Deep Throat #1," "Deep Throat #2," and so on. I sometimes got the impression that she thought she was already in a movie.

The official wouldn't tell her what they planned to do, but he provided a clue. He sent her a press release that had been issued by David Stempler, one of the consumer advocates that Kate had been on a mission to discredit. The official wrote, "Have you guys given any thought to distinguishing yourselves from Stempler?"

Stempler's press release opposed three recommendations made by the task force: slot restrictions, slot auctioning, and congestion pricing. That meant the DOT was going to implement one of those.

"What's a slot?" I asked Kate.

She said she thought it had something to do with the number of flights that can take off. That much I could figure out, but there had to be more to it than that. How were they allocated? Who allocated them? Were there costs associated with them, and what were the consequences of limiting them? There must have been consequences or it wouldn't be controversial. She didn't know either.

Rather than draft a statement or press release that might reveal our ignorance, I wrote to Corbett before we left Albany, provided a list of basic principles, and asked him to draft a statement; "We would be grateful if you could draft a comment – not mine or Kate's area of knowledge of course."

At the Windsor Park in Washington the next morning, Kate and I listened to a conference call held by the DOT and learned that Secretary Peters had decided to reduce the number of scheduled flights that could operate per hour at JFK and Newark – slot restrictions. There were a number of other subjects discussed as well.

"What do you think?" she asked after the conference call.

I said that we didn't have time to understand a fraction of what was going on before our press conference in a few hours. The safest path was to disagree with Stempler and agree with the DOT. That would make us look reasonable and knowledgeable. If we disagreed with everything the DOT did, it could raise questions about our credibility. I also pointed out that it wouldn't hurt to curry favor with Secretary Peters, to help secure a spot for Kate on the upcoming DOT task force on tarmac delays. That cemented her decision, and Kate would in fact be named to the task force in January.

Corbett drafted a congratulatory letter to the Secretary. I used that to write a press release. Kate and I went to the National Press Club and held the press conference. Kate congratulated the Secretary and the DOT for acting in the best interests of airline passengers, and then I took her to Dulles for her flight home.

Two days later, to my complete surprise, New York District Court Judge Lawrence Kahn upheld the New York airline passengers' rights law. Despite my doubts about state-sponsored passengers' rights laws, I wrote a press release that applauded the decision:

> Holiday gifts came early to airline passengers in 2007. Airline
> passengers who travel through New York airports are entitled to
> fresh air, water, sanitation and food according to federal district
> court Judge Kahn. ... Kate Hanni, who attended the court
> hearing in Albany said, 'Clearly the airlines have a callous
> disregard for the needs of airline passengers during long tarmac
> delays. It's incredible that we need a federal court to ensure that
> their essential needs are met.'

ON DECEMBER 28, Paul Hudson filed lawsuits against American Airlines in both California and Arkansas for the December 29, 2006 tarmac strandings that were the genesis for CAPBOR. The lawsuit filed on behalf of Kate in California claimed that the stranding caused her to suffer from "fear, anxiety, mental distress, physical impairment and loss of consortium."

Heaven help us if I ever get subpoenaed, I thought.

Kate made sure that the press was notified about the lawsuits. Dozens of articles were written and one of them appeared in *USA Today:*

> Two passengers who were kept aboard American Airlines jets on the ground for more than nine hours in 2006 have sued the airline, saying they deserve compensation for being imprisoned against their will.
>
> The plaintiffs, Kathleen Hanni of Napa, Calif., and Catherine Ray of Fayetteville, Ark., want courts to certify the cases as class actions covering thousands of passengers stranded on American flights when severe weather temporarily shut Dallas/Fort Worth airport on Dec. 29, 2006, forcing flights to go to other airports[27].

December 29, 2007 marked the one-year anniversary of Kate's nine hour and sixteen minute tarmac stranding in Austin. There were now just over 22,000 signatures on the petition. We had a hotline with which the media was very impressed – especially considering that Kate told them we were getting 70 calls a day from people stranded on tarmacs. We had two stand-alone passengers' rights bills, one in the House and one in the Senate, and we had passengers' rights language in both the Senate and House versions of the FAA reauthorization bills.

The Department of Transportation had rulemaking proposals in place to address tarmac strandings, bumping compensation and airline statistics. The New York passengers' rights law had been upheld by a district court, prompting other states to begin the process of introducing their own. We had conducted three highly successful public events that were covered extensively by the media. And now we had two lawsuits against American Airlines that also generated a fair amount of publicity.

And in the wake of all of that, high level people from a variety of public and private entities had come forward to offer assistance, both secretly and publicly.

If one were to equate the success of all this to the stock market, our rate of gain over the past year would have eclipsed those of the most successful companies. Privately, even knowing what I knew at the time, I had a nagging feeling that I was aiding and abetting some kind of techno-social con game, except all of it was for a good cause – hopefully.

Despite the fact that, at times, I questioned her credibility and judgment, Kate was the face of airline passengers' rights and I would continue to find ways to raise our stock and enhance her public status and credibility whenever and however I could. It didn't take me long to find a way to do just that.

For several months, there had been a controversy brewing between Congress and NASA about an $8.5 million study of commercial aviation that NASA had conducted. NASA had employed a contractor to interview hundreds of flight crews to collect information about bird strikes, near misses, cabin fires and dozens of other issues for which there was previously little data, at least not all in one place and certainly not in a form that was readily available to the public.

The government wanted NASA to release the results of the study, but NASA argued that the results might create undue fear among the flying public. In October, NASA had reportedly told the contractor they used to purge all of the data, but Congress put a stop to that. Following constant pressure from both Congress and the news media, NASA released the data on their website on December 31, but they did so in such a way as to make it incomprehensible.

Imagine starting with a spreadsheet as large as a living room couch, with thousands of columns and rows of numbers – literally millions of data points. Then fold up the paper and cut paper dolls out of it. That's sort of what NASA did. They published the results in about 30 separate PDF files, so it wasn't even in spreadsheet form anymore. That way they could say they released the data, and they were off the hook.

No one in the media could make heads or tails out of it. It was like a Rubik's Cube on steroids. Although the NASA report didn't have anything to do with passengers' rights, I thought it seemed like an interesting challenge. Even better, if I could unravel this mystery, it could propel our stock even higher.

JANUARY 2008

Hanoi Kate

It took me about three days to figure out how all the pieces fit together and convert the data into a spreadsheet. There were 2.6 million cells of data. Because NASA apparently felt that some of the data was too sensitive to release even in the convoluted form that they had, they redacted some of it. That made it more troublesome to recreate the spreadsheet, but not much. They neglected to change the column totals, so if there happened to be only one redacted cell in a column, it was a matter of simple subtraction to re-create the missing value. When more than one cell in a column had been redacted, there were other patterns and clues for how to recreate those.

When I finished with the spreadsheet, I sat back and smiled – felt a devious sense of accomplishment. It seemed as if NASA had gone to great lengths to make it as difficult as possible, and unraveling it had required a certain degree of software knowledge, time, concentration and a level of dogged determination that apparently NASA didn't think anyone had. I also felt a little remorseful. I admired the legacy and accomplishments of NASA, and I hoped no one there would take it personally.

On January 3, I created a new page on the FlyersRights.org website and published the NASA report. Some of the interesting facts that emerged from the report included:

> Hundreds of reports un-commanded movement of aircraft rudders, aileron, spoilers, speed-brakes, etcetera, in flight.

> Hundreds of reports of smoke, fumes or fire in engines, on flight decks and in passenger cabins.

> 2339 instances of air traffic controllers' refusal of pilots' requests to change course due to severe weather.

> Over 4,000 reports that fuel reserves were required to stay in the air.

Kate was on vacation with her family in Florida, so I put my own e-mail address and phone number on the press release. I started to get calls from all over the world – a professor at Stanford, someone from a research center in Europe and several reporters. After the media took interest, NASA re-released the entire study in a readable spreadsheet on their own website.

Still, it was yet another arrow in our quiver, and Kate mentioned it often during interviews, even when subject of the interview didn't have anything to do with the NASA report. She would later appear on CNN's *Larry King* for a segment about reports that airlines were under-fueling planes to save on fuel costs. Why Larry King would have invited Kate on his program to discuss that subject was a mystery to me, and when he asked her if she thought it was safe to fly, she said:

> I believe we're in the land of diminishing returns. Our group
> decrypted the NASA report that was very controversial, that
> finally was released, that showed that the number of
> unauthorized landings, bird hits, near misses were much greater
> than the government was reporting.[28]

What that answer had to do with the under-fueling of airplanes was also a mystery to me, but it was what would sometimes happen, as it had in this case, when I wasn't available to do research and provide sound bites before interviews.

After the NASA publicity died down, I wrote an article in Kate's name that Greg Principato, president of Airports Council International-North America (ACI-NA), offered to publish in that organization's internal quarterly magazine. Headquartered in Washington, ACI-NA is a trade association that represents U.S. airports. Principato also invited Kate to make a speech at their organization's annual meeting in Washington in January.

As I began to work on the speech, I thought it might be a good idea to write it using prose and bullet points from which she could ad-lib, rather than reading the entire speech word-for-word. There were pros and cons to this idea. Letting Kate ad-lib on any subject was dangerous because I never knew what she might say. On the other hand, she was magnificent when it came to looking people in the eye and persuading them to believe what she wanted them to believe, or to do what she wanted them to do. In November, when she announced that we had volunteers at airports all over the country handing out brochures, she was so sincere and said it with such conviction that she almost had me believing it. Reading a speech from a sheet of paper didn't allow that power to be fully realized. The speech would require some rehearsal, but we would have time to do that in Washington the following week.

On Monday the 14th, I drove to Washington for a week of meetings and the ACI-NA speech. Kate's friend from Napa, Annette Hagan, had flown in with Kate. There were no vacancies available at the Windsor Park until mid-week, so Kate and Hagan arranged to share a room at a five-star hotel on Pennsylvania Avenue. For reasons that were never clear to me, Kate tasked Hagan with finding a hotel for me. Hagan put me up in a hotel that smelled like the rooms were rented by the hour. However, the plan was that we would all move to the Windsor Park by mid-week.

On Monday afternoon, I met Kate and Hagan at PIRG and later drove them to their hotel. The three of us went into the hotel bar for drinks and a bite to eat. I took the opportunity to attempt to explain to Kate, for perhaps the tenth time, but the first time in person, why I thought our preoccupation with state laws was a bad idea.

After Judge Kahn upheld the passengers' rights law in New York, the ATA filed an appeal that was scheduled to be heard in early March. Mean-while, legislators from other states began hinting that they might sponsor similar bills. Rubin and Hudson had assured Kate that the state laws would hold up in court. My view was that it was impossible that those laws would survive, despite the fact that Hudson had argued the matter successfully before a district court judge in New York. I worried that our continued focus on the state laws was a waste of precious time and money. The only thing that made sense to me was that it helped keep passengers' rights issues in the media spotlight.

I had done a fair amount of research since the district court judge in Albany ruled in favor of the New York law. I had read a number of legal cases on the subject, including some of the cases cited by the ATA during the hearing and other cases that were pending before other courts. In late December, I had written to Kate and the lawyers that it looked to me like an upcoming U.S. Supreme Court case would settle the matter once and for all.

The case was "Rowe versus New Hampshire Motor Transport Asso-ciation," and it involved the State of Maine's attempt to place certain requirements and restrictions on air and motor carriers that delivered tobacco products to the state. The state's intentions were good – they wanted to prevent tobacco products from getting into the hands of minors. Maine, like the lawyers in the New York airline passengers' law case, argued that federal law does not pre-empt a state's ability to protect its citizens' public health. But the issue, I thought, was larger than that.

The real issue was whether or not states had the power to regulate the services provided by carriers involved in interstate commerce. The U.S. Constitution gave the power to regulate interstate commerce to the federal government, and I was fairly sure that the federal government wasn't giving it back.

Both Hudson and Rubin said I was wrong – that the outcome of Rowe would have no bearing on the New York law. Knowing that I was opposed to our emphasis on the state laws, Kate had recently taken the unusual step of asking one of the attorneys to write a leave-behind position paper for our upcoming Senate office visits. This ordinarily would have been something I would have done, and Kate made it sound like she was doing me a favor by taking it off my hands. When I read the attorney's paper, it was obvious why she asked him to write it. They were going to walk into Senate offices and ask senators to support an amendment that essentially would give states the power to enforce their own airline passengers' rights laws:

> The Congress should also act to correct the muddle of conflicting court decisions that has resulted from the Airline Deregulation Act's preemption provision, 49 U.S.C. §41713(b), by clarifying that ... state regulation of health and safety on board grounded airlines are not preempted.

Kate and I had discussed this at length in instant messages the week before she came to Washington.

8:00 P.M.	Flyersrights: I didn't realize for some reason that you intended to go into senate offices and ask for an exception to preemption of state health and safety laws
8:01 P.M.	Kate: We need one or the other. If they don't strengthen the Fed. Law than we need preemption. But it's more of a lever.
8:03 P.M.	Flyersrights: Nobody is going to buy into ceding that power to the states thru legislation.

In another exchange, I wrote that asking senators to support a federal law that would cede this power to the states would "make us look like idiots." It seemed to me that this was a matter of simple common sense. It would be implausible for airlines to adhere to fifty different state laws, and that's probably one of the reasons why the authors of the Constitution added the commerce clause in the first place. There were no airplanes at that time of course, but there was land and water-based interstate commerce.

Despite contrary opinions from some of our legal advisors, I would eventually be proven correct about the final outcome. On February 20, the Supreme Court would rule unanimously in favor of the carriers in Rowe – citing the commerce clause of the U.S. Constitution. The New York airline passengers' rights law would also be subsequently struck down, relying heavily on the Rowe decision.

However, long before those decisions were made, in the bar of their hotel in January, I tried to explain these concepts to Kate with Annette Hagan looking on. When Kate reminded me that I wasn't a lawyer, the discussion turned into a rather passionate argument – one that I thought was inconsequential at the time, but that would prove to be a major part of this story.

The next morning, Corbett, Rubin, Hagan, Kate and I met with staff members in Barbara Boxer's office. One of the attorneys brought up the possibility of Senator Boxer introducing the health and safety amendment. Boxer's staff said they would discuss the issue with Senator Boxer, at which point Kate shot me a look that I interpreted as, *See, they don't think we're idiots.*

Maybe not her staff, I thought, *but Boxer will,* and the fact was that nothing ever did come of this nonsense.

After that meeting, we all had lunch in a nearby cafeteria. Six days earlier, television news cameras had recorded a tear running down the cheek of presidential candidate Hillary Clinton during a campaign event. Senator Clinton's tear made national news for days. Kate was sure it was contrived. "Shit, I can do that too," she said at the time.

There in the cafeteria, she started to talk about how much she missed her family and how the trips to Washington were such a burden, and then a tear ran down her cheek. She had only been away from home for one day. While the others consoled and sympathized with her, I covered my face with my hands to conceal an insuppressible grin. Peering through my fingers, I saw her shoot me a glance. She loved the action in Washington. This was where she really wanted to be. *If they only knew,* I thought.

Later that evening, Kate and Hagan moved to the Windsor Park. I was supposed to move there the next day when another room would become available. However, I got a message from home about a personal matter that was more important than anything else, so I checked out of my hotel and drove home.

I got a few hours of sleep, and when I awakened, Kate and I exchanged a few e-mails. It was clear that she wasn't happy that I had returned home. Then, except for an e-mail in which she wrote that I should stay home and deal with the personal issue, all communications ceased for the next two days.

Several months hence, Kate would tell me that, sometime during these two days of silence, Annette Hagan told Jack Corbett and Burt Rubin that she thought I was obsessed with Kate and possibly dangerous. She told the lawyers that I was very angry, on the verge of violence in the bar during the argument earlier that week. One or both of the lawyers then allegedly suggested that, if all of this was true, Kate might want to consider filing for a temporary restraining order against me. Kate would also tell me that Hagan then canceled my reservation at the Windsor Park and told the desk clerks to call the police if I showed up to check in.

Naturally, no restraining order was ever sought, but Kate and I wouldn't be seen together again at the Windsor Park for a long time to come. There would come a time when I would question whether Kate had a greater role in this episode than she admitted. Meanwhile, I would march on for several months, unaware of the hysteria that had transpired in my absence.

When I finally talked to Kate on Friday, she said that she hadn't called because she lost her cell phone in a taxi and had to buy a new one. She said she was unable to use e-mail because the wireless connection at the hotel hadn't been working. She asked me to write a press release about a tarmac stranding that had occurred that week, and she said that her speech at the ACI-NA meeting had gone very well.

We knew that there would be ATA representatives at the meeting as well as airline and airport executives. The ATA had been engaged in a campaign to undermine Kate's credibility – challenging the claims she made publicly about the frequency of tarmac strandings and other airline related matters.

We had also heard from some of our press contacts that the ATA privately referred to Kate as a "blonde bimbo" who had no idea what she was doing, or "Hanoi Kate." We took the latter as a compliment. In a sense, I understood the reference. Like the original Hanoi Jane (Fonda) in the 1970s, Kate had made extreme and unsubstantiated claims about current events and the media carried those claims as if they were true. We must have been driving the ATA lobbyists crazy. The ATA never referred to Kate by name in their public statements. Instead they publicly referred to her as "that woman."

It was Kate's first speech before an audience like that, and part of me wondered if she had been invited because they expected her to make a fool of herself. I was determined to not let that happen. I wanted her to leave that audience thinking that she was a commercial aviation genius who presided over a vast, complex organization, and the speech I wrote for her did exactly that. It also meant that, for the first time since I got involved in all of this, I was going to stretch the truth – a lot.

The speech began by having her ad-lib about her tarmac stranding and how she and hundreds of other passengers banded together to form a coalition to lobby for airline passengers' rights. I didn't need to help her with that – she had already told that story a hundred times. The speech went on to describe the departments of a vast, complex organization: legal, information technology, government, research, hotline and others. It talked about a broad range of aviation-related expertise within the organization, listing every discipline needed to operate an airline from baggage handlers to former airline CEOs. The speech concluded:

> The bottom line is, like you, we are trying to help passengers
> get through very difficult situations – situations they do not

understand because unlike the people in this room, they are not well versed in airline and airport operations.

We recognize that you are working to make the situation better and I appreciate the work already underway by airports to help. … The Port Authority of New York/New Jersey developed a set of technical solutions to reduce delays and made a number of useful recommendations for how to help delayed passengers. … This meeting along with the upcoming DOT Task Force on Tarmac Delays is critically important in establishing best practices for handling irregular operations.

We also know that that we need long term solutions, and looking at future demand, it is clear that airport capacity must be increased. We support air traffic control modernization and other initiatives, but without more terminals, gates and runways, airports will become the bottleneck of the future. Like many of you, we are worried that every day Congress fails to act on the FAA reauthorization bill with these provisions is another day ten years from now that more passengers will be delayed because of inadequate terminal and runway space.

The speech was followed by a generous applause. Later, a spokesperson for ACI-NA wrote, "Kate's speech was great and she was quite successful in dispelling some of the negative perceptions about your organization."

It better have, I thought. *It took me over a week to write that nonsense.*

Except for the propaganda in our newsletters, until now I had resisted the temptation to lie or exaggerate on Kate's or CAPBOR's behalf. I was having an affair, and that in itself is a breach of personal integrity. That aspect of my integrity, I thought, was lost the first time I slept with Kate. Conveniently, I subsequently reasoned that it wouldn't matter whether I slept with her once or a hundred times as long as I didn't fall in love with her.

I'd felt enormously guilty after my first night with Kate, but that guilt had waned over time, supplanted by the exhilaration of everything that was happening. I'd been writing most of Kate's quotes for press releases since long before the affair began. Afterward, I had begun to provide her with sound bites for television interviews. There was something intoxicating about seeing her use those sound bites on CNN or Fox News. It gave me a sense of power and satisfaction that I'd never felt before. It was addictive.

Still, the sound bites I provided had been developed from substantive, in-depth research about whatever the airline topic of the day might have been. Kate would often use those sound bites as a springboard to make outlandish claims that no one could easily disprove, such as having CAPBOR volunteers stationed at airports around the country.

At first I worried that one disproven claim could sabotage the cause, but the more the news media ran with her exaggerations, the more interviews she got. No matter what she said or did, it seemed to work. Over time, I learned that whatever ideas I had about doing things with honesty and integrity were misplaced. That's not how things work in Washington. However, I did still have limits.

Chief among those limits was that we couldn't lie directly to government officials. I was quite sure that members of Congress saw Kate on television and that they read the newspapers, but I hoped that they knew what I knew by now; that you can't believe everything you read in the newspaper or see on the television news. It seemed to me that Kate couldn't possibly be the only person in the world who could deceive the media so easily.

AS HER PUBLIC status and credibility increased, reporters began to call Kate for insight on a wider variety of subjects, and I wasn't always available to help with sound bites. On the same day as her ACI-NA speech, a story appeared in the *Los Angeles Times* about an ongoing labor dispute between the air traffic controllers union (NATCA) and the FAA. NATCA officials had begun to issue statements that it was unsafe to fly because there were serious air traffic controller staffing issues at some airports. The FAA disputed those claims. *Naturally*, the newspaper asked for Kate's insight into the matter:

> 'I'm concerned because I'm flying almost every other week,'
> said Kate Hanni, the Napa, Calif.-based founder of the Coalition
> for the Airline Passenger Bill of Rights. 'Planes clearly are not
> falling out of the sky, but there are some problems that appear to
> be creeping up that could become critical.'[29]

Although I loved the fact that the media asked Kate to comment on an increasing range of airline related subjects, I also wondered if some of them should have their heads examined. Marilyn Adams of *USA Today* later explored the phenomenon in a lengthy profile she wrote about Kate:

> News outlets seeking a compelling sound bite transform
> quotable, accessible people into instant media experts. 'She's
> articulate, passionate – and there's a void,' says Robbie
> Vorhaus, a public relations and crisis communications strategist
> in Sag Harbor, N.Y. 'She's doing what nobody else was willing
> to stand up for.'[30]

BY JANUARY 21, Kate, the attorneys and I had completed our final written responses to the Department of Transportation rulemaking proposals for tarmac delays, overbooking compensation, and other consumer-related matters. I had also spent the previous week writing our response for the airline statistics rulemaking proposal. The next day I faxed all of our documents to the DOT for inclusion in the official government docket.

While I was doing that, Kate was appearing before a Washington State Senate hearing in Olympia in support of an airline passengers' rights bill sponsored by a state senator, Ken Jacobsen. In the days prior to that hearing, I sent e-mails to the Washington members to encourage them to appear at the hearing "to support your newly proposed state Airline Passengers Bill of Rights."

On her way back to the airport after the hearing, Kate called me and said that no CAPBOR members had shown up. She seemed disappointed. I consoled her, but I didn't know why she expected anything different. I wondered if she was starting to believe her own rhetoric. Then she asked me to find as many tarmac strandings as possible for the Seattle-Tacoma International Airport (SeaTac).

"Why?" I asked.

"Because I told them we had many tarmac strandings for SeaTac that weren't part of the government statistics," she said. "I need you to back me up."

There was only one three-hour tarmac event at SeaTac that we knew about.

"Kate, we don't have any other tarmac strandings for SeaTac! Where am I supposed to find this stuff?"

"Mark, there have to be. If anyone can find them, you can," she said.

Oh, no, this can't be good, I thought.

The Washington State legislature has a website that provides access to audio and video of hearings. I found Kate's hearing and watched it. At the outset, the chairman of the committee asked her not to read from the written testimony I had sent to her. Apparently, they had allocated enough time for the other witnesses she had promised to produce, but hadn't. He told her to take as much time as she wanted.

Uh oh, I thought.

For the most part, she was informative and even entertaining, moving the committee to laughter at times. At other times, it seemed to me that she had gone overboard to sell the committee on her status as a consumer advocate as well as reasons why they should approve the passengers' rights bill.

Despite not having a single member in the gallery, she grossly exaggerated the number of CAPBOR members from Seattle and the state of

Washington. When asked if she had participated in the drafting of the New York statute, she answered, "Yes, I did. We participated in it to the extent that we were allowed to, although we did ask that arrivals be included in that statute and it did not make it in ..."

I cringed. We didn't even know there was a bill in New York until after it had been approved by the New York Senate. The deficiencies in that law, such as the omission of arriving flights, weren't identified until after Governor Spitzer signed it into law. We had never been consulted on its content.

She went on to make valid points about the fact that there were no federal regulations to protect passengers from being stuck on an airplane for several hours.

A senator then asked her why there were no reports of tarmac strandings at SeaTac. Kate gave a long answer about thousands of flights that weren't counted by the government statistics, and ended with, "We have a lot of reports of things happening at SeaTac that I can get to you. I can get you story, after story, after story, that's happened at SeaTac with a variety of different airlines."

Apparently that was to be my impossible task. She had prefaced her answer by saying, "We have this one gentleman named Mark Mogel on our coalition who used to be in the Air Force and then he worked at Unisys, so he's a geek, and Joe Sharkey affectionately calls him our wonk."

Gee, thanks for another backhanded compliment, I thought. I also wondered if the senators had any idea who Joe Sharkey was. Kate glossed over him as if he was a household name.

In answer to another senator's question, she said, "A number of the *incidences* that have happened at SeaTac have been flights that have landed there [diverted flights] ... the passengers thought they would be sitting there for a half hour, and ended up sitting there for three or four hours ..."

She went on and on. None of it was true, and we never got back to them with any stories of tarmac strandings at SeaTac. Fortunately, Washington's state senators apparently forgot about her pledge to provide those reports.

Two days after the hearing, Kate thought of another way to promote the idea of airline passengers' rights laws – to encourage other states to introduce their own. The airlines had been publicly arguing against the state laws by calling them a "patchwork quilt," meaning that they couldn't possibly adhere to 50 different state laws, which was true of course.

| 6:35 P.M. | Kate: Let's say we have a picture of grandmas making a patchwork quilt, and turn this f...ing phrase on the airlines like this... |
| 6:35 P.M. | Flyersrights: grandmas and f...ing in the same sentence ... no dinner tonite |

6:36 P.M.	Kate: yer sick – Jezuz
6:41 P.M.	Kate: Speaking of 'Patchwork Quilts', has any one of the managers of a major airline ever had to drive in a different State...and I don't mean drunk, I mean abide by different States Traffic Laws? That kind of patchwork quilt?
6:41 P.M.	Kate: Tell me I don't make a good point every so often.
6:42 P.M.	Flyersrights: ur a genius - brilliant - no peer
6:43 P.M.	Kate: Play-Kate
6:43 P.M.	Flyersrights: lol
6:43 P.M.	Kate: Pontifi-Kate
6:45 P.M.	Flyersrights: tolerkate
6:46 P.M.	Kate: mine are actual words dumass
6:46 P.M.	Kate: dedi-kate
6:47 P.M.	Flyersrights: mediKate
6:47 P.M.	Kate: deli-kate
6:47 P.M.	Flyersrights: kaopekate
6:48 P.M.	Kate: you are making up words - adios

I may have been making up words, but mine were germane to how I felt. It was one thing to exaggerate, stretch the truth, or lie to the media or a room full of airline and airport executives, but I was concerned that she had lied to a state legislature. Aside from the possible legal issues, lying to a state legislature to advocate for a state-based airline passengers' rights law was completely unnecessary. I didn't think I needed to tell Kate that she shouldn't lie to government officials; I thought that would be obvious. Surprisingly, Kate drew no distinctions between state senators, the media, airline executives, or anyone else as far as I could tell.

When I did voice my concerns about lying to state senators, she said I was being too critical. I also tried to explain that she kept misusing the word "incidences." I had seen her misuse the word during television interviews just as she had during the hearing, and I was simply trying to help her to be more articulate. She thought I was being too critical about that as well. She had a remarkable ability to deflect any criticism, however well-intentioned or constructively delivered, right back at me.

FEBRUARY 2008

State laws and bubble baths

BY EARLY FEBRUARY, the race for the 2008 presidential election was in full swing. The January caucuses and primaries had Barack Obama leading Hillary Clinton and John Edwards for the Democratic nomination, and John McCain led Mitt Romney and a field of Republican candidates. As much of a stretch as it may have been, it had occurred to me that we should at least try to raise the subject of airline passengers' rights with the candidates. Joe Biden had already withdrawn from the race, but he had issued a formal statement in favor of airline passengers' rights during his campaign.

On February 1, I wrote letters to each of the remaining major candidates and faxed them to every fax number I could find for their Washington, D.C. and state offices. The letters challenged each candidate to state his or her position on airline passengers' rights. We didn't get any responses from the candidates, but it was worth a try. Not every tactic worked, but we just kept plugging away until something did.

BY NOW, IT was clear to me that Kate and the lawyers were hell-bent to keep working on the state-based airline passengers' rights laws rather than concentrating on the federal front. Still believing we were wasting valuable time and money, I decided, *if you can't beat 'em, join 'em*. While I can be obstinate at times, when all is said and done, I'm still a team player.

By the end of December, Burt Rubin had been bestowed with the title "CAPBOR Special Counsel." After the New York law was passed, Rubin had identified several deficiencies in that law and developed a model bill for other states to use. He had also contributed substantially to the argument that prevailed in the Albany district court hearing, although Paul Hudson had delivered the argument in person. Because of that, Kate's earlier concerns that Rubin wanted to "take over" had waned, and he had become a highly trusted advisor.

Rubin and Kate were scheduled to appear before Rhode Island's State Senate Judiciary Committee on February 5. Why Rhode Island, with one 22-

gate airport and no reports of tarmac strandings, needed an airline passengers' bill of rights was beyond me, and why she would waste money going there was equally bewildering. Nevertheless, I wrote her testimony, and sent out a press release and a media advisory.

On the 5th, Kate and Rubin appeared at the hearing in Providence, Rhode Island. We got no media, no articles, no coverage, nothing. The next morning, I asked how the day had gone. Kate said she had gone out to dinner with an elected official and that he had wanted to take a bubble bath with her:

7:08 A.M.	Kate: What would you like to know? About how NAME REDACTED wanted to have me give him a long hot bubble bath?
7:08 A.M.	Flyersrights: sure - start there
7:09 A.M.	Kate: Or...perhaps...how he wanted to "see" my room.
7:10 A.M.	Flyersrights: omg
7:11 A.M.	Kate: Yeah, he came into the hotel and wanted to come upstairs, have a bottle of wine, take a hot bubble bath, and have Me GIVE HIM A MASSAGE. OMG. I had to dance around that like you can't believe not to offend him.

We continued the discussion on the telephone. She said she talked her way out of the situation by telling him she was happily married.

"Where were you all day?" I asked. "I was trying to call you," I said.

After the hearing, the official dropped Rubin off at the airport. Then he took Kate to a wake, she said. After that they went out for dinner. She spent about five hours with the official, much of it drinking. He drove her from the wake to an Italian restaurant, and then later to her hotel. She said he almost ran over a pedestrian.

"Are you *trying* to get yourself killed?" I asked.

"I can take care of myself," she said.

"You're going to drive me crazy," I said.

A WEEK LATER, I flew to San Francisco for a press conference with Kate and California State Assemblyman Mark Leno. Leno had introduced an airline passengers' rights bill and he invited Kate to attend a press conference for the official announcement. I wouldn't have ordinarily flown 3,000 miles for a press conference, but we could only find two other faces to show up for what Kate deemed to be an extremely important event. We got some local news coverage, but it was really just another waste of time and precious member donations.

During my trip back to Philadelphia, I got stuck in the Las Vegas airport for a few hours. Incoming and outgoing flights were halted because of extremely high winds. The airline employees in the gate area made announcements every fifteen minutes to update passengers about the weather situation and the status of the flight. I didn't remember airline employees making announcements with such frequency when I had been delayed in airports during my earlier business career. I wondered if the improvement in customer communications had anything to do with the negative publicity we had brought to bear over the past year.

After a couple of hours in the airport, I decided to call Kate. There was no point in calling the hotline because by then there were no hotline operators. Those volunteers, according to Kate, had all vanished. Still, I was curious what advice she would give someone who was stranded at the gate. She was happy to hear from me at first, but then she seemed uneasy that I had called her to ask what I could or should do.

"What do you want me to do, Mark?" she asked.

"Well, what would you tell anyone else that called?" I asked.

She said she would tell them to sign the petition so that we can get an airline passengers' bill of rights passed by Congress so that these kinds of situations don't happen.

"You're kidding, right?" I asked.

She said she wasn't kidding.

I asked her to check the weather forecast for Las Vegas. One of the things she told the media was that we had people manning the hotline that gave stranded passengers detailed information about the weather.

"How long is this wind going to last?" I asked.

She said she didn't know how to do that and then changed the subject.

"Hey, you're not going to believe this, but I ran out of gas on our way home from the press conference," she said.

Apparently one of the people she brought with her to the press conference told her that he was impressed with how well she maneuvered through the busy highway traffic to get the stalled car safely onto a shoulder.

"He said I was a great driver," she said with a degree of satisfaction.

"They're announcing that my flight is boarding," I said.

"Call me back if you get stuck on the tarmac!" she exclaimed.

"You are too cute to be true," I said.

The next day, a San Francisco television station published an article about a Freedom of Information Act (FOIA) request they had submitted to the U.S. Environmental Protection Agency (EPA) in regard to coliform studies of tap water from airline lavatories and galleys. Later that afternoon, Kate got an interview request from Fox News to discuss the subject on television the following day. She sent me the story, but my internal clock was so fouled up from the trip to California that I was in bed at the time.

The next morning, I read the article and visited the EPA website to read as much as possible about airline coliform studies. Kate called me on her way from Napa to Beyond Pix Studios, the San Francisco broadcast studio where most of her remote interviews took place. She had all of the facts about coliform and the EPA studies backwards. I tried to get her on the right track, but she said that she grew up across the street from a cattle ranch, so she knew all about coliform. She also said that if she didn't make the interview "juicy," they wouldn't invite her back to talk about other things.

A half hour later, I watched her on Fox News. In an interview that lasted nearly five minutes, I wasn't sure anything she said was accurate. Finally the host asked if this was much ado about nothing:

> Trace Gallagher: The truth is we don't have reports of people getting sick on airlines because of water. Are we beating the airlines up here for nothing?
>
> Kate: No we're not. During our event of nine and a half hours on the tarmac in Austin they did not provide us potable water in bottles. We had to drink water out of the bathroom sinks, and there were several people that were stuck in Austin for five days with intestinal viruses because of the water they drank.

Kate had a report from only one person that complained of intestinal problems after the tarmac stranding in Austin. Obviously, he could have gotten a stomach virus anywhere. There was no way for Fox to know that though. What concerned me most was that somebody from the EPA or the airlines might call the Fox producers, demonstrate that Kate had misstated the publicly-known facts, and that might jeopardize her credibility.

I was wrong about the possible negative consequences of the interview though. In the future, cable news programs and other media outlets would invite Kate to do interviews on anything and everything to do with the airlines, from wiring bundles in the wheel-wells of McDonnell Douglas MD-80s to Pitot tubes.

Those interviews, particularly those that involved the safety of airline passengers, would make me wonder if I had gone too far. I had worked to make her famous and increase her public credibility as a consumer advocate, but I hadn't anticipated the possibility that any of that could lead to her having any influence whatsoever when it came to airline passenger safety.

Later that evening, Kate asked me a question that hadn't come up before – a question to which there was no right answer:

9:42 P.M.   Kate: Love me?

9:43 P.M.   Kate: Say it.

9:45 P.M.	Flyersrights: huh?
9:45 P.M.	Kate: Do you love me?
9:46 P.M.	Kate: Don't overthink it. Are you in love with me?
9:46 P.M.	Flyersrights: Yes, Kate - I love you. - e tu
9:46 P.M.	Kate: When did you start speaking Spanish? - Yes - Si
9:46 P.M.	Kate: And I don't know why because I want to kill you a good part of the time
9:47 P.M.	Flyersrights: same here - metaphorically ;-)
9:47 P.M.	Kate: But you are thre for me when no one else is. And I love you for that.
9:48 P.M.	Flyersrights: I am and have been for a long time - here for you.
9:49 P.M.	Kate: Breaking your own code?
9:49 P.M.	Kate: Avoiding the in love with question?
9:49 P.M.	Flyersrights: In love ... that takes more - takes longer.

I wasn't breaking my *code*. In August, just a few evenings after our first night together, we had dinner at Ruth's Chris Steak House in Washington, about six blocks from the Windsor Park. Leaving the restaurant, we walked north on Connecticut Avenue toward the hotel. After a couple of blocks, we crossed halfway across the street and paused on a pedestrian island to wait for southbound traffic to clear so that we could reach the other side.

She had spent the previous few days making sure that I was aware that we needed to be discreet whenever we were in public. She was a public figure and could have been recognized at any time, especially in Washington. Moreover, her long, blonde hair was like a beacon that drew attention wherever she went. Yet there in the middle of Connecticut Avenue, with traffic streaming by in both directions, she pulled me to her for a kiss.

"Don't fall in love with me, Kate," I said.

"Mark, don't put limits on this already. Live a life of possibilities, not limitations," she said.

"Kate, I don't know where this is headed, but I'm not going to fall in love with you. I'm just telling you."

That's what she meant when she now asked, "Breaking your own code?" My *code*, as she put it, was really the certainty that I shouldn't have been involved with her in the first place. I had been happily married before I met Kate, and I hoped to be happily married after Kate was long gone. I knew I had put that possibility at serious risk, but my own selfishness or possibly an ongoing mid-life crisis had supplanted reason.

At 51, I was not only living in a political adventure that was a dream come true, but I was also reliving the typical, adolescent male fantasy of dating the prettiest, most popular girl in school. Kate was the epitome of that fantasy in some ways, and its antithesis in others.

She could be extraordinarily charming and affectionate one week, and self-absorbed, spiteful and paranoid to the point of delusion the next. Our relationship was like a rollercoaster – sometimes up and sometimes down, but never boring. It didn't surprise me that she had already outlived one husband. I thought of her as a spoiled, Machiavellian-like starlet, someone I knew instinctively to keep at arm's length in some ways, and yet drawn to in others.

I enjoyed the time we spent together, and I did care about her, but I was also relieved that I didn't live with her every day. Even still, when we were apart, we were in perpetual contact from early morning until late at night in one form or another. The miracles of modern technology made it possible to be continuously connected by cell phones, instant messages, cellular text messages, e-mail and, by now, webcams.

ON FEBRUARY 20, the U.S. Supreme Court sided with the New Hampshire Motor Transport Association in the Rowe lawsuit. The decision was unanimous and clear-cut. Justice Stephen Breyer, a Clinton appointee, delivered the opinion for the court writing, "Given these circumstances, from the perspective of pre-emption, this case is no more 'borderline' than was *Morales.*"

Morales was a precedent setting case decided by a federal appeals court in 1992. The state of Texas had threatened to sue certain airlines over what the state alleged was deceptive airline fare advertising. The appeals court had ruled that Texas could not sue the airlines regardless of whether or not the advertising was deceptive. It was pre-empted from doing so under the Airline Deregulation Act.

While they concurred that the Supreme Court's decision in Rowe was correct, some of our attorneys sent e-mails to Kate and me to assure us that the decision wouldn't affect the New York airline passengers' rights law.

LATER IN THE month, a spokesman for the International Association of Machinists and Aerospace Workers (IAMAW), a union representing employees of Northwest Airlines and Continental Airlines, contacted Kate to see if she would support their opposition to rumored mergers between Delta and Northwest, and Continental and United.

Soaring fuel prices were costing the airlines billions of dollars, and many financial experts agreed that mergers were a necessary evil to keep the industry healthy. IAMAW feared that the mergers could result in a loss of some of its union membership. According to Kate, the spokesman promised that IAMAW would help her lobby on Capitol Hill if she would support them.

Kate was reflexively opposed to anything the airlines wanted to do, so she wanted to enter into an alliance with IAMAW. In this case, I was ambivalent. It seemed ridiculous to me that anyone would care if Kate endorsed an anti-merger position, but the mere fact that someone would ask was an indication of how far we had come.

I agreed to support the alliance on the condition that IAMAW would let us place an article in one of their newsletters. The article would encourage their union members to join FlyersRights.org, and thus provide a larger base from which we could request donations.

I didn't have direct access to our complete financial picture, but Kate periodically apprised me of our status. With only about $1500 a month coming in from donations, we were hemorrhaging money too.

Kate sent the IAMAW spokesman a draft press release that she had written. She wrote, "I'm sending this to you and Mark Mogel, our VP of just about everything ... so we can get this out today." I probably should have thanked her for the promotion to "VP of just about everything," but her draft was so poorly written that I was embarrassed that she sent it. I rewrote it and sent it back to the spokesman. Four days later, an article about the alliance appeared in the Houston Chronicle:

> A labor union representing workers at some of the nation's largest carriers, including Continental Airlines, joined with a passenger rights group Monday to fight mergers. 'Airline passengers bear the brunt of poor service. Combining two major airlines with diverse corporate cultures is a recipe for disaster,' Kate Hanni, executive director of the coalition, said in a statement.[31]

She had asked me to provide her with a sound bite at the time, but I was busy with something else. I knew little about the dynamics of airline mergers, and intelligent, relevant sound bites took time to create. Kate was usually very good at saying something vague enough to make it sound like she knew what she was talking about, without revealing that she didn't. It was a talent that many in Washington had developed.

A month later, IAMAW ran the article in their newsletter, but there was never a perceptible increase in our petition signatures, and the mergers took place anyway.

This episode was just one example of many similar forays into things that had nothing to do with our goals, but simply increased Kate's growing network of contacts and allies. I had recently begun to realize that I wasn't doing myself any favors.

Her total effort for any one of these things, I thought, amounted to talking to someone on the telephone or writing a couple of e-mails. It was I who then spent a day or more doing background research, writing press releases, speeches, articles or whatever else was necessary to enhance her credibility. I wasn't getting paid for any of this, and while I was busy making Kate famous there was nothing in any of this for me. A degree of resentment was beginning to build.

I didn't want to give up on the cause, but it was time to find a way to make money while doing it. Despite my doubts about what was going on with the hotline, if it was getting even half of the calls she claimed, I thought that there was a potential revenue opportunity there. I told Kate that I wanted to turn the hotline into a new kind of travel concierge service, that I wanted her to sign ownership of it over to me, and that otherwise I was going to leave and find something else to do. She agreed on the basis that she would also be compensated. Over the course of the next month, I would develop a business plan to achieve those goals.

THE DOT'S TARMAC delay task force was scheduled to meet periodically over the next ten months. The first meeting was scheduled for February 26 in Washington, and the DOT invited Kate to make the keynote speech. She wanted to play hotline recordings of tarmac stranding calls at the beginning of the speech. Prior to this, my only involvement with the hotline had been to research a handful of tarmac stranding calls and to assist with system setup. Other than that, I had avoided the hotline like the plague.

As long as I could remember, she had been telling the media that we were getting 70 or more hotline calls per day. An NPR article published on November 19, 2007 said, "Hanni says her hotline fields about 70 calls a day from irate passengers – a number that is growing all the time."[32] In August, she told Fox News that she had received 4000 calls from people stuck on tarmacs in just the previous two months. And there were dozens of other articles with similar claims. I had always suspected that she was exaggerating those numbers. I just didn't know by how much.

Kate and the hotline volunteers had kept a spreadsheet for the hotline calls. I now looked at that and found that the average number of calls wasn't anywhere near 70 per day. I thought maybe this was just a lack of diligent documentation, so I logged into the hotline's online system and found a comprehensive, automated, historical record that listed every call since the inception of the hotline the previous June.

It turned out that the hotline was getting approximately seven calls per day, but most of those were hang-ups, media people trying to reach Kate and other non-airline passenger issues. Between the spreadsheets and the automated records, I determined that the hotline got an average of about three calls per day from airline passengers.

The vast majority of those calls involved ticketing complaints, baggage issues, and canceled flights. According to the spreadsheets, there was an average of only one or two calls per month from a passenger stuck on a tarmac. It was rarer still for those calls to come in when a passenger was still on the airplane – they usually called a day or two later. If I had previously had any doubts that perhaps it was me with the distorted view of reality, this revelation put those doubts to rest. When I asked Kate where the other thousands of calls were, she said she got a lot of calls on her cell phone that weren't accounted for in the spreadsheets or the automated logs.

"I'm not very good at documentation," she said.

We spent a week trying to find hotline recordings about tarmac strandings to play during the task force speech. We managed to find about fifteen, of which only eight were useful.

A few days later, I met Kate at Dulles International Airport as she arrived from California. She had arranged for us to stay at a Holiday Inn in College Park, Maryland. When I asked why we weren't staying at the Windsor Park, she said they were full.

The next morning, I set up my laptop in front of a room full of over fifty airline and airport executives at the first DOT tarmac task force meeting in Washington. Kate stood at the podium while I played the eight hotline calls through the sound system. When the last audio finished playing, she held up her I-Pod and said she had "9000 more calls from passengers whose needs were not met while stuck on aircraft."

I glanced over the screen of my laptop and saw heads turning, airline executives looking at one another as if to determine which airline was the worst culprit. I looked back at Kate at the podium. She was still holding her I-Pod in the air the way a golfer holds her finish after a great shot.

She is unreal, I thought.

After the task meeting, Burt Rubin, who had also attended, accompanied Kate and me to the Metro station across the street from the DOT. I couldn't put my finger on it at the time, but it seemed as if Rubin was hovering – *minding* us. Of course, I didn't know about the restraining order discussion in January, and he didn't know that Kate and I were staying in the same hotel room. I heard him tell Kate that he would probably have to switch trains soon, but it sounded more like a question – as if he wanted to know if he should stay on the train. I heard Kate say, "It's okay."

"What was that all about?" I asked after Rubin got off at his stop.

"I don't know," Kate said.

The day after the task force meeting, we held a press conference in the Rayburn House Office Building on Capitol Hill to release our 2007 airline report card. Once again, despite numerous requests for other coalition members to appear, there was only Kate and me. The night before, Kate pleaded with Ed Mierzwinski of US-PIRG to attend and he had agreed.

I talked about airline statistics, contracts of carriage, customer service plans and the types of food service provided by each of the major airlines. Kate talked about the pages of the report card that she had developed; including unsubstantiated claims of callous and inhumane treatment of airline personnel toward sick and elderly airline passengers. Then she announced that Delta and American tied for the worst airlines. Later that day, articles appeared in the media that said the claims Kate made in her parts of the report card were "baseless and not constructive." In a *Travel Weekly* article, the author wrote:

> The Air Transport Association fired back with a statement declaring that it was 'well aware of the serious but complex problem of extended flight delays,' and that it does give priority to the health and safety of its passengers and crews. The ATA pinned part of the blame for lengthy delays on an 'antiquated air traffic management system' and blasted Hanni for a 'rush to judgment based on conjecture and sensationalism' not only on tarmac delays, but also on topics such as airline mergers and onboard medical emergencies.[33]

I had worried since June 2007 about some of the claims she made in her pages of the report card. "Maybe it isn't true, but let them prove it," she would say, and none of them ever did. One of the advantages that she had seized upon after I discovered that airlines weren't required to fully report tarmac statistics, was that she was free to make whatever claims she wanted about the number of tarmac strandings and their durations. There was no easy way for the airlines to disprove anything. The airlines were lying so she was responding in kind. I was beginning to understand the logic.

After the press conference, we headed to Pittsburgh in my car. We were going to spend the following week traveling through Pennsylvania, New Jersey and finally to New York City, a 7-day, 650-mile road trip. I had arranged a series of press conferences along the way.

A Pennsylvania state representative, Douglas Reichley, had sponsored a passengers' rights bill in the statehouse, and he was having trouble getting the bill considered by the consumer affairs committee. Our trip through Pennsylvania was designed to apply media pressure to get the bill moving. It was also an excuse for Kate and me to spend some extended time together without raising any red flags.

Over the next five days we held press conferences at the Pittsburgh International Airport, inside the state capitol in Harrisburg and in center-city Philadelphia. We got very good press turnout at each one, and the media rewarded us with plenty of print and television coverage. The remarks I wrote for Kate to use in Philadelphia, with Independence Hall and Constitution Hall in the background, read in part:

> We've come here to the birthplace of the Constitution and the
> Bill of Rights to plead with the governor and lawmakers in
> Pennsylvania to pass the airline passenger bill of rights now
> stuck on the tarmac in Harrisburg.
>
> On Wednesday, we will be at a hearing in the Second Circuit
> Court of Appeals in New York City, where the airlines are once
> again trying to use our great Constitution to deny passengers
> basic needs such as a granola bar, water, and working toilets
> when we are held on the ground for hours on end. We don't
> think that's what the founding fathers and authors of the
> Constitution had in mind.

Having now observed Kate in action for several months, I had learned that enticing the media and the public didn't have anything to do with my two best friends, facts and logic. It had to do with emotion, exaggeration and victimization by large, evil corporations.

ON THE 29TH, Congress passed another extension to fund the FAA – this time until June 30, 2008.

MARCH 2008

Hillary Clinton weighs in

ON MARCH 4, we continued our road trip at the New Jersey State House in Trenton. State Assemblyman Sam Thompson had sponsored an airline passengers' bill of rights in New Jersey and we went to hold a joint press conference with him. After the press conference, Thompson bought us lunch in the cafeteria and told us that he thought the Speaker of the House was being bribed by Continental Airlines to prevent his bill from being brought to the floor for a vote.

Later that afternoon, we arrived in New York City and checked into a hotel in midtown Manhattan. Then we started working to get people to show up for the following day's federal appeals court hearing for the New York airline passengers' rights law.

Kate and I had not been getting along very well for the past two days. We had consciously avoided conflict for the first several days of the trip, but after a full week with her, she was driving me crazy. Apparently I was doing the same to her. We hadn't shared a kind word for some time, and it wasn't about to get any better.

Like the court hearing in Albany in December, Kate thought the final decision of the federal appeals court judges – there are three of them at this level – would be influenced by the number of CAPBOR members that would show up for the hearing. This time she wanted to entice members to show up by offering a prize – a free trip to her house in Napa. It was so absurd that I couldn't even argue about it; I just sent it out.

> New York residents! The airlines are trying to overturn your New York State Passengers' Rights Law. Please join us at 10:00 AM on March 5 in Lower Manhattan at the Daniel Patrick Moynihan U.S. Courthouse, 500 Pearl Street, New York, NY 10007. We need as many people as possible to attend this hearing. Show your support for your rights!

> The 50th Coalition member that shows up will get a free trip to
> Napa, CA including a wine tour and golf. And you'll stay at
> Kate's house!

We got no takers, only more unsubscribers and complaints. Kate called
a woman from Philadelphia and convinced her to take the train to New York.
I called someone in Queens. He agreed to come too. At the courthouse the
next morning, the guards made all four of us remove our CAPBOR buttons.

Ted Olson, a former U.S. Solicitor General, was the lead attorney for the
ATA. It seemed to me that the recent Supreme Court ruling in Rowe formed
the basis for the main argument made by the ATA, and it was obvious that
Olson made the better case. In the wake of the Supreme Court's decision, the
lawyers for the state seemed to only half-heartedly defend their passengers'
rights law. Between the substance and tone of the judges' questions, it was
obvious that the state would lose the case.

The press was waiting for us outside the courthouse after the hearing.
Kate got to perform her Hillary Clinton tears act on camera for the first time
– implored the judges to uphold the law. It was very impressive, but it didn't
make national news.

Later that afternoon, I took her to JFK for her flight home. By that point,
Kate and I could hardly wait to get away from one another. Nine straight
days and nights together had been about three too many. When I pulled up to
the curb at the airport, she got out of the car and headed inside without a
word.

"Going to take your bags?" I called after her. *Apparently not.* I thought.
Your chauffeur is supposed to get them for you, eh? I popped the trunk,
removed her bags and wheeled them toward the door, at which point she
reappeared. I handed her the bags.

"Seeya," I said.

"Bye," she said, and off she went.

"You're welcome," I muttered to myself, and then began my long drive
home. Usually, she would call and talk from the time she got through airport
security until the announcement on the plane that the passengers had to turn
off their electronic devices. This wasn't one of those times. Our relationship
would return to normal in a few days, but for now the silent drive home gave
me a chance to reflect upon the past weeks and months.

It had been almost exactly one year since I got involved with airline
passengers' rights. In that time, we had made countless requests for coalition
members to help with lobbying, appear at press conferences and to assist in a
variety of other ways. Except for the lawyers, there had been nary a soul to
pitch in or do anything on a consistent basis.

I had just spent nine straight days and nights with Kate. She hadn't
received a single distress call on her cell phone, so I was now certain that the

hotline, at least on the scale that Kate claimed, was either an illusion or a delusion – I wasn't sure which.

We had run a poll in December to get people to give us a simple yes or no answer in regard to our comments for the DOT rulemaking, and we received only 175 responses to send to the DOT from our then, 20,000 active and dedicated members. At the time, I worried that the miniscule response might have affected Kate's chances of being named to the tarmac task force, especially since it had been me who faxed all of the documents to the DOT. I was wrong about that too. *Maybe the people at the DOT can't count,* I thought.

Yet as far as public, media and governmental regard for Kate and CAPBOR were concerned, we looked like we were a thriving coalition of airline passengers' rights activists. *How insane is this?* I wondered. *Can this really be happening?*

A DAY LATER, back in Napa, Kate received a call from a woman who had seen a news report on a local television station about a tarmac stranding at Dallas-Fort Worth International Airport. A winter storm had dumped seven inches of snow, snarling the airport's operations for hours. None of the stranded passengers called the hotline. The next day, Kate got the phone numbers for three of the passengers from a reporter that covered the story.

This stranding incident was particularly noteworthy because it was just the latest of many since American had pledged in early 2007 that they would abide by a voluntary four-hour limit. After Kate talked to the passengers, I wrote a press release titled, "Up, up and away goes American Airlines promise not to leave passengers stranded on tarmac; Incident underscores why voluntary measures won't work."

> 'We weren't able to physically move aircraft.' That's the explanation hundreds of angry passengers got from American Airlines a day after the carrier stranded 17 flights on the tarmac at Dallas/Fort Worth International Airport (DFW) on Thursday, March 6th.

According to one of the passengers, American served peanuts and water after four hours on the tarmac, but the passengers had to pay for them.

BY MID-MARCH, I finished with the hotline-concierge service business plan. I had researched costs for everything from credit card processing, to taxes and legal fees. I had developed a set of tiered services and prices that should attract subscribers. For every 2200 annual subscribers, we would net a profit of approximately $22,000. Forty percent would go to Kate and sixty percent to me. The hotline operators would be paid, thus solving the ongoing problem of finding people to tend to it. I would own and run it. Most importantly, Kate would be responsible for promoting it. She may not have promoted the hotline as well as she could have in the past, and I was sure that, regardless of previous hotline statistics, we could turn it into a cash machine if she would promote it better. She agreed to everything.

I interviewed several lawyers to find the right one to deal with legal work and contracts, and retained one who offered additional ideas for how the hotline could be made more profitable. He said he had contacts in the hotel and travel industry that could make that happen. I arranged a conference call between Kate, myself and the lawyer. After the conference call, Kate told me that she wanted to retain her own lawyer and accountant in California. "Fine," I said. "Just do it soon, please."

ON MARCH 26, the United States Court of Appeals, Second Circuit, struck down the New York airline passengers' rights law, putting a permanent end to all state-based airline passengers' rights laws. The three judges cast a unanimous decision. In their opinion they wrote, "This conclusion draws considerable support from the Supreme Court's recent unanimous opinion in Rowe ..." The next morning, Kate asked me to write a press release.

> 11:43 A.M.   Flyersrights: k - Looks like they relied heavily if not explicitly on Rowe in their decision. I don't suppose any of the experts will now admit I was right about that case and its affect on the outcome since December - before the Supreme Court even ruled on it.

She didn't respond to that. It didn't take long for a media firestorm to flare up and we spent the next two days managing it.

> 12:41 P.M.   Flyersrights: Kate - can you do CNN at 8:15 AM tomorrow. 5:15 AM for you?

> 12:44 P.M.   Kate: If they will send a car for me and have makeup I'll do it. I just got a call from Fox saying that the AP is reporting that no state can pass a law that it's the Feds that must pass the law.

> 12:44 P.M.   Kate: Is that true?

I yelled, "Are you kidding me?" at my computer screen. At the same time, I was glad that we could finally put the state law sideshow behind us. I could only hope that we hadn't squandered too much precious time and money when we should have been concentrating our attention on the DOT and Congress.

After I wrote a press release, I spent the rest of the day returning calls from reporters and producers from several media outlets. I arranged for CNN to send a car to take Kate to San Francisco for their early morning telecast and for a makeup person to meet her at the studio. When Kate got to the city later that night, there were two local news crews waiting for her. She called to tell me.

"I'm so excited," she said.

"Great, here's the thing," I said. "We have a golden opportunity right now to get the attention of the presidential candidates on this issue. Every newscast you go on, you have to say something like, 'It's time for the presidential candidates to step up and support our bill. Biden has already come out in support. Where is Hillary Clinton?' Something like that."

She nailed the presidential challenge when she appeared on CNN the next morning, although she only mentioned Hillary Clinton by name. I regretted that I had been so specific. After her early morning television appearances in San Francisco, she returned to Napa.

While I was right about the hopelessness of state-sponsored airline passengers' rights laws, I never anticipated the enormous amount of media coverage we would get when the federal appeals court put an end to them.

9:55 A.M.   Flyersrights: Kate - you have a 9AM radio show with Spud McConnell in New Orleans. What is the 8am show?

10:07 A.M.   Kate: OK, Jim Bernstein from News Day just called and i just did another interview in Albany for the Gazette. Busy f...ing morning for being 7 am.

10:09 A.M   Flyersrights: u love it

She answered that she did love it, but that she needed to go to a pharmacy to get a pregnancy test. She said she might be pregnant and that I was the father – something she previously assured me wasn't possible. I tried not to let that distract me from all of the work that needed to be done, but it wasn't easy. Care about her though I did, the possibility was nothing short of a nightmare. There was nothing I could do about it, so I stayed in denial for the rest of the day.

Later, I was listening via Internet feed to a radio show in New Orleans that I had arranged for Kate. During a commercial, without telling me, Kate decided to call into another radio show. When the New Orleans station returned from their commercial, Kate was gone. She had gone on a nationally syndicated radio program out of Irving, Texas, and it didn't go well.

11:45 A.M.   Kate: Salem Radio. They F...ed me. He said he was completely against everything we were doing how dare we ask for legislation, he accused me of lying and it's a nationally syndicated show 5 minutes of radio. I want that show stopped.

I found an audio file of the show on the station's website. The host was Mike Gallagher, and despite the fact that he had given her a difficult time, I thought Kate had done a pretty good job of deflecting his negative comments. It seemed to me that the interview was fine, and I told her there was nothing to worry about.

On the other hand, I was concerned that she kept applauding Judge Kahn, the New York district court judge who upheld the law in December, as a liberal, while she chided the three judges of the appeals court as being conservatives, as if that was why they opposed the law. Sometimes I felt like I was engaged in a perpetual battle to maintain her public image while she was hell-bent to undermine it. I wrote to her:

> Labeling judges as liberal or conservative or right wing does not help our cause. It detracts from the real issues and can alienate people who would otherwise be on our side. People (like me) who believe that the states should not be able to regulate the airlines may still believe in federal legislation and our cause. But if you blame conservative judges for doing the wrong thing, you may alienate these supporters. This is a bipartisan issue but you are making it a liberal issue when you say these things and you're also giving the opposition unnecessary ammunition.

She agreed to stop labeling the judges as liberal versus conservative, "no matter how painful," she wrote.

Later that day, presidential candidate Senator Hillary Clinton issued a statement in support of airline passengers' rights: "The federal government has a responsibility to protect the health and safety of millions of travelers who utilize the airline industry every year."

8:20 P.M.	Kate: This is a statement, finally, from Hillary. Guess we are making a little bit of progress.
8:20 P.M.	Flyersrights: you made the ask. you got a response. Awesome!
8:21 P.M.	Kate: It's not enough I want to hear her say I support the Senate passing the FAA Reauthorization bill before June 30th. Period.
8:22 P.M.	Flyersrights: ok - but its progress. She was listening.
8:22 P.M.	Kate: She'd better f...ing listen. Wait 'til I call out your boy McCain. He's Naval lint.

Later that night, after I had gone to bed, Kate wrote, "You want a boy or a girl?" Fortunately, she was only teasing. The test had come back negative.

FOR SEVERAL MONTHS we had been using Google Alerts to collect articles on a variety of airline related subjects. One of my Google Alerts was set up as "Kate Hanni," so whenever an article containing her name appeared on the Web, Google automatically sent me a link to it.

Three days after the New York law was overturned, I awoke to find a Google Alert for an article in which Kate was quoted as being opposed to airline pilots having guns in cockpits. This was precisely why I told her in October that I needed to be consulted on policy decisions, and once again, I wasn't.

> Kate Hanni, executive director for the Coalition for an Airline Passenger Bill of Rights, said she opposes having a gun in the cockpit. If there must be one, she said, it shouldn't be on the pilot's body during flight, but rather within reach in case of a threat.[34]

One advantage of the time difference between the East and West Coast was that it gave me plenty of time to research issues long before she woke up in Napa. I wrote to her:

> Why are we opposed to pilots having guns in the cockpit when 75% of all pilots polled in 2002 were in favor, the House passed overwhelmingly 307 of 435, and in the Senate it passed 87 to 6? If the pilots had guns in the cockpits on Sept 11, the World Trade Center would probably still be there and thousands of lives would have been saved. We probably would not be in a war in Afghanistan or Iraq, we wouldn't have 4000 dead soldiers, and the country would have saved billions of dollars. This is an enormously unpopular position to take, so splain to me why we're opposed to having guns in the cockpit!

She called and said that she didn't know the reporter was going to ask her about guns in cockpits, so she "just winged it." She said that her father taught her about guns so she knew what she was talking about when it came to guns. "They can be dangerous if they aren't handled properly," she said.

"Next time, please tell the reporter that we haven't formulated an official position and that you'll get back to them. You don't have to answer every question that a reporter asks you," I said.

KATE AND I were scheduled to tape a half-hour Comcast talk show on March 28 that was based out of Philadelphia; *Larry Kane's Voice of Reason.* I would be at the Comcast studio in Philadelphia, and Kate would appear by satellite from San Francisco. The show would be seen by Comcast cable subscribers from Virginia to New England.

I had done a number of print interviews and had appeared briefly in some television newscasts, but never in a situation like this. I preferred being in the background, doing research and providing sound bites. I wasn't a seasoned performer like Kate, and I wasn't looking forward to doing a public duet with her. Kate and I disagreed about so many things, so often, that I worried that we could easily get into an argument right there on the show. Unfortunately, when I had pitched the idea for the show to its producers in February, they insisted that somebody from the Philadelphia area appear on the broadcast. I was the only option.

The night before the taping, Kate asked me to provide some talking points. I wrote and e-mailed them to her the next morning.

At the Comcast studio in Philadelphia later that afternoon, I was nervous about appearing on a television show for the first time. I looked at my reflection in the mirror in the makeup room. Nearly bald, the little bit of hair I still had on the top of my head stuck straight up. *I hate this,* I thought.

While a makeup woman sprayed some kind of makeup on my face, Larry Kane appeared in the door of the room with a spectacular blonde whom he later said was Victoria Zdrok. The makeup woman warned that if I didn't keep my head still, she'd spray me in the eye. After Zdrok left, Larry came in and introduced himself. He said that Zdrok was one of only two women ever to appear as a centerfold in both *Playboy* and *Penthouse* magazines. He had just interviewed her for another show.

"Tough job, Larry," I said.

Larry and I walked down a hallway and into a studio to tape our show. Inside, I could see Kate on a television monitor reading the talking points. They came in handy, but Larry would take us into a direction that I hadn't anticipated. As one of the segments ended, he said that he was going to come back to me after the break to ask if our legislation addressed the quality of air in an airplane when it is stuck on the tarmac.

That's going to lead to a question about airline water, I thought. *If he asks **me** about that, there's going to be a big problem.*

I had been trying to educate Kate on the facts about the EPA airline water study since the Fox News interview in February, but that tutelage hadn't gone well. She continued to tell reporters that all of the airlines were flying around with E. coli in their water. I wasn't worried about answering the question accurately if Larry asked me about airline water. I was worried that Kate would disagree with me, and that could lead to the on-screen argument that I had feared from the onset of this project.

After someone in the studio signaled that they had stopped taping, I tried to tell Kate that she should take the next set of questions. What followed was akin to an Abbott and Costello *Who's on First* comedy routine, except that it wasn't funny. Because Kate, Larry and I were all talking through the same audio system, we were all talking over one another.

"Can you tell me how much time we have?" Larry asked his producer, who was hidden from view somewhere in a control booth. Only Larry could hear the producer.

"Kate," I said, trying to get her attention in San Francisco.

"Not Kate," Larry said.

"I don't know," Kate said.

"No, this is for the producer," Larry said.

"How long – oh you're finding out," Larry said to the producer.

"Kate," I repeated.

"No, I'm talking to the producer," Larry said.

Apparently still talking to the producer, Larry said, "We're going to talk a little about air, fresh air …"

"Yes, that is in the bill," Kate interrupted.

"I was thinking that Kate might be better off – uh – she might be better suited to talk about that," I said.

"OK, I just want to know how much time we have remaining in the program," Larry said.

"Mark, you know that's written in the bill," Kate said.

Larry gave me a look – to shut up so that he could hear his producer. We could see Kate on the monitor, but she couldn't see us. She kept talking.

"OK, we have four minutes," Larry interrupted.

Now talking to Kate and me, Larry said, "The first thing I want to talk about is fresh air and the fact that a lot of people get sick on airplanes …"

"Yes," Kate interrupted. "How about the E. coli in the water?"

Larry said we would talk about that too. Then, he and Kate started to talk about the weather in San Francisco. I couldn't get a word in edgewise.

"OK, we're back for a lightning round …," Larry said as they resumed taping.

A bolt of lightning would be a blessing right now, I thought.

Fortunately, Larry only asked me about air quality, and then turned to Kate to ask about airline water. Kate said that all airlines had coliform in their water and that meant there were feces in the water.

One of the things I had tried to explain to her since the Fox News interview in February was that the presence of coliform in the water did not mean there were feces in the water. It meant that it was *possible* that there were feces in the water. The 2004 EPA study had found that 49 of 327 samples from airplane lavatories or galleys tested positive for coliform, but only two tested positive for E. coli/fecal matter.

I didn't want fecal material in any airline water, but her continuous, gross exaggeration of publicly available facts, I feared again, would sink the ship at some point. By and large, the media relies on credible sources, and she seemed hell-bent to risk our credibility over things that had nothing to do with our main objectives.

Earlier in the show, Larry had asked me why it was taking so long to get airline passengers' rights laws passed. I explained that we were outgunned by the airlines' political machine, and that we were only able to lobby in Washington once a month while the airlines were there every day.

Larry turned to Kate for her opinion. "So Kate, there's a lot of political opposition to what you're trying to do?" he asked.

Reflexively, as she did so often, she just had to disagree with me, except this time it was on television.

"Well actually there's not a lot of political opposition," she said.

I thought I'd have a coronary. We didn't have a three-hour rule in either the House or Senate FAA reauthorization bills specifically because of political opposition, and she said there wasn't much opposition – on a television show that would be rerun about ten times in the largest combined cable television market in the United States, including Washington, D.C. And then she criticized Senator Jay Rockefeller's support of user fees, the small-plane taxes that LMG had been retained to fight against.

Later, as we chatted in his office, Larry told me to tell Kate that she had done a great job during the program.

"I'll do that," I said – *right after I strangle her,* I thought.

APRIL 2008

Seventy calls per day

IN EARLY APRIL, Kate was featured in an article published by CNN-*Money* magazine. The reporter wrote, "Hanni has collected more than 9,000 voice mails from stranded passengers, which she has played at press conferences and to Department of Transportation (DOT) officials."[35]

While articles like that served our goals, they also made me worry about the credibility of the media at large. I had certainly heard others question the reliability of the news media, but I had always suspected that those questions were raised by pundits or others with self-serving agendas.

By stating that Kate had collected 9,000 voice mails from stranded passengers, the reporter implied that this was a verified fact. Had the reporter attributed the claim to Kate, the article would have been accurate and true even though Kate's claim wasn't.

In our world of airline passengers' rights, it might very well have been that the ends justified the means – only history would tell. But in a broader sense, I wondered how much I'd previously seen and read might have been partly an illusion perpetrated by individuals and organizations with hidden agendas and then served up by the media as true and accurate.

I also wondered how much Congress was affected by the news media, if they too were manipulated by its coverage, or did they already know or suspect that much of what was reported wasn't true.

A claim such as "9,000 voice mails from stranded passengers" helped make the tarmac stranding situation appear to be far more prevalent than it really was. It also helped to bolster the appearance that CAPBOR was a large, flourishing organization – there would have to be a small army of trained volunteers answering the phones, and people managing those volunteers and processes.

None of it was true, but by now, partly with my help, Kate had convinced everyone that she presided over a vast organization composed of legal, lobbying, administration, communications, information technology and research departments, each teeming with armies of volunteers. As far as I could tell, the other members of the inner circle, the lawyers, believed most of this too. All they knew was what Kate told them along with articles she sent to them, which just repeated her exaggerations.

While Kate and I may have had different motives, we didn't have a hidden agenda. We were genuinely trying to get airline passengers' rights laws enacted. Kate had apparently taken an ends justifies the means approach from the beginning. It had taken me a while to catch on and willingly join her in that strategy, but I still had limits.

She was scheduled to appear before the House Aviation Subcommittee on April 9, and that presented a dilemma in my mind. *How do we maintain the public illusion in the face of possible probing questions from elected federal representatives?* I thought I had heard of people going to prison for lying to Congress. I wasn't going to go to prison for a three-hour tarmac rule, and I didn't want Kate to go to jail either.

I spent the first days of April writing the testimony for the upcoming hearing. I started by looking at the September 2007 testimony that I had also written. To my dismay, that testimony said the hotline got 70 calls per day. I had no way to know at the time that it wasn't true. There would be no claims of 70 calls per day in this testimony. I worked on the draft for three days. Corbett applied his usual professional polish, and then I sent the testimony to the committee.

Fishing for ideas to round out her oral testimony, Kate talked to a senior member of the committee's professional staff. According to Kate, one of the suggestions made was for her to talk about "how many hotline calls we've gotten since June [2007]."

Sometimes I felt like I was playing the arcade game "Whack-a-Mole." Just when I thought I had solved one problem, the varmint would stick its head up somewhere else. I wrote a lengthy e-mail to Kate about the tone and subjects that I thought we should have in the oral testimony. I specifically objected to the suggestion that she talk about the hotline: "I think this is a waste of valuable time. And remember, you're under oath."

They didn't administer an oath during the hearings when Kate testified, but it seemed possible to me that there might have been some kind of law against lying to them anyway. Even if there wasn't a law, there were moral issues at stake. Unfortunately, I couldn't figure out a way to ask any of our lawyers about the legal consequences of making false statements to Congress without raising other questions I didn't want to answer.

Corbett agreed with my suggestions about the tone and direction of the oral testimony, and suggested that Kate follow that course.

I had gone out to play golf, and when I got home I received an outline for the oral testimony that Kate had written. We discussed the outline via instant messages. For the most part, she had followed my original suggestions, but she also wanted to talk about the slot restrictions that the DOT had previously ordered for the JFK and Newark airports. She had a penchant for wanting to weigh in on every conceivable airline related issue. It added to the public illusion that she was well informed, but it diverted time and attention, usually my time and attention, from the ultimate goal; a three-hour tarmac limit.

5:54 P.M.   Flyersrights: This is not our immediate problem. Passengers rights! Deplanement. Essential needs. Unenforcement of contracts! DOT crapola!

5:54 P.M.   Kate: If you totally re-write it I may not be able to memorize enough. Agreed that's the problem. And I'm going to be in the f...ing hot seat so let's make it hot.

After Kate had been named to the DOT task force on tarmac delays, we had returned to a tried and true method of getting publicity by criticizing the DOT and everything they did. Because of that, Kate had been getting a lot of flak from one of her "deep throats" at the DOT. Reluctantly, to help preserve her relationship with him, I had softened the written testimony in regard to the DOT, and had even complimented the department for some of its recent actions.

5:57 P.M.   Flyersrights: Here's what will make it hot ... you've pressured yourself into making nice with the DOT , and saying all these nice things because politically you're afraid they will be all consumers are left with because Congress won't f...ing act. So you have to say all these nice things but sitting here now, I can't do it. In tears. Please act!

5:57 P.M.   Kate: Exactly. Perfect.

I wanted her to disavow the written testimony, testimony that I had written, and say that she had only submitted that under duress from the DOT. Knowing that she could shed tears on cue, it could work. I worked on her oral testimony for an hour and then we resumed our conversation. Kate was scheduled to fly to Washington the next day.

7:11 P.M.   Kate: I want my oral before I leave so I can study it, memorize it, practice crying.

7:12 P.M.   Kate: You know the things that are really important in a relationship are honesty, integrity and a good sense of humor..................if you can fake those things you're in good shape.

7:12 P.M.   Flyersrights: lol

Unfortunately, I was coming down with a cold or the flu, and it was becoming increasingly difficult to think or stay awake. The best I could do was to send her a draft before she left for the airport. Corbett had taken a stab at writing it too, but neither Kate nor I liked his version.

Kate flew to Washington on Sunday, and I drove down to meet her on Monday morning. She had reserved two rooms at a Howard Johnson's in Cheverly, Maryland. When I asked why we were staying there, once again, she said that the Windsor Park was full.

Kate would share her room with Jennifer Shirkani on Monday and Tuesday. Shirkani would be replaced by Anjum Malik on Wednesday. I stayed in a room a few doors down the hall. Shirkani and Malik had made congressional appointments with their senators and representatives for the upcoming week. With their help, we were beginning to get a bit more organized when it came to making appointments.

By Monday night I was desperately ill, which made it impossible to concentrate on the oral testimony. It was all I could do to drive Kate and Shirkani to Capitol Hill on Tuesday morning. I went back to the hotel to sleep. Later that afternoon, Corbett inquired about my health and the status of the testimony, which by then I had conceded I couldn't finish. I replied:

> Seems like I'm improving. As for the oral ... Kate is requesting
> support from a 3rd party and I think she's back on the safety
> issue. I think maybe we need to try a hybrid approach ... Yours
> doesn't sound like her. Mine did but went awry. Only problem is
> I'm running out of gas ...

The next morning, Kate sent me a copy of the oral testimony that had been revised by someone at LMG. In the e-mail string, LMG founder Julian Epstein had written to Kate, "Thanks again for all the great work."

Thanks for what great work? I wondered. *Thanks on behalf of your general aviation clients?*

That same morning, American Airlines canceled hundreds of flights around the country to comply with an FAA airworthiness directive for how wiring bundles were installed in the wheel-wells of its fleet of McDonnell Douglas aircraft. Kate hadn't talked to me or polled anyone else, but was nonetheless ready with a sound bite for the *Los Angeles Times*:

> 'Passengers are definitely worried,' said Kate Hanni, founder of
> the Coalition for Passengers' Bill of Rights, Health and Safety, a
> traveler advocacy group. 'People are afraid.'[36]

I wondered how a newspaper like that could publish a nonsensical quote like that but, more importantly, despite my previous objections she had added "Health and Safety" to the CAPBOR name. Ever since former DOT inspector general Ken Mead had suggested that we get involved in health and safety issues, she was hell-bent to do so. Shoehorning those words into the name of the organization seemed to be the most important step, and apparently adequately substituted for the fact that we knew very little about those subjects.

This incident, along with the forgone 25 percent of proceeds from a possible book, the hotline plan for which she still hadn't retained a lawyer, and the seemingly continuous flouting of the pact we made in October to confer on policy issues, made me resolve that Kate and I needed to have a long talk about her definition of an *agreement*.

That afternoon, she testified before the House Aviation Subcommittee. I was still sick, but I went to the hearing anyway. I sat next to Ed Mierzwinski. Anjum Malik and Burt Rubin were also there. After she thanked Chairman Costello for his introduction, Kate's oral testimony began:

> The active members of our coalition number 22,074 as of
> yesterday and growing. Among many coalition activities, we
> now operate a state-of-the-art, around-the-clock hotline to talk
> with people in real time who are stranded on airline flights …

This wasn't going to turn out well, I just knew it.

"As recently as last month, American Airlines kept 17 aircraft on the tarmac at DFW for several hours beyond that airline's own non-binding four-hour limit. I know this because we get the phone calls from the passengers inside those aircraft," she continued.

We never got any phone calls from those passengers. I had mentioned the incident in the written testimony and in the oral testimony draft because it was important to demonstrate that airlines' voluntary commitments weren't worth the paper on which they were printed. I deliberately avoided the details about how we found out about the incident. I wondered if the reporter who gave the names of those passengers to Kate was watching the hearing.

Finally, she got to the substance of why a passengers' bill of rights needed to be enacted, and that was good, relevant testimony based upon what Corbett and I had written. Then she mentioned the danger of off-shore airline maintenance and inspections, another hot topic that had been in the news lately, but that we didn't know much about. *What is she going to say if they ask her more about that?* I wondered.

Finally it was over. I breathed a sigh of relief. *Okay, that wasn't so bad*, I thought. She had fibbed here and there, but nobody would go to jail over any of that – but it wasn't over.

During the question and answer session, Chairman Costello asked Kate about the hotline; "Your organization has a hotline, an 800 phone number for passengers and people who have complaints to call. How many calls do you get in a given period? You must have statistics?"

The gallery was full of many of the same reporters that she had been telling that she got 70 calls a day. *Please say you'll get him that information later,* I thought.

"Our average is 70 calls per day ..." she said with a heavy emphasis on the word "average."

I'm obviously not a saint, but I believe that people should not lie to Congress. It isn't just a legal question – our democracy depends upon it. Without accurate information, people can't make sound decisions, and Congress already has enough trouble making sound decisions without people lying to them.

Members of Congress lie all of the time; not all of them but many. They lie to each other, they lie to the media and they lie to the public. The difference is that everyone knows that somebody is lying. It's all part of a well understood game. But when a citizen sits in one of those witness chairs and purports to give factual testimony so that Congress can make a decision about something, I believe they must tell the truth.

Nobody, not even Kate, had worked harder than I during the past year to achieve some level of airline passenger protections. The effort I devoted to airline statistics was intended to give Congress and others a more accurate picture of tarmac strandings. Everything else I did was to make her famous and credible, and to increase the volume of discourse in regard to tarmac strandings so that the subject stayed in the public conscience. I didn't do any of it to give her a license to lie to Congress.

I had no idea whether three calls or seventy calls a day would cause the government to do something different. Maybe it didn't matter, but what if it did? They had specifically asked for that information, so there must have been a reason. As I sat there at that moment, for all I knew Kate had just committed a federal crime. *What if they ask her for proof?* I wondered. *What if you end up in jail, Kate?*

Chairman Costello smiled, listened intently. "Seventy calls a day," he echoed. He seemed impressed.

Then Kate said, "Yes, now that goes up at holiday times and down during slower travel periods, but the average is 70 a day."

She told more lies in the next five minutes than in five Washington State testimonies put together.

"The first day we started our hotline I got 900 calls in three hours," she continued.

Costello asked Kate what she did with the hotline calls.

Kate said, "First we take care of their immediate need – like if an eight year old daughter has been told to get off a plane without accompaniment ..."

There was only ever one incident like that, and the woman called to complain two days after the airline temporarily lost track of her daughter. Nobody helped her in real time.

She went on like this for what seemed like an eternity. Four days earlier, I specifically warned her to stay away from the subject of the hotline, not to lie. Two days after the hearing, I quit. I sent an e-mail to Corbett and Rubin to let them know, although I didn't tell them why.

SUMMER 2008

No good choices

I WAS UPSET when Kate lied during the hearing on April 9, but that wasn't the only reason I quit. It might not even have been in the top ten.

After the hearing, Anjum Malik, Kate and I went to Union Station – first for a bite to eat and then to retrieve my car. Later, in their room at the hotel, Kate and I had a couple of drinks and talked about a press conference that we were scheduled to attend the next morning at the Capitol. Eventually, Malik and Kate said they were going to turn in. I said goodnight and went to my room. About twenty minutes later, there was a knock at my door.

"Kate, I'm still sick," I cautioned as she entered my room.

The next morning, I awoke to hear a loud gasp. Sunlight streamed through the curtains. Kate stood beside the bed. Her hands covered her mouth – her eyes were as wide as saucers.

"What am I going to tell Anjum? Shit, shit, shit."

"Tell her we were working on the press conference statement and you fell asleep." I said. "What's the big deal?"

She looked at me as if I was crazy. "This has never happened to me before," she said, and out of the door she went.

I watched with a mix of concern and amusement as she scurried down the hallway in her pajamas. When I saw that she was safely inside her room, I started to get ready for the day ahead.

What has never happened to you before? I wondered.

It was our last day in Washington, so I packed Malik's, Kate's and my luggage into my car. We checked out of the hotel and headed to Capitol Hill. We were scheduled to have a press conference with Senators Boxer, Snowe, Schumer, and Lautenberg at the Capitol later that morning, and then we were to have a meeting with Senator McCain's office immediately afterward. I spent the drive to Capitol Hill arguing with Kate about her addition of "health and safety" to the CAPBOR acronym.

I wasn't as passionate about that particular issue as I was about others, but I thought if I engaged in an argument with Kate in front of Malik, it might help to ease whatever awkwardness had occurred when Kate got back to her room. That is, if Kate and I argued about something, Malik would be inclined to believe that Kate had inadvertently fallen asleep in my room and that there was nothing more to it.

I dropped off Malik and Kate in front of the Senate Hart Office Building, and then drove to the Union Station parking garage. It took me about fifteen minutes to walk back to Senator Boxer's office. When I got there, my intuition told me that something was wrong. Malik seemed nervous. Kate was unusually quiet and distant. Rubin took me aside to try to assuage my concerns about Kate's addition of "health and safety" to the CAPBOR name, but it seemed as if he was trying to keep me occupied.

Eventually, someone from Boxer's staff led us to the underground train that would take us to the Capitol for the press conference. I walked to the train in front of the others and, when I boarded one of the cars, Rubin, Malik and Kate boarded another car behind. Except for Boxer's staff member, my car was empty. When we reached the press conference room in the Capitol, I milled around and found myself chatting with one of Senator Lautenberg's legislative aides. The room was crammed with reporters and cameras. "They really show up for Kate, don't they." he said.

Kate Hanni, April 10, 2008, U.S. Capitol,
Washington D.C.
Copyright © 2008 Associated Press

Each of the senators made speeches in support of airline passengers' rights, and Kate read the remarks I had prepared for her. After the press conference, Kate answered a couple of questions from reporters and then disappeared through a side door. *Where is she going?* I wondered.

Malik approached me and said that Kate had to go to a last minute, unexpected meeting. Malik said that Kate wanted me to meet with Senator John McCain's office myself – McCain who had already clinched the Republican nomination for the upcoming presidential election!

"You're kidding, right?"

"That's what Kate asked me to tell you," Malik said.

"When was this?" I asked.

"On the train on the way over," she said. "It can't be helped."

Something is wrong, I thought. Kate never gave other people messages like that to deliver to me.

I waited in McCain's office for about a half hour before his staff canceled with an excuse about an emergency of some kind. I knew before I got there that they probably wouldn't meet with me since I was neither a constituent, nor a well-known public figure like Kate. The only reason we got the appointment was because Kate's mother lived in Arizona.

Later that afternoon, I met with a staff member for another senator's office. Burt Rubin showed up – an unprecedented event. Rubin had sometimes attended meetings when Kate was present, but he had never before attended a meeting with only me. Afterward, as we walked to Union Station, Rubin asked where I was going. I told him that I needed to find Malik because I had her luggage in my car, and then the same for Kate – to take her to the airport. Rubin said he was going home to Alexandria, just outside of Washington.

I located Malik on Connecticut Avenue. When I pulled up to the address she had given me, she was standing on the sidewalk in front of a clothes store. I rolled down the passenger window.

"C'mon, get in," I said.

"No, I don't want to trouble you," she said. "I'll get a taxi."

She said she was going to a friend's house in northwest Washington, and she repeated that she didn't want to trouble me, that she would get a taxi.

"It's no trouble," I insisted.

Finally, she got into the car and I drove her to her friend's house. Then I headed back into town, to the National Press Club where Kate had last told me she would be. I called her when I got to the lobby.

She said that I should leave the luggage with the guard because the security people wouldn't let me come up to the studio without an escort, and she said that the network had arranged for a town car to take her to the airport. It was a quick, perfunctory call, not at all like Kate.

"Don't get paranoid, Mark," I said to myself. "Just leave the luggage and go home."

When I was just a few miles north of Washington, Kate called and asked where her luggage was.

"I left it with the guard at the National Press Club," I said.

"But I'm at Bloomberg," she said.

"Shit! Do you want me to come back and get you?" I asked.

"No, Burt is here. He'll help me. Gotta go." She hung up.

Burt? But he said he was going home, I thought. Now I was sure something suspicious was going on. I tried to call her back. She didn't answer.

A few minutes later I got a call from Marilyn Adams, a reporter for *USA Today*. Adams was writing a story – the premise of which was that Paul Hudson and Kate were leading the fight for passenger's rights.

Kate had been talking about this story for the past two weeks, and I had mixed feelings about it. Kate's purpose for this publicity angle, she said, was to reward Hudson for assuming the financial burden for the lawsuits against American Airlines.

Hudson had made a contribution to the passengers' rights cause, but he hadn't contributed a fraction of the time and effort that either Corbett or I had, at least not since the formation of CAPBOR. Based upon my observations, it was arguable that Rubin had invested more into the effort than Hudson. Rubin's idea for the Strand-In alone was priceless.

I didn't know how Rubin or Corbett felt about the story angle, but I didn't want the publicity so I was willing to go along with it. The problem was that I didn't have anything substantive to say about Hudson. I couldn't even figure out on what possible basis Kate had pitched the story angle to Adams. On top of all that, I suspected that I had been thrown under a bus. I told Adams that it wasn't a good time to talk because I was driving.

"Let's talk tomorrow," I said.

The next day, Kate was back in Napa, and I was in Collegeville. I called her. The first thing I wanted to know was what happened when she got back to her room the previous morning. She tried to change the subject, stalled and asked me why I hadn't called Adams back. I persisted, and Kate finally said that Anjum Malik had been very worried about her whereabouts when she awoke to find Kate missing. According to Kate, Malik suggested that I might have slipped something into Kate's drink the night before.

"Anjum said that I should call the police and get a rape kit," Kate said.

The word "rape" exploded in my brain like a cluster bomb.

"Rape kit!" I yelled into the phone. "What did you tell her?"

Kate said, "I told her that everything was alright, that I trust you and it was just bad judgment for going to your room in the first place."

This doesn't sound right to me, I thought. *Why would Malik jump to the conclusion that a rape had occurred?* I assumed that Malik must have said something similar to Burt Rubin before I got to Boxer's office. That would have explained his actions.

"What was with all the sudden changes in plans – me not taking you to the airport? Why was Burt at Bloomberg?" I asked.

"Mark, they love me. They want to protect me. They want to make sure I'm safe."

How true that was. They all thought she was some kind of a saint.

"Kate, you need to fix this and you need to fix this now," I said loudly. I hung up. I had no way of knowing what really happened when Kate got back to her room, but I knew I couldn't have one person, let alone two, wondering if I might be a rapist. I couldn't talk to her further because I had a golf and dinner date scheduled with my wife and some friends. I shot about 50 over par on the golf course. I'm not sure I could even see the ball.

Later that night, Kate and I had a major argument in e-mails and instant messages – an argument that lasted until the early morning hours of Sunday, April 12. I had given her ample opportunity to find a way to resolve the situation. She told me that she had been doing a radio interview earlier and she hadn't had time, that now it was too late. She continued to try to change the subject, kept asking why I hadn't returned Marilyn Adams' calls about the *USA Today* article.

She didn't grasp the enormous gravity of the rape situation. It was as if it meant nothing. I thought I was going to have an aneurism, while she remained cool and detached. I told her that if she didn't find a way to mitigate the problem, I would tell Malik and Rubin about the affair. She said they would never believe me.

It was possible that she was right. I had plenty of personal e-mails, instant messages, pictures and videos that would constitute evidence of the affair in a courtroom, but I couldn't share any of that with Malik or Rubin. Much of it was far too personal. Without those things it would be my word against hers, and that was a fight I didn't want to have.

It was obvious that Kate wasn't going to tell Malik or Rubin the truth, or make any attempt whatsoever to mitigate the situation. All she seemed to care about was the *USA Today* article. In her mind, it seemed, she had told Malik that everything was fine, and therefore there was no reason for me to be upset about anything. In my mind's eye, I saw my friend being raped 40 years earlier. Male or female, I perceive rape as a more horrendous crime against another person than any other. I couldn't have been more distressed, but I was in a box.

If I pressed the issue with Malik and Rubin, I worried that things could get out of control – that my wife would learn the truth. There were only two options left: I could either move forward as though nothing had happened, which is what Kate seemed to want to do; or I could withdraw from the field. *That's* when I quit.

After two weeks of silence, Kate began to send me e-mails in which she claimed that I hacked her computer to have it send personal videos to my e-mail address – videos she had sent to me months earlier. There was nothing of consequence in the videos. They were short videos of Kate, fully clothed, saying "I love you" and things of that nature. She knew I had other pictures that were far more risqué, but in her e-mails she seemed transfixed on the videos. It was obvious that she was worried that I might use any or all of those things to retaliate against her in some way, but I would later learn that this was only one of her motives for concocting the hacking allegation. She was also worried that, if Hudson, Corbett or Rubin found out about the affair, they would stop assisting her. More importantly, her husband would soon discover some of this evidence on her computer, and she would tell him that I had hacked into her computer and planted it. It was her perfect explanation for everything.

I replied that she had no need to worry. I assured her that I would never let anyone see anything and that I just wanted to move on in peace. Not only did that not satisfy her, but she escalated the situation to blackmail. She threatened that, if I were to tell anyone anything, she would see to it that I was thoroughly embarrassed by a media campaign that she would mount against me – something I knew from experience that she was more than capable of doing. She also threatened to tell my wife, not that we'd had an affair, but that I was an obsessed stalker who had hacked her computer.

I continued to write reasonable, dispassionate, conciliatory responses, but nothing seemed to appease her. She was really scaring me. I became increasingly stressed and worried about what she might do. She seemed to have come apart at the seams.

ALTHOUGH I HAD quit in April, I continued to follow news reports about airline passengers' rights. On May 16, I received a Google Alert about airline statistics. The U.S. Department of Transportation announced that, beginning in October, airlines would be required to report more complete tarmac data. With me gone, Kate had to write a press release about the announcement herself. I could tell from her misuse of the word "incidences" and several incorrectly capitalized words. Also, in what seemed like spite directed toward me, she minimized the significance of the new rule:

> 'Today's DOT Announcement is a small but important victory for airline travelers who've found themselves stuck on the tarmac on a diverted or canceled flight,' Hanni said. 'At least the Government will force the airlines to document and report these incidences where people leave the gate and fly at tarmac level for hours on end. Our Coalition discovered that diverted and canceled flights were not counted for Time on the Tarmac and we can take credit for this victory.'

It was, in fact, a major victory – the first governmental rule issued as a direct result of our actions. I should have been able to celebrate, but I was so ill from stress that I found it difficult to eat or sleep.

On that same day, Joe Sharkey wrote a column in his personal blog about the new rule and the book he was working on with Kate. He also took the opportunity to take potshots at David Stempler and Paul Hudson:

Kate gets a lot of media attention, especially on television, because she is the real deal – unlike other often-trotted-out so-called passenger spokesmen who have been the go-to people for reporters over the years. ... The other two media favorites, David Stempler, the self-described president of the so-called Airline Passengers Association, and Paul Hudson, the self-described executive director of the so-called Aviation Consumer Action Project, actually represent no one but themselves. Both 'groups' are one-man operations, with no real constituencies (or even offices) – even though the credulous media often refer to Hudson as a Ralph Nader associate (as if poor old Ralph Nader has any credible standing, or associates, anymore.)

"One-man operation" and "no real constituency" was how Kate often spoke derogatorily about Hudson behind his back. It was particularly ironic that Sharkey deleted his blog entry two days later, because on that day, *USA Today* published Marilyn Adams' article about how Paul Hudson and Kate had been leading the fight for airline passengers' rights. I hadn't contributed to the article. I had ignored Adams' phone calls. The article wasn't entirely positive:

Hanni clearly enjoys the media spotlight. A theater arts major in college, Hanni says she always wanted to be a rock star, 'to be in front of a gazillion people with their lighters on' in concert. 'That's why this media stuff has been so easy for me,' she says. The coalition has brought her far more notoriety than any of the local rock bands she ever performed with. But she sometimes struggles with accuracy. [37]

You have no idea, Marilyn, I thought. *No idea at all.*

Meanwhile, I tried to move on with my life. I was doing some website development for a client, and I also happened upon an idea based on a local tragedy. The Philadelphia news media reported that students from a local high school had been killed in a one-car accident because the driver had been sending text messages from his cell phone while he was driving. This was a problem that I knew could be solved through technology.

Having worked for Motorola for ten years, I had a general knowledge of how cell phones worked. My idea was simple; install a device in the car to interfere with a cell phone's radio-frequency (RF) communications. When I conducted a search to determine if a patent already existed for such a device, I found that one did and that the patent owner lived about thirty miles from me. I also found that there were federal laws that broadly prohibited the use of RF jamming devices for civilian use, so I thought the patent was probably useless unless the law could be changed.

If the law could be changed, not only would it potentially save the lives of teenage drivers who might otherwise be killed using cell phones while driving, but it could also be a financial success. With the experience I had gained lobbying Congress and Department of Transportation officials, and working with transportation-related news media, I thought this would be a perfect match. I might be able to help the patent owner get the law changed.

I retained a law firm that specialized in intellectual property to determine if the patent owner had a lock on the technology and, if so, possibly negotiate an agreement with him that would give me a percentage or interest in the patent in exchange for a public relations campaign and lobbying effort.

Unfortunately, Kate seemed to be determined to not let me move on with my life. She continued to harass me with e-mails containing threats of blackmail for the entire summer. By the middle of June it was obvious that she was determined to publicly destroy my character and reputation, and that she was going to do it soon.

Everything I had done to make her famous and credible had backfired on me. The dream had become a nightmare. In desperation, I wrote to a prominent travel reporter who was one of the few who didn't seem to be one of Kate's friends. She had left me with no alternative but to try to fight back. I had no intention of telling him about the affair or other personal matters. My only chance of survival, I thought, was to expose her deceptions about the membership and the hotline, lying to Congress, her association with LMG and other things. It was, I thought, possibly an award-winning story, even though it might also put an end to airline passengers' rights.

The reporter never responded to me. Unlike Kate, I hadn't developed relationships with the reporters we had worked with. She had their ears, I didn't. I had trusted her with all of that power, and I now knew that trust had been misplaced.

Two days later, Kate started to make good on her threat to mount a media campaign against me. On June 25, a Google Alert led me to a blog for Chris Elliott, a travel reporter for MSNBC and other media outlets. Elliott was one of the reporters we had worked with in the past. He had written an article that was critical of the House version of the airline passengers' bill of rights. Kate had posted a rebuttal to the article on Elliott's blog. In it she also wrote:

> I've had to file 2 sherrif's reports for stalking, and one FBI
> report because my computer was hacked by a nutt who joined
> our Coalition.[38]

Despite the fact that she didn't mention my name in the blog, I knew that she would have told Elliott, off the record, she was referring to me. I wrote to Elliott, told him that Kate was the "nutt" and that there was no way she would ever report me to the police or the FBI. At the time, despite the fact that she seemed willing to lie to just about anyone, it seemed implausible to me that she would lie to law enforcement officials.

Kate called me soon thereafter. It was the first time we had spoken on the telephone in three months. She said she knew I had written to Elliott. He had apparently told her, but he hadn't told her what I said. She demanded to know what I said to him.

"I told him you were the nut," I said.

She said she didn't believe me and that, if I was any kind of a gentleman, I would destroy all of the videos and pictures I had. I asked her how, even if I destroyed them, I was supposed to prove that to her. She warned me that if I continued to correspond with Elliott that I would "live to regret it," and she hung up.

She then resumed her unilateral e-mail war. The e-mails became even more disturbing and were obviously not meant for me. Most of them didn't make any sense to me. She was laying the groundwork for a character assassination by sending me e-mails filled with wild, false accusations, but blind-copying others – probably reporters, I thought at the time.

Terrified, I wrote to Elliott again. I made the same offer I had made to the other reporter. Elliott wasn't interested. It was obvious she had already destroyed any credibility I might have had with him.

I couldn't have felt more alone, more isolated. I was living in a virtual prison of my own making. I tried one more thing. I told her I was going to retain a lawyer. It wasn't true, but it seemed to work. It silenced her until August 23 when, astonishingly, she sued for peace.

From: Kate
Sent: Saturday, August 23, 2008 8:50 PM
To: Mark Mogel
Subject: Are you ready to declare peace?

I'd like to propose something to you.

But first I need to know if you can let go of the past and move on. I also need to know that you have no legal action that you are taking or intending to take against myself or the Coalition.

I'll repair any relationships or make any meetings happen if we can come to an agreement.

Let me know.

I wasn't sure what she had in mind, but in subsequent e-mails she made clear that she wanted me to come back to work with her again – as an equal partner. I was deeply troubled that our lawyers, Kate's reporter friends and others might have thought I was a computer hacker or possibly a rapist, and heaven only knew what else she might have been saying. If I returned, Kate would have some explaining to do. They would all realize that whatever claims she had made couldn't be true, and I wouldn't have to say a word.

I also considered the fact that I had helped set the stage for a historic change in how airlines treated their passengers, and I did have a desire to see that through to the end – a peaceful end I hoped. Furthermore, if she were to return to the irrational, destructive path she had been on, she would destroy any chance I had of following my personal goal of lobbying for the cell phone jamming device.

There were no good choices. It took me two days to make a decision – I accepted her peace invitation. Ultimately, I thought that would be the only way to fix whatever she had broken, to make right whatever wrongs she had committed.

Within hours, she gave me new passwords for the FlyersRights.org website and e-mail accounts, including hers. She asked me to modify the website, write a newsletter, and meet her in New York City the following week. She also asked me to talk to a ghostwriter for her book. Apparently, the book deal with Joe Sharkey had evaporated over the summer.

I agreed to everything except meeting her in New York. I had no intention of renewing the affair and there was no other reason for me to be there. I didn't even understand why she invited me. Based on her behavior during the summer, it was inconceivable that she wanted to renew the affair either.

SEPTEMBER 2008

Rape kits and restraining orders

BY THE TIME I returned, Kate had changed the name of the organization to "FlyersRights.org" to match the name of the website, although it would take years for the transition from CAPBOR to be fully completed.

On September 5, a detective from the Napa County Sheriff's Department sent an e-mail to Kate that apparently summarized a conversation they had on or about August 8, two weeks before she asked me to return. The subject line of the e-mail said, "Extortion Investigation." Detective Joseph Jones of the Napa County Sheriff's Department wrote to her:

> Kathleen-
>
> Please reference the paragraphs below and ensure they are an accurate reflection of the events that have occurred thus far. This is only a summary but will be used to obtain a court order for records related to this investigation. Please feel free to respond with any corrections or changes you see fit.
>
> Thanks
>
> On or about March 16th 2007 Hanni received her first email from suspect Mark S. Mogel. Hanni established a business relationship with Mogel who agreed to provide her organization with business and technical assistance. On or about June 12th 2007 Hanni had been experiencing technical problems with her America Online email system. Mogel agreed to assist her remotely with her problem. Hanni provided Mogel with remote access to her laptop computer, with the agreement that he would only log in and assist her with this technical issue. Mogel was able to assist Hanni with her technical problem. Hanni is unsure how Mogel was able to obtain remote access.

Throughout the remainder of Mogel's involvement with
Hanni's organization he would frequently travel to Washington,
D.C. and other locations to assist in business related matters. On
several occasions Hanni and her business associates felt Mogel
was becoming overly attached to her. Mogel became possessive
and defensive of Hanni and publicly displayed this on several
occasions.

On or about July 30th, 2008 Hanni reached a decision that it was
in her best interest to release Mogel from any involvement with
her organization. Immediately after calling Mogel and notifying
her of her decision she noticed that her home computer systems
'crashed'. This included her laptop, and desktop computer along
with other computers attached to her home wireless network.
Hanni suspects Mogel caused this technical collapse due to his
previous access and knowledge of her network. Hanni spent
several days with the assistance of other [sic] to restore her
home network and computer components.

In the following weeks Hanni received email messages from
Mogel expressing his anger and frustration with her decision.
Mogel also made note of a personal video of Hanni's that he
[sic] was in his possession. Mogel further proclaimed that he
had contacted reporter, Chris Elliott, at MSNBC and threatened
to release this video to him. Hanni described the video as a
personal video she had made for her husband in which she
exposes herself sexually. Hanni had previously saved this video
on her computer, and had not released it to anyone else. Mogel
also related that he had stored a copy of the digital video in a
safe deposit box. Hanni believes that the last email message she
received from Mogel was on July 14th, 2008.

There had been no extortion, no sex video and, while I had helped her
with a technical problem in 2007, I had no remote access to her computer or
knowledge of her home network. I had used a well-known online meeting
service to access her computer. If her computer network had gone down, that
could have been caused by any number of reasons, but I wasn't one of them.
All of the allegations set forth in the e-mail were half-truths and outright lies.
     Perhaps the biggest lie of all was the lie of omission – that she had
obviously not told the detective that we had been having an affair since July
2007, an affair that she initiated, nurtured, and as I was soon to learn, an
affair she intended to resume.
     Kate sent several e-mails to me on this day, September 5, 2008, but she
never mentioned the Napa detective's e-mail, and I wouldn't see it until April

2010. Ironically, I didn't respond to any of Kate's e-mails on this particular day because a deadly hurricane named "Hanna" was moving up the Eastern Seaboard and was forecast to hit Collegeville the next day. Knowing that it would be several days before I would get another opportunity, I spent the entire day playing golf with my wife, followed by a late dinner. Because I hadn't responded to any of Kate's e-mails, later that night she wrote, "You die or something?"

The next morning, I wrote to let her know that I had not died, and throughout the day we exchanged over fifty e-mails on a variety of subjects – none of them having to do with the detective's e-mail. As Hanna's hurricane-force winds and torrential rain lashed against the windows of my house, Kate asked for my opinion on several news media articles. She also asked me to write a newsletter, make some changes to the website and write a press re-lease. In one of her e-mails she wrote, "Hanni is over Collegeville. Every hurricane has an i."

ON SEPTEMBER 11, Kate asked me to write a press release regarding an airline passengers' rights bill that she said had been passed in Canada earlier that week. I had a fair amount of historical knowledge about the subject, so I didn't do any research. I relied entirely on what Kate told me in addition to a press release that had been issued by the Ministry of Transport, Canada's equivalent of the U.S. Department of Transportation. My press release read, in part:

> Kate Hanni today commended the Canadian government on the first airline passengers' bill of rights enacted on the continent. Canada's bill of rights is more comprehensive than even the European Union regulations, and specifically addresses strandings, allowing passengers to deplane after a 90 minute tarmac delay, with the option to re-board the plane.
>
> 'If it's good enough for Canada, why isn't it good enough for America?' asked Hanni. For several months, Ms. Hanni has been assisting Mayor Woodrow French (who first proposed the bill) and House of Commons officials on background for the bill. 'Now it is time for Congress to act!' added Ms. Hanni.

Several news outlets picked up the story, including MSNBC:

> The government just passed an airline passengers' bill of rights (PBOR). Among its provisions: If your plane is delayed for four hours, you're entitled to a meal voucher. If it's delayed for eight

hours, you're entitled to a voucher for a hotel stay. And if the delay occurs once you're on board, you have the right to disembark after 90 minutes have gone by. Too bad you have to be in Canada to take advantage of the plan.[39]

Two months later, I found out that it wasn't true. While it was true that Canadian airlines were required to provide vouchers under certain circumstances, those requirements had been on the books for years. There was no right to deplane after 90 minutes, and nothing had been passed by the Canadian government in September.

This time it was my own fault. Although the press release credited Kate with working with House of Commons officials, it was actually me who had been working with them.

Six months earlier, in March, a Cubana Airlines flight was stuck on the tarmac for twelve hours in Ottawa. Soon thereafter, a Member of Parliament, Gerry Byrne, asked the Library of Parliament to conduct research on U.S. and European passengers' rights legislation. A lawyer for the Library was assigned to conduct that research, and he got my name and phone number from the FlyersRights.org website. Over the span of a couple of months, we exchanged many e-mails and spoke on the telephone often. I provided him with information about the bills pending before Congress and other passengers' rights information. I had continued to support his research even after I quit working with Kate in April.

In November, two months after I wrote the press release, the lawyer called me again.

"Mark, I'm looking at a press release on your website that is completely wrong. There's no airline passengers' rights law in Canada," he said.

"Please, tell me you're kidding," I said.

I spent the next two days researching the matter. Reading through Canada's air transport regulations and laws that govern air carriers, I found that no new bills, laws, rules, regulations, or anything of the kind had been passed in September. Canadian airline passengers didn't have the right to deplane after 90 minutes.

When I looked at it more closely, I found that the "Flights Rights" program announced by the Canadian Transport Minister in September was little more than a brochure that informed Canadian airline passengers of their existing rights. The ministry had also announced a set of recommendations for what it thought Canadian airlines should do to improve customer service. It had been nothing but a publicity stunt designed to thwart Byrne's call for legislation. Byrne had subsequently issued a press release that called the ministry's actions "trickery," and Canadian consumer advocacy groups publicly agreed with him.

I tried to explain all of this to Kate, but it was an exercise in futility. For months she continued to tell reporters, radio hosts and others that Canada enacted a passengers' bill of rights in September 2008. The strangest thing was that reporters never checked. Nobody ever thought to pick up the phone and call someone in Canada. They just believed Kate.

I continued to work with the lawyer for the Library of Parliament for the next five months. Kate was convinced I was wasting my time – right up until the day when another Member of Parliament contacted her in March 2009 and told her he was introducing an airline passengers' bill of rights in the House of Commons.

ON SEPTEMBER 13, Kate invited me to attend the inaugural meeting for an "advisory committee" in Washington on September 23. The meeting would be held at Jack Corbett's law firm's offices on DuPont Circle. I wasn't quite sure how an advisory committee would function with Kate, but I welcomed the idea. Rather than having Kate and me making all of the decisions and arguing about most of them, there would now be others, theoretically, to help break the ties. I doubted the committee would last for very long though.

In the list of attendees that she prepared, she expanded my title to "Director of Research and Information Technology." There were no other directors on the list except for Kate. I was a little disappointed that I had been demoted from the "VP of just about everything" title she bestowed upon me in February, but I was relieved to see things were getting back to normal.

On the morning of September 23, I checked my e-mail before I left my house to attend the meeting in Washington. I received a Google Alert that was the most shocking to date. Kate had attended a meeting of the DOT's tarmac delay task force in Washington the day before, and the Google Alert contained an extremely strange and inappropriate snippet about that meeting. Among other things, she had written that an executive for the Air Transport Association was "an herb."

The alert led me to a blog that Kate and her husband had started in January 2007. There, plastered across the home page of the blog, was an instant message conversation between Kate and someone named Mike Collins, a public relations strategist from Washington. Kate had written about the task force members:

> They treat me like some blonde barbie doll that doesn't know
> what she's talking about, but are they ever wrong. I've proved
> that I've mastered operational issues and understand the airline
> issues better than any of the pundits who purport to knowing
> this industry.

I didn't have access to the blog, so I called Kate and told her to delete the blog entry. While she did that, I continued reading the instant message conversation. About DOT Secretary Mary Peters, Kate had written, "She is a driveling idiot," and "she rides a Harley Davidson which is her best attribute and I wouldn't be surprised if she had massive body piercing's and tattoos."

Kate later wrote to me that Mike Collins, the person with whom she'd had the instant message conversation, was responsible for the success of a couple of well-known news reporters. "You know who Leslie Sanchez is? He made her famous. Anderson Cooper? Him too."

I didn't know if any of that was true but, unlike me, Collins wasn't going to make Kate famous for free. She was going to have to pay him. The instant message conversation continued on the blog:

> I am going to be borrowing from peter to pay Paul on this and
> hiding a bit from my hubby just to make this happen, but I
> believe in what I'm doing and I want to become the new Ralph
> Nader of the Skies and hopefully of TV and everything else.

For personal reasons, Kate rarely consumed alcohol when she was in Napa. However, I had observed that whenever she was away from Napa, she sometimes drank more than she should. She also sometimes took a prescription sleeping pill when she had been drinking. This cocktail sometimes led to erratic and potentially dangerous behavior. She could remain awake and somewhat functional for hours, although her judgment was extremely impaired. Fortunately, I had usually been present in the past to ensure that she didn't do anything harmful to herself or the cause.

Whatever the reason this time, she had posted an inappropriate instant message conversation on the blog. If Secretary Peters or anyone else mentioned in the conversation had Google Alerts configured for their own names, they might have already seen the post. After I read the entire conversation, I sent Kate an e-mail:

From: Mark Mogel
Sent: Tuesday, September 23, 2008 7:51 AM
To: Kate Hanni
Subject: omg

You called Mary Peters a driveling idiot. Jeezus. We need damage control. Even though you deleted this from the blog, it will show up in Google cache for a while – long enough for people to find it. OMG, OMG OMG

Maybe put something up there now that says someone hacked into the blog last night and posted scandalous and untrue information. You have the deepest respect for the task force and the DOT. Etc etc etc. **Don't mention names!**

She replied, "I have no recollection of posting that and for the life of me can't imagine commiting suicide, but it's possible." She posted a disclaimer on the blog:

> Our post was hacked last night with strange postings that were
> not generated by us. Clearly there are forces at hand that would
> like to destroy our credibility. We will figure out who did this
> and protect ourselves from future attacks.

Meanwhile, I drove to Washington for the advisory committee meeting. When I arrived at Jack Corbett's law firm, Corbett, Burt Rubin, Kenneth Mead and a member of LMG were present. Paul Hudson and Ed Mierzwinski were on conference call lines. Cindy Bouchard, a volunteer who had attended the Strand-In and our first report card press conference, was also present.

I wore a golf shirt, jeans and sneakers. Kate came to the meeting dressed to kill. I wondered what the others were thinking. *Is he a rapist? Is he a computer hacker? Why did Kate invite him back?* I was still trying to figure out the answer to that last question myself.

There were a number of subjects discussed, but I thought the meeting was really just a show for the sake of appearances. Despite the fact that others participated in the meeting, the day-to-day advisory committee would be primarily composed of Kate, Corbett, Rubin and me.

After the meeting, Kate invited me to have a drink with her and Cindy Bouchard at a nearby street-level bar. At every brief opportunity when we were alone, she told me that she was sorry for everything she had done over the summer. She also apologized for not handling the situation better when she got caught spending the night in my room in April. She said that Anjum Malik had overreacted. Kate said she thought I had overreacted to the rape allegation too – that it wasn't her fault that Malik jumped to conclusions.

"What about that hacking bullshit with Chris Elliott?" I asked, referring to the post she made on his blog.

"I didn't mention your name," she said.

"Why did you post that thing at all?" I asked. "Why were you accusing me of hacking your computer all summer? Why were you sending me all of those nasty f...ing e-mails – threatening me?"

She said that soon after I quit in April, her husband found evidence of the affair on her computer. She told him that I hacked into her computer and planted it, and that I had fabricated it to make it look like we were having an affair. She was also worried that I might be angry enough at her to publicly reveal the videos or pictures I had and, if I did, she wanted to make sure her husband was convinced that I had stolen them. Most of the e-mails she sent to me, and the sentence she put in Elliott's blog, were intended to convince her husband that I hacked her computer, she said.

There was something about all of this that didn't make sense to me, but between the Margaritas and trying to keep Bouchard from hearing what we were talking about, the discussion was difficult and fragmented. Kate asked me to get a hotel room so that she and I could talk privately. She said she would figure out a way to lose Bouchard, who was staying with Kate in her suite at the Windsor Park. I told Kate that I wasn't going to get a hotel room – I was going home.

"Then come back to my room," she said. She said that, based on the past few nights, she was certain that Bouchard would go to bed soon after we got there, and then we would be able to talk privately.

The three of us walked to Ruth's Chris Steakhouse on Connecticut Avenue where we ate and had more drinks. There, Kate took me aside and said there was something I needed to know before we got to the Windsor Park. She said that it would be awkward for her and me to walk into the hotel together. She asked if I would be willing to climb one of the fire escapes, and then she would let me into the hotel from the inside.

"Fire escape!" I exclaimed. "Why?"

Kate said that, the day after I left Washington in January, Annette Hagan told our lawyers that she thought I was obsessed with Kate and possibly a danger to her. Hagan told them about the argument Kate and I had in the hotel bar a few nights earlier, the passionate argument about the state-based airline passengers' rights laws. According to Kate, Hagan also told them that I had driven down two dead-end streets on the way to the hotel, a hotel that none of us had ever been to before.

Except for the *obsessed* and *dangerous* parts, all of that was true but, "How did Annette turn our argument in the bar and my getting lost on the way to the hotel into the possibility that I was dangerous?" I asked.

"I don't know," Kate said. She said that Hagan was so convincing that the lawyers suggested that Kate might want to file for a restraining order.

"What!" I exclaimed. "What were you doing while all this was going on? Why didn't you defend me?" I asked.

"I tried," Kate said, "but I didn't know what to say. I obviously couldn't tell them about us."

She said that Hagan had backed her into a corner in front of the lawyers, and she didn't know how to get out of it.

I tried to figure out what Hagan could have been thinking – how she could have interpreted my behavior as dangerous. Perhaps she was shocked to hear me talk to Kate as I had, swearing at her at times. Hagan probably thought that it was highly unusual for a run-of-the-mill volunteer to behave that way toward the famous founder and spokeswoman for CAPBOR. She couldn't have known that Kate and I routinely had spirited, passionate arguments, and she obviously didn't know about the affair. But I still couldn't figure out how Hagan could have concluded that I was obsessed or dangerous. I considered that it was possible that Kate had more of a role in all of this than she was telling me, but I was so relieved that the war was over that I decided to give up trying to make sense of all of it.

One thing that did now seem to make sense was why Burt Rubin had been hovering over Kate and me on the subway after the first task force meeting in February. He probably thought he was protecting her. He couldn't have known that we were staying in the same hotel room.

I asked Kate how she had since squared all of this with the lawyers. She said she told them that she trusted me and that Hagan had overreacted.

"What does all of this have to do with climbing a fire escape?" I asked.

Kate said that Hagan told the desk clerks at the Windsor Park to call the police if I showed up at the hotel during the rest of that week in January.

I shook my head, couldn't help but laugh. The crazier it got, the more I was drawn to it, even more determined to make everything right.

"And *that's* why we haven't stayed at the Windsor Park since January?"

"Yes," she said.

"Well, it may be awkward, but I'm not climbing any fire escapes. You and I are going to walk into that hotel together," I said.

An hour or so later, the desk clerk on duty at the Windsor Park was visibly startled to see Kate, Cindy Bouchard and me walk through the lobby of the hotel. It was the first time he had seen Kate and me together since January. I had been there so many times that the three desk clerks, who worked rotating shifts there, knew me as well as they knew her.

Soon after we got to Kate's suite, Bouchard retired to the bedroom and closed the door. I wanted to hear more about why Kate had acted as she had during the summer. She said she was sorry and that she wanted us to move forward, to forget about the past. She said that she had been upset because I quit and that she had missed me so much that it made her crazy. She didn't want to *talk* about how much she missed me though. She wanted to *show* me.

When I left the hotel a few hours later, I told the desk clerk that whatever had happened in January had been a "big misunderstanding." "Apparently," he said, "I assumed that when I saw you and Kate walk in together."

Driving home, I thought, *if I were not living through this, I would never believe it. Rape kits and restraining orders – what next?*

THAT WEEK, CONGRESS passed yet another extension to the FAA reauthorization bill – this time until March 31, 2009.

OCTOBER 2008

The hits keep on coming

ON OCTOBER 19, Kate flew to Dallas. A member of the tarmac delay task force from Southwest Airlines had invited her to visit their operations center in Dallas to learn how the airline planned for irregular operations such as extended tarmac delays. In an instant message conversation two days earlier, Kate had tried to convince me to meet her there, and it wasn't so that I could take the tour. She had fallen back into our relationship even more deeply. "I'm at a different level now. ... This is serious," she wrote.

Kate, I now understood, saw relationships in black and white. There was no middle ground. I was either with her, or I was against her. She had more than amply demonstrated the benefits of peace and the consequences of war. Nevertheless, I told her that I'd see her the next time she returned to Washington, but that I wouldn't meet her in Dallas.

Meanwhile, back in Napa, Kate's husband logged onto her home computer and found e-mails and instant messages about Dallas and our reunion in the hotel in September. He also found some rather embarrassing e-mails from earlier in our relationship. He sent several of them to Kate and me with a predictably unhappy commentary.

For the next several days, I found myself in the peculiar role of peacemaker in an e-mail war between Kate and her husband. Kate had told me in 2007 that she wasn't worried about her husband finding out about us, and she now made it clear why. Rather than show any sign of contrition, Kate hurled accusations at her husband that made it sound as if our relationship was his fault. Shockingly, they both copied two other people on some of their e-mails – one their long-time family therapist, the other a male family friend.

I tried to appeal to some sense of compassion and empathy for Kate to stop her attacks, but those tactics didn't work. I finally managed to persuade her to end the war of words when I suggested that FlyersRights.org couldn't continue without her husband – there simply wasn't enough money, and separate households would have created an unsustainable financial situation. That seemed to have a positive effect. I also wrote to her husband, downplayed what he had read as meaningless banter, apologized for events that were indisputable, and told him that there was no ongoing relationship.

Meanwhile, Kate went to stay in the guest quarters of their family therapist for a few days to try to figure out how to move forward. She had apparently told her therapist how she felt about me, and that she did not intend to give me up. According to Kate, the two of them developed a plan – an insane plan I thought – that Kate and I would simply inform our spouses that we were going to have open marriages.

It occurred to me that her therapist was trying to show her that it was possible, if not probable, that I wasn't as committed to the relationship as she was, or as much as she thought I was. Her therapist was right about my level of commitment, but I knew I had to be careful how I responded.

> 7:31:16 PM   Mark: i got that this was a discussion. And I get that my answer is important. The game here is that the other guy (me) is not committed or is committed. Test me – right?

She said that it wasn't a test. Maybe she didn't know it was a test. It took me five minutes to replace the open marriage plan with an alternative – one that I knew her therapist would be able to see through like glass.

> 7:37:52 PM   Mark: ... I want you to live your dreams ... if that means you have to leave me out, then that's what should happen. It's more important to me that you live your dreams than anything else. I want to be there, but not at the expense of your success.

I let her know, explicitly and implicitly, that I was not her *knight in shining armor*, especially where money and a long-term relationship were concerned – two of the things with which she seemed most concerned. Her husband, I said, was in a much better position to provide those things. I also told her that there was "no way in hell" that I was going to tell my wife that we should have an open marriage.

I don't know what her therapist told her, but Kate seemed to have made a decision by the 27th. She wrote to me, copied her husband, and said that our relationship was over. She wrote that we would continue to work together, but that she was cutting off all direct communications with me. She also wrote:

> I know this will be awkward for awhile, but I'm sure we can deal with it. The Coalition needs your skills and no one can replace you. You have contributed so much to the Coalition without asking for anything in return.

Again, I just need to re-iterate no more IM's, no more phone calls, I must save my marriage which means more to me than anything in the world.

I replied, "I completely understand. Your priorities are in the right place."

Shortly thereafter, she sent me a cellular text message to ask me to change my instant message name so that we could communicate covertly. That's why my instant message name changes to "Frantic Flyer" in the instant messages below. Kate would soon learn that she hadn't attributed the level of intelligence to her husband that he deserved.

LATER IN OCTOBER, Kevin Mitchell, whom Kate tried to assassinate (metaphorically) exactly one year earlier, sent her an e-mail to let her know that Terry Trippler, a frequent media commentator on travel issues, had posted a video on the Internet that accused FlyersRights.org of having a secret agenda to re-regulate the airlines.

When I went to Trippler's website, I found an e-mail that Kate had sent to a third party during the summer. She had written to someone who was advocating that alcohol should be banned from all airline flights. She wrote, "We need to get our first piece of legislation passed so it can be amended later with laws like yours."

Re-regulation of the airlines was an extremely controversial issue, and any hint that we were headed in that direction could be politically damaging to our main objective – the three-hour tarmac rule. I could only imagine what else she had done while I was gone.

I wrote a new comment on the third party's blog, in Kate's name, to spin her earlier comment away from re-regulation and the banning of alcohol on airline flights. Our conversation about Kevin Mitchell resumed the next day:

5:35:05 PM   Frantic Flyer: ... and since when are you and Kevin Mitchell best buddies?

5:35:54 PM   Kate: Not best buddies. Just able to communicate. Did you see the stuff he sent me? It's amazing. I was hoping you could do stuff like that for us?

5:36:08 PM   Frantic Flyer: bite me

5:41:19 PM   Frantic Flyer: There was a time when you wanted me to go thru his garbage to find out what he was up to ... etc. I'm just a little surprised you guys are buddies now. A lot has changed since I left.

A more significant change was that Kate had by now attained a level of public status that even the Law Media Group (LMG), who launched her passengers' rights career in early 2007, now came to her for help.

On October 28, LMG asked Kate to send a letter to Secretary of Transportation Mary Peters. The letter, written by LMG, called for the DOT to reverse an earlier approval for a Chinese airline, Hainan, to have landing rights in the U.S. Kate sent the letter to me and asked what I thought. I told her I would get back to her as soon as I figured out what was going on.

One of the first things I learned was that a liquidating trust, run by a Washington, D.C. law firm, had obtained a $14 million judgment against Hainan on behalf of a bankrupted company, Dornier Aviation-North America (DANA). The DANA trust had recently petitioned the DOT to reverse the landing rights decision. It didn't take long to put two and two together. Someone, probably the trust, was paying LMG to employ a well-known tactic used by public relations firms – get third parties to support your agenda. The agenda was to pressure the DOT to deny Hainan its landing rights in the U.S. unless Hainan paid its debt.

That the DOT would have acted on the DANA trust's request is un-likely. The DOT is not in the business of collecting debts. But if other organizations were to weigh in on the issue, third parties without an obvious financial incentive such as FlyersRights.org, the DOT might be inclined to take the request more seriously. Getting third parties to weigh in on issues on behalf of their paying clients was apparently one of LMG's specialties.

By now, there was more information available on the Web about LMG than I had been able to find in 2007. In mid-2008, a reporter for a high-tech periodical, *CNET News*, had apparently been bewildered by the fact that a coalition of corn farmers had written letters to the U.S. Justice Department and Congress to oppose a joint advertising venture between Yahoo and Google. The *CNET* reporter, Declan McCullagh, had written a series of articles about this odd alliance.

The anti-Google letters had been sent in PDF file format to members of the press. When McCullagh examined the metadata for one of the files – data not visible in the letters but present in the file – he found the name of an LMG staffer as being the author of the letter. Interestingly to me, it was the same Southpaw/LMG staffer that Kate told me had been leading her from office to office when she first went to Washington in early 2007.

McCullagh's *CNET* series suggested that LMG had written the letters on behalf of Microsoft, essentially creating a "fake coalition" of corn farmers and others to oppose the Google-Yahoo alliance. Microsoft admitted that they used LMG as a consultant and that it was no secret that they were opposed to the Google-Yahoo deal. The point was that LMG had been able to convince grassroots organizations to petition the government on behalf of their client. In one of his articles, McCullagh quoted someone familiar with how this works in Washington.

> One person who has been involved with creating fake coalitions
> said it was trivial to organize letters to politicians. 'You go
> down the Latino people, the deaf people, the farmers, and
> choose them,' said the person, who requested anonymity. 'You
> say, I can't use this one--I already used them last time... We had
> their letterhead. We'd just write the letter. We'd fax it to them
> and tell them, You're in favor of this.'[40]

Despite the fact that the LMG staffer's digital fingerprints were all over the letters, spokesmen for the corn farmers and LMG itself denied that LMG had any role in the letters that were sent to Congress, but that was precisely what LMG was trying to do in the case of Hainan.

LMG's Hainan letter would make it look like Kate was submitting the request on behalf of her vast coalition and all U.S. airline passengers. The letter said, "Airline passengers in the U.S. should not be subjected to the delays, cancellations and general inconveniences that would inevitably result from Hainan's irresponsible corporate misbehavior." Neither LMG nor the name of their client was mentioned in the letter. It was to be submitted to the DOT solely on the behalf of FlyersRights.org.

In one of his articles, McCullagh wrote about something I hadn't heard of before; "astroturf" coalitions. He also raised questions about Op-Eds that had supposedly been written by Rainbow Push coalition leader, Jesse Jackson, Charles Steele, Jr., president of the Southern Christian Leadership Conference, and a former MIT professor. McCullagh suggested that all of the Op-Eds were written by LMG. He drew financial links between LMG clients and their interests, supported by the Op-Eds. He also wrote:

> Op-eds of dubious provenance are nothing new in political
> circles, and fake grassroots 'astroturf' campaigns enjoy a long,
> although hardly distinguished, history. One of the most
> influential practitioners of this art is the LawMedia Group ...[41]

The hits just keep on coming, I thought.

I found that "astroturfing" was a term that is believed to have been coined by former U.S. Senator Lloyd Bentsen of Texas. It is used to describe organizations that fashion themselves to look like grassroots coalitions composed of concerned private citizens, but that are really organizations financed by large corporations, politicians or private entities.

On Wikipedia, I found a definition of astroturfing that hit me like a ton of bricks: "Astroturfing is a form of propaganda whose techniques usually consist of a few people attempting to give the impression that mass numbers of enthusiasts advocate some specific cause." *By that definition, we could be considered to be an astroturf organization,* I thought.

Whatever had been the history of astroturf coalitions when Bentsen coined the term, LMG had taken that concept to an entirely different level. They had apparently figured out how to make an astroturf organization look like a grassroots organization.

The small-plane alliance, for example, was run by LMG and financed by general aviation trade organizations. The spokesperson for the alliance worked for LMG.

Still, the alliance seemed to have gained real people as signatories to their organization. As I perused its website, I found a list of individual citizens who had apparently joined the organization. And then I happened upon a name I recognized. One of their so-called members was Bloomberg News reporter, John Hughes, the same reporter who revealed the connections between CAPBOR, LMG and the small-plane alliance over a year earlier. *He's no more a member of that alliance than I am,* I thought. The names of other individuals and member companies were easily traced to small-plane owners and private pilots – all with an ax to grind against the user fee issue.

The more I perused the Web for other public relations firms and their activities, the more alarmed I became. A book I found, *Toxic Sludge is good for you*[42], co-authored by John Stauber, founder of the Center for Media and Democracy, described how the Gulf War was sold to the American public by U.S. public relations firms hired by the Kuwaiti Royal Family. Stauber credited much of the research from this particular incident to a book written by John MacArthur, *The Second Front.*

The year was 1990. Iraq had invaded Kuwait. Two months after the invasion, a 15-year old Kuwaiti girl, identified only by her first name, Nayirah, appeared before a human rights organization in Washington. Sobbing, she testified that she had witnessed Iraqi soldiers removing babies from incubators and leaving them to die on a cold hospital floor. The story was heavily covered by the news media and was oft repeated by government officials and proponents of a war against Iraq – including President George H. W. Bush.

It was a story that I remembered well, one so atrocious that it altered my opinion about U.S. involvement in that conflict. It was also, as the author noted, quite possibly the tipping point for U.S. public opinion and the U.S. Senate, which narrowly voted to authorize the Gulf War.

After the Gulf War ended, no other witnesses could be found to corroborate Nayirah's story. It was later discovered that she was the daughter of the Kuwaiti ambassador to the U.S. It was also learned that the human rights organization, before which she testified, occupied the same offices as the public relations firm that had been paid an estimated $11 million by the Kuwaitis.

I was learning about a side of Washington politics that I hadn't seen on C-SPAN. Public relations firms spin much of what we see on the news and read in newspapers. In a sense, they are the Orwellian *Ministry of Truth* except, rather than generating propaganda intended to protect the government, they work on behalf of wealthy clients to deceive the public and the government, and they do much of it by using the news media.

The more I read, the more I questioned my own values. *Maybe I was wrong to be upset when Kate lied to Congress?* I thought. *Is this really how it all works? Is this the accepted way of doing business in Washington?*

Certainly everyone in our democracy, including large businesses and firms like LMG, have a right to advocate for issues, but I wondered if there wasn't something fundamentally wrong with how they do it. I also wondered how long our democracy could survive with a news media so easily manipulated.

When I finished with my Hainan research, I wished I had never started. There was a time – that now seemed so long ago – that I thought I knew something about Washington politics. I now knew that I never had any idea and probably still didn't. I felt so naïve.

Kate said she felt indebted to LMG, and she wanted to send the Hainan letter on that basis alone. I couldn't have cared less what she thought she owed them. We had no way to know what the other side of the story was or what the possible political backlash might be.

The DOT had approved Hainan's landing rights, and it didn't make sense to criticize a decision that had nothing to do with airline passengers' rights. There was also a risk that we might offend someone at the DOT who would later have a say in our primary goals. I said that we should stay out of the issue. Corbett and Rubin agreed.

I never asked Kate if she sent the letter. It was, I knew by now, a pointless question. She would have told me that she didn't send it, even if she had.

NOVEMBER 2008

Peace

BY NOVEMBER, I had re-immersed myself fully into the politics of airline passengers' rights. While personal dramas continued to play out in the background, airline passengers' rights continued to move on in the fore.

The tarmac delay task force was scheduled to wrap up its work in mid-November. For all intents and purposes, that meeting would be a formality. The final task force report had already been completed.

On the legislative front, we were trying to get the National Air Traffic Controllers Association (NATCA), to sign a letter that would indicate that they were in favor of a three-hour rule. In September, Chairman Costello had said that the FAA claimed that a three-hour rule was unworkable because planes couldn't just turn around and go back to a gate. Buses wouldn't work either, he said – they couldn't drive buses out to planes on active taxi-ways to deplane passengers.

Corbett had been pressing Kate to use her relationship with an air traffic controllers' union official to get NATCA to write a letter to Costello that would say that a three-hour rule *was* workable. She had written to the official and asked if he would meet with her the following week when she would be in Washington. The official replied that he could "probably" meet with her. She didn't like that answer.

This was the union official who had written to Kate in November 2007 to tell her that he had arranged for air traffic controllers to contact us whenever they observed a long tarmac stranding. Kate was extraordinarily adept at getting men to do things and then pushing for more. Now she expected him to get a letter from NATCA that would endorse a three-hour rule. However, in this rare instance, she would fail to get what she wanted.

Meanwhile, Kate's husband sent Kate and me an e-mail that gave us the green light to work together in the clear. Predictably, he had discovered that we were still communicating with instant messages. In a compromise Kate worked out with him, there would be limitations on our communications going forward. Everything had to be in writing – no telephone calls.

After we received his consent to work together in the clear, I changed my instant message name permanently to "Peace." The choice was no accident – *peace* was all I really wanted.

The next day, someone from the DOT asked Kate if she planned to make a presentation during the final meeting of the tarmac delay task force in Washington later that week. She forwarded the e-mail to me and asked, "I am doing a presentation right?"

There was nothing specific in the final task force report that we could point to and disagree with. It seemed to be a good faith effort made by all of the participants to develop airline and airport contingency plans for handling long tarmac delays. Earlier in the week, I had polled a few of the consumer-friendly members of the task force, and they each indicated that they were going to vote in favor of the final report. Kate, Corbett and Rubin were inclined to vote in favor of the final task force report as well.

But that morning I had awakened with a brainstorm: If we cast the only dissenting vote, we could clean up on the media coverage. FlyersRights.org would stand alone from the media's perspective, and we could demagogue the task force report to death. It would be a publicity bonanza handed to us on a silver platter. I wrote back to Kate, "You are giving a speech," and I explained the plan.

At first she was worried that we might offend some people at the DOT – a curious concern. She didn't mind destroying the people she professed to love, but she was worried about offending a few bureaucrats. When I explained the media angle, she was all for it. I also told her not to worry about offending her DOT deep-throats from the Bush administration. Barack Obama had been elected a week earlier, and all of the political appointees would be replaced in January. I spent the rest of the day working on her speech, and then I sent it to Corbett and Rubin. It read, in part;

> After thousands of miles traveled, thousands of dollars of hard-working coalition members' money spent, I feel as though we've accomplished very little. ... On February 26th I was personally honored to represent our coalition and deliver the first member's speech before this task force. In the course of that presentation, we played just a few of the more compelling hotline calls from stranded airline passengers that have called our hotline asking for help. We feel as though those desperate cries for help have fallen on deaf ears. ... Finally, Mr. Chairman, we greatly appreciate the opportunity to participate in this task force, but regretfully, the Coalition for an Airline Passengers' Bill of Rights must dissent.

Corbett said we were the media experts so he would defer to us. Rubin agreed with the strategy. Kate sent the speech to reporter Joan Lowy of the Associated Press.

On the afternoon before the final task force meeting, I drove to Washington and checked into the Churchill hotel on Connecticut Avenue. Kate checked into a suite at the Windsor Park, six blocks away. I had taken her at her word when she wrote that she was rededicating herself to her marriage – I didn't expect to see her until the task force meeting in the morning. But shortly after I arrived at the Churchill, she called from a hotel phone and said she was coming to the Churchill for dinner. After dinner, she said she needed to use the landline in my room for a radio interview. She never left.

At 12:30 a.m., with Kate asleep in my room at the Churchill, I found myself explaining to a bewildered desk clerk at the Windsor Park – not the clerk I talked to in September – that I was checking Kate out of the hotel and collecting her luggage. I also told him that whatever had happened in January – when Annette Hagan allegedly told the clerks to call the police if I showed up to check in – was a misunderstanding.

The next morning, Joan Lowy's Associated Press article had already been published before we arrived at the DOT for the final task force meeting:

> The task force wasn't even able agree on what constitutes a
> 'lengthy delay' — one hour, two hours or 10 hours. Kate Hanni,
> a task force member and passenger rights advocate, said
> Tuesday there is nothing in the draft document that requires
> airlines or airports to provide additional services for passengers
> stranded aboard airplanes going nowhere.
>
> 'We were hoping at a bare minimum to come out of this task
> force with a definition of what is an extensive on-ground delay,'
> Hanni said, but that didn't happen because the airline industry
> 'doesn't want anything that is remotely enforceable.'[43]

At the task force meeting later that morning, Kate, Burt Rubin and I were introduced to DOT Secretary Mary Peters. Peters said she was very impressed with what we had accomplished and that we should be very proud of ourselves. Apparently, thankfully, Peters hadn't seen Kate's blog posting in which she had written that Peters was a "driveling idiot."

The chairman of the task force wasn't nearly as impressed with us though. Referring to the AP article, he opened the meeting by stating that defining a lengthy tarmac delay was not a task force objective – that the task force had been formed to develop plans for avoiding tarmac delays and for what airlines and airports could or should do when they occur.

What he didn't understand was that that was a minor detail. What mattered was that Kate said the task force was a ten-month long exercise in futility, and the media ate it up. There were television cameras waiting for her the second she walked out of the door. We spent the rest of the day traveling from one television news studio to another. It was the largest media bonanza since the New York airline passengers' rights law was overturned in March, and we would ride this new media wave for weeks.

ON THE EVENING of November 24, twelve days after the final task force meeting, I received a telephone call from a detective with the Napa County Sheriff's Department. He said he wanted to talk to me about a complaint that had been filed by Kate in August. I decided that I'd better talk to Kate before I talked to him, so I asked him to call me back the next day.

A *normal* person may have been surprised or shocked by such a call, not to mention everything else that had taken place up to this point, but I am, admittedly, atypical. The rape incident involving my friend hadn't been my first association with drama, nor was it my last.

In 1962, when I was five years old, my parents were in the midst of a bitter divorce, something I wasn't aware of at the time. All I was knew was that my father wasn't around anymore. People began coming to our house to remove furniture – repossessed I would come to learn. At times, we didn't have electricity or heat. In desperation, my mother asked my paternal grand-parents keep me at their home in northern New Jersey – 100 miles away – until she could get back on her feet. While there, my grandparents brain-washed me into believing that my mother was evil and dangerous – that she would kill me. Unbeknownst to me, they had also refused to return me to her, leading me to believe that she had abandoned me.

One sunny afternoon, as I sat on a swing in their backyard, I spied my mother hiding behind a decorative outdoor fountain and fauna in a neighbor's yard. As I had been instructed, I screamed and ran toward the safety of the house. I wasn't fast enough. My mother caught me before I reached the back door. She swept me up under one arm, ran to the front of the house and threw me into the back seat of a waiting car. I didn't recognize the male driver.

Coincidently, relatives from my father's side of the family were arriving at my grandparent's house and witnessed much of this. A car chase ensued that led out of town and onto an interstate highway. As I sat in the back of that car with my mother, the other car just inches from ours, horns honking, angry, distorted faces in both cars screaming and yelling, I couldn't possibly have been more terrified, more traumatized.

"Why are you doing this?" I cried at my mother.

After what seemed like a half-hour into this nightmare, the driver of our car pulled into a police station. As I sat in the back seat of that car with people screaming and banging on the car windows, all of them people I had depended upon for my safety and welfare, I decided that they were all crazy and untrustworthy, including my mother. Unable to locate my father, the state police let my mother take me with her. I told her that I would run away as soon as I was old enough. It was a vow I never forgot.

There would come a time when I would understand what a terrible thing my grandparents had done – to alienate me from my own mother. Even still, I would forgive everyone involved. They had acted in varying degrees of ignorance and selfishness – human frailties in which I am not in a position to judge. Despite the genuine fear of her in which they had indoctrinated me, my mother would eventually become my primary role model – someone I grew to love and admire again. Nevertheless, sadly for me and most of the women in my life, all of this had a profound effect on my ability to have meaningful, personal relationships. I love and respect women. I'm just not able to fall in love easily – to take that emotional leap of trust.

After living for 12 years with a stepfather who didn't like children, and possibly subconsciously driven by the vow I made to my mother years earlier, I left home shortly after high school graduation. Working at menial jobs for little money, I lived in cheap apartments and hotels for a few years, sometimes slept in cars or vacant buildings when money was scarce. By the time I enlisted in the Air Force at 20, I'd survived two violent car crashes and a train derailment. I'd also been shot at and had knives pulled on me.

I emerged from all of that being rarely shocked or surprised by anything. I'd been desensitized to drama long before Kate came into my life. I held fast to a notion, perhaps naively, that people are innately good and well-intentioned, but get sidetracked by greed, ignorance or traumatic events in their own lives. I felt as if I had survived all of that with little more than a few minor physical and emotional scars, and I had gone on to build a successful, happy life for myself.

So far, except for Anjum Malik's alleged concern that I might have raped Kate, and Kate's threats of character assassination during the summer – either of which could have destroyed everything I had worked so hard to achieve over the past thirty years – most of the drama was child's play to me.

When I got off the telephone with the Napa detective, I was worried about only one thing; that whatever was going on, it would lead to my wife finding out about the affair. My wife, an otherwise intelligent, independent and sane person, had married me despite my history. Nobody else in their right mind, with her spirit and temperament, would have. That was one of the reasons why I didn't want our marriage to end. I loved her as much as it was possible for me to love anyone, but that love, as one might suspect from the life I've lived, is not the kind of love that *normal* people are able to feel.

I sent Kate an instant message to tell her about the detective's call:

9:10:30 PM	Peace: hey - well - just got an interesting call. Det Jones from Napa Valley Sherriff's dept.
9:10:42 PM	Kate: [expletive deleted] - really?
9:11:13 PM	Peace: told him this was a bad time ... talk to him tomorrow at 11AM my time. yes really.
9:12:08 PM	Kate: just say I'm dropping thecase.- I'll e-mail him now - WHat did he say?
9:12:43 PM	Peace: Just said he wanted to talk to me. I told him to call back tomorrow. That was it. He said OK
9:12:53 PM	Kate: This is not a good time to talk about this, can you put him off?
9:13:13 PM	Peace: ok - I'll try

Kate was scheduled to appear on CNN from San Francisco early the next morning. She said she planned to go to bed early – which was why it was "not a good time" for her to talk about it. I pressed the issue. She wrote that she wouldn't discuss it in writing via instant messages – she would only talk about it on the telephone. Despite the telephone restrictions imposed by her husband, I called her.

I already knew much of the background. Seven months earlier, in May, she told her husband that I had hacked into her computer to plant whatever evidence he had found about our affair. She told him that I had fabricated everything he found, and that I was a crazy, obsessed volunteer. She was also paranoid that I would do something to harm her with some of the pictures I had, so she spent the entire summer threatening me with a public character assassination.

In early July, when Chris Elliott of MSNBC told her that I had written to him, she became even more paranoid – thought that I was trying to sell those pictures to MSNBC. She didn't believe me when I told her that I hadn't offered any of those things to Elliott or even told him about them. This paranoia hadn't ended after we resumed our relationship in September. She had asked me about this on at least one occasion since.

Knowing full well that I hadn't hacked her computer to obtain anything I had, she had filed what I assumed was a computer hacking complaint with the Napa County Sheriff's department. Based upon what I knew at the time, I assumed her motive was to try to get the authorities to compel me or Elliott to reveal the content of our communications through a criminal investigation.

What I didn't know, and wouldn't know until 2010 when I would see the detective's September 2008 e-mail, was that she had told the sheriff's department that I was trying to extort her over a sex video, a video that she knew never existed.

I did know that I hadn't done anything that was remotely illegal, and she knew it too. In her October 27 e-mail she had written, "You have contributed so much to the Coalition without asking for anything in return."

Now on the telephone, I asked her if she had thought any of this through to its likely conclusion; that I would have to tell the sheriff's department about the affair and the true origin of the pictures.

"Kate, did you tell the sheriff's office about the affair?" I asked.

"Why would I tell them that?" she asked.

"What the hell do you think I'm going to tell them?" I asked. "You told these people that I hacked your computer to steal those pictures. Did it ever occur to you that I'm going to have to tell them how I got them? You seriously need to get a lawyer," I said.

I told her that she could end up in jail for lying to the police. I also said that I would try to protect her, but that I wasn't going to take a fall for her either. She said she would call me back.

She had dug yet another hole for herself, and this time I had no idea how to help her out of it. Perhaps inappropriately, I actually felt sorry for her. I thought she had acted out of paranoia, emotion, and fear that I might try to do something to harm her public image. Had she thought about that from my perspective for one second, she would have seen that my doing such a thing would have resulted in Armageddon for me, too. Because she hadn't given any rational consideration to any of this, the thing that we both feared most, that the affair would become public knowledge, was now almost a certainty.

Later, she sent me an instant message that she was on the phone with her family therapist trying to figure out what to do, so I went back to some research on airline policies regarding obese passengers that I had been doing before the detective called.

Kate called me an hour later and put her husband on speakerphone. That conversation was civil, but convoluted. Her husband didn't understand why Kate needed a lawyer. He thought I needed one. He didn't know that I knew with absolute certainty that Kate had fabricated whatever she told the sheriff's office. I also couldn't explain how it was that I had personal images of Kate without getting into details that neither Kate nor I wanted him to know.

Conversely, her husband knew what I didn't know at the time; that Kate had made an extortion allegation as well as an allegation that I stole a sexually explicit video she said she made for him. It was therefore little wonder that her husband thought I needed a lawyer although, even if I had known, I still wouldn't have retained one for any of this nonsense.

Kate, the only person on the call who knew everything, was uncharacteristically quiet during the conversation. Consequently, the call wasn't very productive. Later that night, I sent an e-mail to Kate and her husband to ask what they wanted me to do when the detective called the next day.

Kate had already gone to bed to get some sleep before her early-morning appearance on CNN. Her husband replied, "Kate has requested that the investigation be terminated. If they call tomorrow please refer them to Kate and the e-mail she sent this evening."

I talked to the detective the next day and told him, uncomfortably, that Kate had apparently made a mistake, and that we were "working together again in peace and harmony." Between that explanation and whatever Kate sent to him, he seemed satisfied.

I was glad for this particular bout of insanity to be over. I was in an impossible position. Forcing the issue would have been devastating to both Kate and me, publicly and personally. Doing so might have also dealt a severe if not fatal blow to the future of airline passengers' rights.

DESPITE THE FACT that her husband had conceded that Kate and I could continue to work together, we still had communications limitations. Except in an emergency, we still couldn't talk on the telephone. For some reason, our ability to use instant messaging was an on-again, off-again proposition. Sometimes we were allowed to use it and sometimes we weren't. Our inability to communicate freely, to discuss the subjects of media interviews in advance, would have an immediate impact on her effectiveness.

The day after I talked to the Napa detective, Kate appeared on Fox News in a spot in which she was supposed to talk about how airline passengers could get refunds on airfares. Oil prices had dropped from $147 per barrel to $50, resulting in lower ticket prices. Airlines were allowing passengers to get refunds on the difference. Fox News had been promoting the spot for two days – telling viewers they would be able to save hundreds of dollars.

Kate thoroughly botched the interview. It was so bad that host Megan Kelly said, "Just so our viewers understand, you and I are a little off page." Kelly then explained to viewers what Fox expected Kate to talk about. Kelly went out of her way to spare Kate from embarrassment, but it was really bad.

After that fiasco, Kate decided that she had to risk telephone calls. She asked me to configure my cell phone so that my number would be blocked from her caller-ID and so it wouldn't appear on her telephone bill. Reporters often blocked their numbers when they called her, so it was normal for her telephone bill to show blocked telephone numbers. When she wanted me to call her, she would call my cell phone, let it ring once and then hang up. That call wouldn't appear on her telephone bill either.

DECEMBER 2008

Pin-ups

BEFORE A NEW administration takes office, the president-elect creates transition teams within each of the agencies of government to learn about issues that the previous administration was working on. Jack Corbett had arranged a meeting with President-elect Obama's DOT transition team so that we could ensure the new administration knew who we were.

Corbett and I prepared a two-page paper that summarized our primary goals. We asked that the incoming DOT Secretary require airlines and airports to develop contingency plans for long tarmac delays, set a federal tarmac time limit of three hours, and establish a hotline for airline passenger complaints.

We also asked that the new DOT secretary establish a permanent advisory committee for aviation consumer protection. The plan had long been that Kate would be named to that committee, but I now had grave concerns about her serving on a committee that could have a broader influence over ongoing airline issues. Unfortunately, this had been a part of our platform almost since the beginning, and I couldn't tell Corbett to take it out without getting into an impossible discussion with him.

On December 1, I sent the summary to the DOT transition team leader Robert Rivkin and told him that Kate, Corbett, Rubin and I would be attending the transition team meeting the next day.

Kate arrived in Washington that afternoon and checked into a room at the Churchill hotel. I had, by this time, assured two of the three desk clerks who worked at the Windsor Park that whatever had happened in January was a misunderstanding. Despite that, Kate said it was too awkward for us to stay there. In fact, for the remainder of my association with Kate, we would never again stay at the Windsor Park.

Soon after she checked into the Churchill, a CNN producer called and asked Kate to appear on CNN the following morning to talk about baggage and other airline fees. Some airlines had begun to charge passengers additional fees for luggage, seating preferences and even pillows. When I learned that she would be on CNN the following morning, I knew I could leave her alone that night. Kate always wanted to look her best on television, so she wouldn't get herself into any trouble the night before an interview. Despite the fact that I would have loved nothing more than to attend the presidential transition team meeting, I told her that I wasn't coming to Washington that night.

The call with the Napa detective six days earlier made me suspect that Kate was more dangerous and unpredictable than I had ever dreamed possible. Unlike 2007 and 2008, when we spent entire weeks together, I would now limit our time together to just enough to keep the peace.

Later that evening, we discussed the CNN interview and other subjects over instant messages. She planned to say that FlyersRights.org disagreed with the unbundling of airline fees such as baggage and seating preferences. I was concerned that we shouldn't take a position that conflicted with the majority of airline passengers, and naturally we hadn't polled anyone to develop an informed position.

It was certainly wrong that airlines were not disclosing some of these fees at the time of ticket purchase, but I thought they had every right to charge for ancillary fees. Also, all of the surveys I found on the Web indicated that the majority of airline passengers preferred a la carte pricing. Kate's opinion was that the federal government should outlaw a la carte pricing altogether. This was a fundamental difference that fueled many of our disagreements over policy during the past two years; I believed in free market forces with a minimum of government regulation, while Kate believed that government regulation was the answer to everything.

We discussed the issues for several minutes through instant messages, although we didn't reach an agreement on sound bites. Finally, she said she was tired and, before we signed off, she said she would talk to me again in the morning prior to the interview. She didn't. She went to the studio without talking to me. When the CNN host asked her about a la carte pricing, Kate said she didn't know of anyone who thought the airlines should be permitted to continue the practice, and it was all downhill from there on subjects ranging from fuel prices to airline profit margins.

Terry Trippler blasted Kate and CNN in a video he posted on his website later that day:

> She doesn't like to let the facts get in the way of a good story.
> Kate certainly left the facts out, and CNN did nothing to
> challenge her, nothing to even ask a question. Kate said, and I
> quote, 'that fuel costs have been at an all time low for the last
> year and a half.' Now we all know the truth is just the opposite.
> Fuel costs have been at an almost record high for at least the
> past year and a half. And it looks like the only people that don't
> know that are Kate Hanni and CNN.[44]

In regard to her answers about airline fees, Trippler continued, "Kate said it was all about money and airlines increasing their profit margins." He pointed out that that airlines were losing billions of dollars, asking rhetorically, "Where are the profit margins?"

Meanwhile, Kate and the others attended the transition team meeting and met team leader Robert Rivkin. It was an important meeting if for no other reason than it gave Kate face time with Rivkin who would later be appointed as DOT general counsel, a position that reports directly to the secretary of transportation.

I arrived in Washington later that evening and found Kate working on her laptop in the bar at the Churchill. She said the Internet access didn't work in her room. When we got to her room, I logged onto the Internet within about two minutes.

"Well, it wasn't working earlier," she said.

Many questions had been troubling me since I talked to the Napa detective a week earlier. In September, I accepted Kate's explanations and apologies about the restraining order and rape kit incidents – she had seemed sincere. I knew she wasn't telling the whole truth, but I was weary of conflict – wanted to put it behind and move forward. But after I talked to the Napa detective, knowing that Kate was entirely responsible for making whatever false allegations she had made, I had begun to wonder if she was also entirely responsible for the restraining order episode, and if she, not Anjum Malik, had brought up the subject of rape in April.

I also wondered what might happen when Kate and I severed ties again – it was inevitable that we would. I wondered if, when that day came, she might resurrect any or all of those things for a future, public character assassination campaign against me – a campaign designed to disavow the existence of the affair and its artifacts, and to discredit me.

I wasn't worried about having to prove the existence of the affair in a legal setting – that would be easy though extremely embarrassing. My concern was, if faced with the need to prove the existence of the affair outside of a legal setting, how I would do that without having to rely on embarrassing, graphic e-mails, pictures or instant messages.

Kate was stretched out on the bed, fully clothed. I turned on my webcam, pressed the record button, turned and walked toward her. She slid to the side of the bed and sat up. I leaned over. We kissed. I tucked her hair behind her ears and then stood up, looked at her, hoped I was wrong.

"That's it?" she laughed.

"Let's go back down to the bar," I said.

I returned to my computer and turned off the webcam. I didn't know if it was legal and I didn't care. I just hoped that I would never have to use that video to defend myself against a future character assassination.

TWO DAYS LATER, back in Napa, Kate was obsessed with the Terry Trippler video that bashed her appearance on CNN. A few weeks earlier, on the day of the final DOT tarmac task force meeting, someone from the ATA sent a text message to Associated Press reporter Joan Lowy that accused her of "drinking the Kate Hanni Kool-Aid." Lowy showed the message to Kate off the record, a journalistic term that clearly meant it should never be repeated. Kate told almost everyone she talked to afterward.

Based upon that text message and Trippler's video, she was convinced that the ATA was engaged in a conspiracy to discredit her. Paul Hudson suggested that he would draft a cease and desist letter to warn the ATA and Trippler to stop attacking Kate. I thought that if Hudson had any idea what Kate had been up to for the past two years, he would see that it paled in comparison to anything the ATA or Trippler might be doing.

A debate ensued between Kate, Corbett, Hudson, Rubin and me as to whether or not we should send the cease and desist letter to the ATA. I wrote to Kate:

9:32:15 PM   Peace: Writing a letter like that will make you look crazy. You and I know you are ;) but let's not let the rest of the world know. Seriously though, you have only one piece of evidence against the ATA, and if you use that, you are f...ed with AP. joan showed you that in complete confidence, and you've already told WAY too many people about that.

The cease and desist letter was abandoned, but Kate had Trippler in her sights and she wasn't going to forget about him. She enlisted a family friend from Napa to investigate him. Nothing was ever found about Trippler that could embarrass him, and his character assassination was later abandoned, but the cause would occupy Kate's mind for months.

ON DECEMBER 5, a glowing article about Kate appeared in the Financial Times. The title was "A champion for America's airline passengers."[45] The article was accompanied by a photograph of Kate that made her look like a 1940's-style pin-up girl.

She said that the author of the article had been talking about working with her to write a book and develop a screenplay for a movie about her. She described the theme of the movie as, "Kate the pin-up advocate movie, how to be a hot rock star chic[k] flick, overcoming all odds."

10:58:01 PM   Kate: Now the pedal hits the metal with Obama - Everyone knows the Big O is a consumer friendly guy - Everyone knows that we have our best shot NOW

10:59:12 PM   Kate: Do you agree?

10:59:34 PM   Peace: how can I disagree with a pin-up?

Two days later, the movie was still our main topic of conversation. Apparently, the Financial Times' reporter thought that actress Felicity Huffman should play Kate. Kate didn't think that Huffman was pretty enough. She thought that Gwyneth Paltrow was pretty enough, but she wrote, "I'm not sure Gwyneth can capture the complexities of my personality."

7:19:02 PM   Kate: Who else could play me?

7:19:08 PM   Kate: How about you? Not Brad Pitt

No, not Brad Pitt, I mused. *He wouldn't be able to capture the complexities of my personality.*

IN MID-DECEMBER, the BTS published the first month of airline statistics under the new reporting rules. It was an intensely satisfying moment for me personally. Twenty-eight percent of the first month's three-hour tarmac delays were attributable to the reporting rules we had worked to change.

I set out to determine if the new data were valid. The overall numbers were still low. The airlines had been publicly claiming that, even with the new reporting requirements, extended tarmac delays were still rare. After a few days of analysis and crunching spreadsheets, a pattern emerged that showed the airlines weren't reporting the new data correctly. I wrote to the BTS and explained the problem. They acknowledged there were serious errors, and they promised to investigate the matter. It was another important news item and we already had several reporters interested in the story. One of those reporters was Mike Fabey of *Travel Weekly*. It was the first time I worked with him on a story. In his article he wrote:

> It appears airlines and others in the aviation industry might have
> popped the cork a little too early on a recent Transportation
> Department report showing only 50 tarmac delays in October,
> the first time the DOT included such delays in its monthly
> airline report card. ... "Internally, we were missing a key data
> check," said Anne Suissa, the DOT's director of airline
> information. "The checks and reviews of this data were not as
> thorough as they should have been. I can't say the tarmac delay
> number is correct." ... "It looks like the airlines are just filling
> in numbers," said Mark Mogel, Flyersrights' research director.[46]

Meanwhile, Kate, Corbett, Rubin and I had been engaged in a debate over the need for airlines to provide food and water on the airplane during extended tarmac delays. The requirement was vague in Senator Boxer's passengers' rights language. Boxer's office had asked us to suggest something more specific.

Kate thought that airlines should have to provide food and water anytime a passenger needed or asked for it, beginning from the time they set foot on the plane. My opinion was that airlines shouldn't have to provide anything until the three-hour limit was reached, assuming they hadn't deplaned passengers by then.

Boxer's bill would eventually say that adequate food and water would have to be provided "in any case in which the departure of a flight is delayed." As illogical and unfair to the airlines as that seemed to me, not to mention the fact that the cost would be passed on to airline passengers, it wasn't worth arguing about. Besides, I always had a nagging feeling that we didn't have any business commenting on this in the first place. We weren't nutrition experts.

While working on the airline statistics article with *Travel Weekly* reporter Mike Fabey earlier in the month, we learned that we shared a common passion; Philadelphia Eagles football. Fabey, who lived in Virginia, was originally from Philadelphia and some of his family still lived in the area. I had four season tickets, and Kate encouraged me to sell two of them to Fabey for an upcoming game so that I could pitch another story to him in person.

11:20:13 AM   Kate: We should tease him with things like - 99% of the statistics appear to be corrupted - This is MUCH deeper than it seems

11:20:55 AM   Peace: k - so I'm not just going to a football game to have fun. This is a mission. ;)

While I had talked to many reporters during the past two years, none of them had given me a second thought. To them, Kate was the star and I was just one of the hundreds of volunteers she told them she had. This had led to the predicament I found myself in during the past summer. She had their ears, I didn't. I didn't realize it at the time, but spending a few hours with Fabey at the football game would be three hours well spent – he would get to know me personally, something no other reporter had done.

December 28, the day of the game, turned out to be one of the most dramatic in Eagles history. Two teams ahead of the Eagles in the playoff race unexpectedly lost earlier in the day. The underdog Eagles then went on to defeat the Dallas Cowboys and made it into the playoffs. In the midst of all that excitement, I wasn't able to interest Fabey in writing another article about statistics or even discussing the subject. The only thing he asked me in regard to passengers' rights was, "What's it like working with Kate Hanni?"

"She's a piece of work," I said, "I wouldn't even know where to start."

The next day, I sent out another FlyersRights.org newsletter. I checked the newsletter statistics minutes later. Whenever we got complaints, which meant that people were reporting our e-mails as SPAM, Kate blamed the airlines. The only problem with that conspiracy theory was, if true, thousands of our members were planted by the airlines.

4:19:43 PM	Peace: we got 7 complaints already. That'll get us blacklisted again. What is wrong with these AOL people.
4:34:15 PM	Kate: Probably the airlines
4:35:05 PM	Kate: Today is...guess what? - 2nd anniversary of my stranding. In fact I'd be sitting on the f...ing tarmac right now.
4:39:02 PM	Peace: missed the news cycles for today - the stats thing can wait a day but we should have done something
4:39:22 PM	Kate: We can do it right now
4:40:01 PM	Peace: do what?

And then I wrote our last press release for 2008:

Passengers Remember Ghost of Christmas Past

Napa, CA - December 29th: Flyersrights.org, formerly the Coalition for an Airline Passengers' Bill of Rights, is troubled by Congress' inaction regarding an airline passengers' bill of rights. On December 29, 2006, Kate Hanni and her family were trapped on a plane in Austin Texas for over nine hours. Passengers had no food or water and the restrooms were inoperable. Young mothers ran out of baby formula and had to make diapers out of T-shirts for their babies. The treatment of the passengers was both callous and avoidable.

By the end of February 2007, one month into the existence of CAPBOR, there were 14,000 signatures on the petition – members. My projection at the time was, at that rate of growth, we would have 140,000 signatures by the end of 2007. Now, nearly two years later, we only had 24,000 signatures and at least a third of those were of questionable origin. Even more telling, only a fraction had donated money to the cause.

A 2007 petition to free actress-model Paris Hilton from a California jail, where she served two days because of a DUI, got over 30,000 signatures – in one week.

JANUARY 2009

Media heals all wounds

ON JANUARY 1, Kate and I started working on the 2008 airline report card which we planned to release in February. One of the incidents Kate wanted to include in the report card was from January 16, 2008 when an ice storm hit Atlanta's Hartsfield-Jackson International Airport causing tarmac delays due to long deicing queues. In the days following that incident, two passengers had called the hotline.

Using the accounts from those two passengers, along with three articles that appeared in the *Atlanta Journal Constitution* and the *Washington Post*, Kate applied her unique mathematical skills to determine how many planes were affected and how long they were on the tarmac.

One of the articles mentioned that 90 jets had been in line for deicing, and it also mentioned that a passenger said that it took 25 minutes to deice his plane. However, neither article mentioned how many deicing lines there were. Using the two data points she did have, she calculated that all of planes sat on the tarmac for four to ten hours. Because the articles were published over the span of three days, she multiplied 90 by 3, and then rounded up to come up with "approximately 300 jets" that sat on the tarmac for "four to ten hours."

Kate and I argued about this formula for two hours over instant messaging before I gave up. I reasoned that whether it was 30 or 300 airplanes, the grading system that we had used since 2007 would still only assign one "F" to Delta Airlines in the report card, so it wouldn't affect the final outcome.

On January 4, Jack Corbett suggested that we might want to submit a letter to the FAA in favor of an FAA proposal that would ask carriers to voluntarily reduce flight volume at LaGuardia in New York City. Either Kate or Corbett had inserted this sentence into the draft:

> The facts included in the Federal Register notice mirror the
> experiences of airline passengers travelling to or from
> LaGuardia as reflected in calls to CAPBOR's manned hotline.

A quick look at the hotline records showed only five calls from passengers that had anything at all to do with LaGuardia since the inception of the hotline a year and a half earlier. That wasn't enough to support an argument about the number of delays at LaGuardia. I was worried that the DOT would get the letter, challenge Kate to provide specific data to support her claim, and then she would have to tell them she only had five calls. That could lead to other questions about her truthfulness about hotline claims that she had made in the past to both Congress and DOT officials. It wasn't worth the risk.

I sent an e-mail to Corbett and Kate that said we should delete the sentence. Naturally, that precipitated yet another argument between Kate and me. After an hour of arguing about that, she insisted that we keep the sentence.

> 12:08:14 PM   Kate: Last thought. But this is the final word on this. I think the more we let the government know that our hotline is still effective the better. I think it's OK and they'll never challenge us as to the total number of calls.

She was right. Nobody ever challenged *us* about anything.

In November, I had seen an excellent editorial in *USA Today* that a Lee Wallace had written about passengers' rights. I tracked him down to find out if he might be willing to write some newsletters and fundraisers. Even though I had recently returned to the fold, I had lost my enthusiasm for doing many of the things that I had done before I left in April. Writing newsletters and fundraisers were among those things. Thankfully, Wallace agreed and wrote a few afterward.

After Kate and I finished our argument about the LaGuardia hotline calls, I reviewed a draft newsletter that Wallace had written. One of the sentences that Kate had given him was, "Canada recently passed legislation to safeguard the rights of its citizens whenever they fly." I wrote to Wallace and told him to take the sentence out. Kate's delusion that there was a Canadian passengers' rights law passed in 2008 was intransigent. She insisted that we keep the sentence.

> 7:26:57 PM   Peace: ok - makes you look naive is all. Misinformed. - Plays right into ATA hands - with Trippler etc - k - i'll leave it- go right ahead - keep saying theres a law.

Between this disagreement and others we'd had over the past three days, Kate blew a gasket – said she would kill me if I kept arguing with her:

> 7:59:12 PM   Peace: whoa nellie

> 7:59:34 PM   Kate: no I will - seriously - kill you

8:00:00 PM	Kate: don't second guess me
8:00:07 PM	Kate: You underestimate my fury - my power - my will
8:00:19 PM	Peace: no i don't. - I rely on your compassion, empathy, and love - to overcome your anger, and desire for murder
8:00:46 PM	Kate: And when I kill you it will be with compassion, empathy and love
8:01:13 PM	Peace: lol
8:02:13 PM	Kate: Really - I have no murderous rampages, except with you - I wonder why?
8:02:42 PM	Peace: bring out the best in you
8:02:50 PM	Kate: My killer disposition
8:03:04 PM	Peace: the real Kate

I harbored no real fear that Kate would literally kill me, although I'm certain her rage and desire to kill me may have been real at times. To me, the more salient aspects of this conversation were the subjects of compassion and empathy. These were personality traits that Kate had often attributed to herself in previous conversations. That seemed quirky to me. The traits were there or they weren't – demonstrated by behavior, not words. She had certainly not shown any compassion or empathy for either me or her husband as far as I could tell. Yet she often reminded me how well endowed she was with those traits. She went to great lengths to portray this as part of her public image as well.

A week earlier, on New Year's Eve, a cancer patient in a wheelchair was denied boarding of her flight at an airport in Eugene, Oregon. There had been some kind of disagreement between a gate agent and the patient. Someone in the terminal observed what was happening and called the hotline. Kate called me and asked what she should do. By this point she had purchased a service that allowed her to call me directly from her computer, calls that were easily concealed.

"This will make a great story if we can do something," she said.

I happened to be standing at the deli counter in a grocery store, so there wasn't much I could do to help at that moment. I suggested that she find the phone number for the airport's operations manager, and call him or her to see if there was anything they could do. She did, and the net result was that the patient was put on a later flight and eventually made it to her destination.

The actual circumstances of this incident were sketchy, and eyewitness accounts varied. Some assigned fault to airline personnel, some faulted the behavior of the patient. Nevertheless, Kate apparently played some role in getting the woman to her destination.

Had I been the one who called the airport to call attention to the woman's plight, I would have let it end there, personally satisfied that I had helped someone. But Kate wouldn't let an incident like this end that way. She exploited each of them with calls to reporters, YouTube videos and fundraising letters that described the incidents, and her empathetic and compassionate role in them, in melodramatic detail. I didn't have a problem with that – it benefited the cause. But I also knew what others didn't – that it was all part of the act.

The day after she threatened to kill me, the BTS pulled all of the new tarmac delay data off of their website as a result of the discrepancies I had found in December. They replaced the data with this message:

> Tarmac times for cancelled flights, diverted flights at the diversion airport, and those with multiple gate departures have been removed. BTS is reviewing the data reported by carriers for October and the following months. Data will be released when the review is completed.

5:51:30 PM   Kate: We need to pounce on this

5:51:36 PM   Kate: POUNCE

And pounce we did. Upset with me though she had been, whenever we could generate media attention around factual issues, it seemed to heal all wounds. We got articles in *Travel Weekly*, *Bloomberg News* and the *Wall Street Journal*:

> The DoT's Bureau of Transportation Statistics has removed data on tarmac delays from its Web site following complaints from a consumer group that the numbers were unreliable. 'It is clear that you have uncovered problems with how the air carriers are submitting their data and our internal edit checking process,' said a DOT official in an e-mail to Mark Mogel of the Coalition for a Passengers Bill of Rights.[47]

Once again, we would ride the statistics story for months to come. No matter what the statistics said, we could keep saying that the government and the airlines were lying.

The statistics issues, combined with the few people who did call the hotline, gave Kate just enough ammunition to give to reporters to prove that that at least one or two tarmac strandings were not among those counted by government statistics. She would tell the reporters that there were thousands of other people and flights that she could give them. She knew that the reporters didn't have time to follow up and would be satisfied with the two people she gave them. They wrote articles, and those articles led to others, and those led to still others. Kate could make one or two incidents multiply like rabbits.

ON JANUARY 15, US Airways Flight 1549 crash-landed in the Hudson River. All 155 passengers and crew survived. News reports later that day indicated that the plane may have hit a flock of geese. Kate didn't believe that was possible and she desperately tried to find a way to interject herself into the story. She said that it was unusual for geese to be in New York in the winter because it was too cold. She was convinced that the pilot of the plane, Sully Sullenberger, was engaged in a conspiracy with the airline to cover up for *deferred maintenance* issues, another subject in which she had been determined to involve us since early 2008.

News reports indicated that the jet's engines were not attached to the wings as the airplane floated in the Hudson River, and she was sure that at least one of the engines, if not both, had fallen off before the plane hit the water. Finally, after arguing with her for two days to stay out of the incident, photographs surfaced that showed both engines were attached to the wings before the plane hit the water.

12:08:01 AM	Peace: do you believe at least one of the engines went out as a result of a bird hit?
12:08:06 AM	Kate: yes - can you show me the photo
12:08:40 AM	Peace: then you must also believe that an incredible coincidence occurred that caused the other engine to fall off or fail independently of that. - at the same exact time - a maintenance problem
12:10:32 AM	Kate: photo
12:10:52 AM	Peace: in yer email

Apparently a picture *is* worth a thousand words. The photograph I sent to her concluded FlyersRights.org's two-day investigation into the incident – leaving the National Transportation Safety Board on its own to determine the cause of the accident and unravel the non-existent conspiracy.

THERE IS A congressional election every two years and, before the new Congress is seated, all of the bills that didn't pass in the previous Congress die. That meant that the stand-alone passengers' rights bills in the House and Senate had to be reintroduced. After almost two years of working with Senator Boxer's office, tweaking the language one way or another, we all thought Boxer's stand-alone bill in its current form was the best we were going to get, and the best one to use for both the House and the Senate.

Boxer's bill required airlines to provide adequate food and potable water, working restroom facilities, cabin ventilation and comfortable cabin temperatures, and access to necessary medical treatment whenever a flight was delayed on departure or arrival.

It also required airlines to provide passengers with the option to deplane three hours after passengers boarded the aircraft and the aircraft doors were closed. The same limit applied to a flight that had landed. Assuming that the airline hadn't canceled the flight, the bill also required the airline to offer passengers the option to deplane once every three hours thereafter.

There were exceptions; if the pilot thought that it was likely that the flight would depart within 30 minutes after the three-hour limit, he or she could override the three-hour limit; if the pilot thought that deplaning passengers would jeopardize their safety or security, then the rule would be waived. The bill also called for the Secretary of Transportation to assess civil penalties if the law was violated, although no dollar amount was specified.

On January 15, Senator Boxer introduced her new passengers' rights bill in the Senate. Mike Thompson followed suit in the House the next day. This time, Thompson's and Boxer's bills were identical. There was still very little chance that these individual bills would ever pass, but if we could get their language incorporated into the new House and Senate FAA reauthorization bills, we thought airline passengers' rights would have a much better chance – despite the endless series of FAA extensions we had seen since September 2007.

On January 23, I flew to Florida for a golf trip with friends. Except for the summer of 2008, it was my first break from airline passengers' rights in nearly two years.

FEBRUARY 2009

All about appearances

I RETURNED HOME from Florida on February 1, two years to the day from when I had first seen Kate on C-SPAN. We were scheduled to be in Washington the following week to unveil our annual airline report card and for Kate to testify before the House Aviation Subcommittee.

While I was in Florida, Jack Corbett had apparently suggested to Kate that she compile stranded passenger stories for her oral testimony. Kate sent us what she had done in response to that suggestion, including a dozen or so hotline calls. When she told me that this was Corbett's idea, I wrote to him and asked what he had in mind. He responded:

> What's riveting about Kate's five-minute testimonies before
> Congress are the human stories she mentions. Everybody gets
> quiet when she tells those tales.

That may have been true, but Corbett didn't know that Kate was usually lying or grossly exaggerating when she told those *tales*, and I wasn't going to sit through a repeat performance of the April 2008 testimony. Even the hotline calls she produced this time were cajoled and scripted. Half of them were recorded in the previous three days, but the events described by the callers had occurred months or years earlier, many of them unconfirmed.

Corbett had already started on Kate's written testimony and he circulated a draft amongst Kate, Rubin, Hudson and me. I reconciled the comments from everyone. A couple of days later we had a final version and I sent it to the committee.

Soon after, Corbett sent me an e-mail in which he asked if I thought it might be a good idea to have a dinner in Washington the following week in honor of Kate and her family. In the two years since the founding of CAPBOR-FlyersRights.org, no one from her family had ever accompanied Kate to Washington. Corbett was also going to invite Rubin, Hudson and Mierzwinski. I thought the dinner was a great idea, but that my attendance would be a *really* bad idea. I wrote to Kate:

3:05:49 PM	Peace: well - all i can think to tell jack is that I won't be there - can't make a dinner. - obviously not a good idea
3:08:35 PM	Kate: Yes, you should absolutely make dinner - You need to suit up, show up, as the nicest, formidable person in the world - Not being there would make it doubly awkward right?
3:09:33 PM	Peace: LOL - yer a pip Kate. I don't know which will make it more awkward.
3:11:51 PM	Kate: I've survived far worse my friend - I need your help here
3:12:02 PM	Kate: It's all about appearances

Her point was that if I were to attend the dinner it would be more convincing to her husband that she and I weren't still having a relationship. If I didn't go, that would look more suspicious – possibly to Corbett and the others as well. I replied to Corbett and told him that the dinner was a great idea.

Meanwhile, there was a lot of work to do. It was clear to me that the airlines still weren't reporting the new tarmac data correctly, and I wanted to see the correspondence between the airlines and the BTS in regard to the new statistics collection rules. I spent the next couple of days writing a Freedom of Information Act (FOIA) request to obtain that correspondence.

The FOIA request would also give Kate more fodder for the media – the media loves it when someone questions the credibility of the government. Anytime we could stir up controversy, it generated media attention.

The next day, Kate said she retained Mike Collins to pitch media and write press releases for the upcoming week. Collins was the public relations consultant with whom she'd had the inappropriate instant message conversation in September – the conversation she had posted on the blog. She said she was paying him $2500 for the week. I wasn't happy that someone was going to get paid for doing things I had been doing for free for two years, but we needed help and there were no other options.

On the 9th, I picked Kate up at Dulles International Airport. She checked into a room at the Churchill. I checked into a room across the street at the Hilton. With her family scheduled to arrive the next day, we couldn't stay in the same room or even the same hotel. Later, she joined me in my room for dinner. She said she was worried that she was being followed by private investigators – presumably hired by her husband – and she didn't want to be seen alone with me in a restaurant. Her logic escaped me.

Once again, she fell asleep in my room. With her family arriving sometime the next day, I thought I'd better get her back to her room across the street. They weren't due to arrive until the next afternoon, but I wasn't taking any chances. Her husband might decide to take a red-eye and show up early. If he couldn't find her when he got to the hotel, I was pretty sure who would get thrown under a bus. The events of April 2008 were never far from my mind. I still had "rape kit" banging around inside my skull almost every day.

I managed to get her back to her room at the Churchill, a task made all the more difficult because she had difficulty walking. I had to practically carry her most of the way. I wasn't sure what was wrong with her. She'd only had a couple of glasses of Pinot noir during dinner – not nearly enough to account for her current state.

I got her into her hotel room, laid her on the bed and covered her with a blanket. She seemed to be semi-conscious. I watched her for several minutes. Something seemed very wrong. I glanced into an adjoining room, noticed a tall, empty glass on a coffee table. I smelled it – a Mimosa or Margarita from room service, I guessed. The glass was flanked by two prescription pill containers.

Shit, Kate. What have you done? I sat on the edge of the bed and wondered what to do. *What if she overdosed? How can I tell? Maybe she's just drunk, but what if she isn't?* I didn't want to overreact, but I didn't want to under-react either.

I shook her, "Kate, are you okay? Do you need to go to a hospital?"

"Help me, Mark," she murmured.

"Help you do what, Kate? Do you need to go to the hospital?" I repeated.

"Yes," she said.

"Nine-one-one, what's your emergency?" the operator asked.

"I don't know. I have a very sick woman here and I think she needs an ambulance," I said.

I gave the 9-1-1 operator the hotel address and answered other questions. I ran down to the street to wait for the ambulance. My heart was pounding. The street was deserted. It was probably around midnight. I hadn't checked the time. The first vehicle that arrived was a massive fire engine, complete with a team of firemen.

"Holy shit!" I exclaimed, "I only asked for an ambulance. There's no fire!"

The driver sat in the truck and glared at me. I envisioned the scene turning into a circus. *What if a reporter shows up - some insomniac journalist monitoring the emergency bands?* I was worried about whether or not Kate might die, but I was also worried about her public image, the law, and everything else we had worked for.

About a minute later, an ambulance arrived with two paramedics. I led a parade of paramedics and firemen through the hotel lobby and up to the room. The paramedics got Kate onto a gurney, checked her vital signs, and off we went. I rode with her in the back of the ambulance, held her hand until we reached a hospital emergency room.

After about five hours in the hospital, Kate was awake and lucid. A doctor came into the room and asked me to wait outside so that she could have a private conversation about the blood tests they had run. When the doctor left, Kate called me back into the room and told me we were leaving "now."

She asked me how to remove the IV from her arm, and then she pulled it out herself. I grabbed some gauze from a nearby counter and applied pressure to stop the bleeding. I gave her my jacket – it was cold outside. For some reason, she didn't want to leave through the emergency room. Instead, we left the hospital through an alternate exit and then hailed a taxi.

Soon after we got into the taxi, she asked "What would have happened if you and I had met first?"

"I think I better take you back to the hospital," I kidded.

She didn't think that was funny.

"Kate, if you and I had met in our twenties or thirties, gotten married or something, one of us would be dead by now and I'm pretty sure that *someone* would be me," I said.

"You're probably right," she said, "but just think what we could have accomplished together."

Dawn was breaking as the taxi pulled up in front of the Churchill. I walked her to her room and then I returned to my room at the Hilton. I looked out of my hotel room window at Connecticut Avenue and the Churchill's entrance beyond. Washington had come to life. Dozens of pedestrians bustled over the same sidewalk where I had stood alone hours earlier as I waited for the ambulance. It was all so surreal.

Kate was scheduled to testify before the House Aviation Subcommittee in less than thirty hours and nary a word had been put to paper for her oral testimony. We had a major press conference scheduled for Thursday morning and the centerpiece of the event, the 40-page report card, was far from finished. We had meetings scheduled with congressional and DOT offices throughout the week. Media advisories and press releases needed to be written and distributed. We weren't ready for anything.

I called room service, ordered breakfast and two pots of coffee. The final airline statistics for 2008 had been released by the BTS a day earlier and I began the arduous task of incorporating them into the report card. Kate woke up a few hours later.

| 11:18:09 AM | Peace: think that IV bruise on your arm might be noticed? |
| 11:20:49 AM | Kate: barely noticeable |

11:20:52 AM	Kate: tiny red dot
11:20:55 AM	Kate: no bruise
11:21:09 AM	Kate: I hate hospitals

I wondered silently how much she remembered and what might have happened had I not called for the ambulance – questions that would go forever unanswered. We never spoke of that night again.

Normally, despite all of the work that needed to be done, I would be able to manage. I work well under last-minute pressure. But this time, with her husband arriving later that day, Kate would be mostly incommunicado with me and that wasn't good.

Except for media-related work, I wouldn't usually let Kate have responsibility for anything that was a critical component of a project. With all of the work that had to be done, this time it was a necessary risk. I knew that there was no way she could write her own testimony, but I hoped that she could at least make an effort – produce something that I could clean up later. Another critical task was to secure a location for the report card press conference with Senators Boxer and Snowe. She told me that she had taken care of that:

| 1:58:01 PM | Kate: We got confirmation of Boxer and Snowe |
| 1:58:06 PM | Kate: They told me not to worry about the room |

I didn't know what their staff members told her, but I had a feeling that the arrangement was doomed. It was inconceivable to me that the senators would attend that press conference if their staffs read the drafts of Kate's pages that I had sent to them days earlier. I could only assume that nobody in their offices had read them yet. Meanwhile, Kate kept getting distracted by things that were not in the critical path, like reporters asking for non-existent hotline calls.

| 3:17:20 PM | Peace: ok - here's the thing - testimony is tomorrow. Stop doing anything that doesn't have to do with getting the oral done. Your family will be here soon and then yer f...ed. Testimony is TOMORROW! |

She got a call from yet another reporter. Finally, she responded.

3:28:55 PM	Kate: ok - But I need more New Jersey calls. I only found one on this computer. I don't have a lot of them on this computer.
3:34:58 PM	Peace: i see 6 calls on the spreadsheets for Newark - ho - i'll email them to you. Then you just need to find those calls
3:39:19 PM	Peace: actually - except for one of these, they pretty much suck
3:39:33 PM	Peace: i think you're looking for calls that don't exist.

This wasn't going to turn out well, I just knew it. Next, I got an e-mail from Mike Collins. He had written a draft press release that included a quote he wanted to attribute to Kate:

> Would Captain 'Sully' Sullenberger have been able to land
> safely in the Hudson if he'd had to spend the previous 9 hours
> cramped in the cockpit, waiting on the tarmac?

That touched off a series of e-mails debating the issue of whether or not to include anything about Sullenberger and the Hudson River landing. I thought it was exploitative, not to mention the fact that nobody had any idea whether Sullenberger, by now a national hero, would endorse our positions, and heaven help us if he didn't.

Collins had no idea who I was. As far as he knew, I was just one of Kate's hundreds of non-existent volunteers, so I was wasting my breath with him. I told Kate to tell him that we weren't using Sullenberger in the press release, and that was the end of that.

Later in the afternoon, Kate sent a draft of her testimony to Corbett and me. It wasn't good – not even an honest effort by her standards. Corbett wrote a concise and accurate rebuke, "Start over."

By 9 p.m., Kate only had a few hours of sleep, I'd had none, and she was scheduled to testify the next day at 2 p.m. Kate's family had arrived at the hotel a few hours earlier. I had purchased a bottle of Chardonnay at a store across the street. It was terrible.

9:17:13 PM   Peace: ewww Three Blind Moose Chardonnay - if only
               there was somebody around here that knew something
               about wine

She spent the next several minutes explaining the concept behind triple-blind wine tasting. She said it had to do with wine tasting contests where people are blindfolded so they can't see the color of the wine, the wine labels are removed, and the wine is in a bag. I didn't understand why it needed to be in a bag and the labels removed if the person was already blindfolded, but I didn't want to ask. I was already sorry that I brought it up.

Then came the request that I knew would eventually come. She hadn't made any progress at all on her oral testimony. She asked me to write it.

9:33:10 PM   Peace: huh? jezuz for some reason i thought you were
               doing that .. and then sending me what you had

9:33:16 PM   Peace: [expletive deleted] - ok

I used the testimony that Corbett had written days earlier as a starting point and worked on her oral testimony until 2 a.m. By the time I finished, I had been up for almost 40 hours. It had been one hell of a day.

The next afternoon, I got word that Senators Boxer and Snowe weren't going to attend the report card press conference after all. That meant we lost the room for the press conference – if we ever had one. A room in the Senate office complex can only be used if a senator appears. I tried to get Senator Lautenberg's office to help, but he couldn't make it either. I spent two hours exploring every conceivable option to find a free room for the press conference, but I hit dead ends at every turn. I considered reserving a room at the National Press Club, but I didn't know if we had enough money to pay for it – especially considering our travel expenses and paying Mike Collins.

I had been watching the House Aviation Subcommittee hearing on an Internet feed in my hotel room. The committee members had gone to the House floor for a vote about something and the hearing was in a recess. I could see Kate sitting at the witness table talking to someone. I sent her a text message. Her phone must have been turned off – she didn't respond. *Shit, I'm going to have to go down there*, I thought.

At 4 p.m., I could see that the committee was reconvening. I knew from past experience that the administrative office at the National Press Club would close soon, and I wouldn't be able to reserve a room for the next day if I didn't act quickly. I grabbed a taxi and headed to the Rayburn House Office Building where the hearing was being held. Except for a trip across the street to the wine store, I hadn't been out of my hotel room in 34 hours.

Kate was being introduced just as I got to the hearing. I sat in the gallery on the opposite side of the room from Kate and her family. It was their first time to see Kate testify in person and I didn't want to spoil the moment, but there was no getting around the fact that I was going to have to go over there and talk to her.

I listened to her read the testimony that I wrote the night before. I no longer felt the sense of excitement and pride that I did when she first read my words during the hearings in 2007. I looked at her family sitting on the other side of the room. I felt sorry for any angst I had caused them. I also thought they could have done worse. I had protected Kate from others and I had protected her from herself. I made sure that she returned to them safe and sound after each trip. But as I sat there, I wondered how much longer I could keep doing it, how much longer I *wanted* to keep doing it.

I also wondered, again, if it had been Kate who brought up the subject of rape when she returned to her room the previous April. It was a question that had haunted me perpetually since I first heard the words "rape kit." If she, not Malik, had made the allegation, it would cause me to wonder about the veracity of her June 2006 assault story.

That she knowingly filed a false complaint against me with the Napa County Sheriff's Department, regardless of her excuses and motives, contributed to my growing doubt about her 2006 assault claim. *If she could make serious false claims against me to cover up her own actions, she could have done it to someone else,* I thought.

The pain, trauma and long-term consequences of rape or attempted rape are not to be trivialized, so I risk censure if I question the legitimacy of any victim's claim. But just as these are crimes of psychological violence, so are unfounded accusations of those crimes. There was no way for me to know who broached the subject of rape in my case without asking Malik or Rubin, and I couldn't bring myself to do that. I'm not sure I even wanted to know. I still wanted to believe that this airline passengers' rights icon that I had helped to create was incapable of inflicting that kind of pain.

All I knew was that if it had been Kate who brought up the subject of rape in April, her claim was unfounded. I leave it to readers to draw their own conclusions, fully aware that suspicion and disbelief of women who accuse men of rape or attempted rape is a taboo subject. There are no winners in this debate.

I refocused on Kate and listened to her read the testimony. I had intentionally omitted any mention of hotline calls, numbers of coalition members, or anything else that could be considered remotely untrue. There was some demagoguery, but that was okay – that's part of the game. The basic message was that we disagreed with language in the FAA reauthorization bill that would allow airlines to set their own time limits for tarmac delays:

> We applaud the provisions recently introduced in H.R. 915 by Chairmen Oberstar and Costello, but … we hope you would consider Congressman Mike Thompson's HR 624: Passenger Rights Act of 2009. It has 24 co-sponsors already and mandates effective minimum standards for water, food, working toilets, tolerable temperatures, and an option to deplane after three hours if it can be done safely.

She ad-libbed at one point, said that sitting behind her was a GE engineer who got a blood clot caused by a three-hour tarmac delay. In advance of the hearing, she and Collins had distributed media advisories and press releases that said she was going to be surrounded by "a number of airline passengers who have sustained blood clots, diabetic shock and other complications as the result of tarmac delays as long as twelve hours."

The number of airline passengers surrounding her was one, and his tarmac delay was three hours. *Close enough,* I thought.

Thankfully, none of the committee members asked her any questions during the Q&A, thus avoiding a repeat performance of the April 2008 hearing.

When the hearing adjourned, I took a deep breath and made my way to the other side of the room. Kate sat at the witness table and chatted with the stenographer. Kate's husband stood a few feet behind. There was no getting around it – I introduced myself to her husband, shook hands, was humble, apologetic. We had spoken on the phone and exchanged some e-mails a few months earlier, but this was the first time we met in person. It was an extraordinarily awkward moment. I had an overwhelming urge to tell him that he should always be here with her, or that he should hire someone to look after her.

Just then, Kate finished talking to the stenographer, stood and turned to find herself, her husband and me standing within a few feet of one another. She looked at me, her husband, smiled, and without a word, made a beeline for the exit. *Appearances, Kate!* I thought. I caught her at the door.

I told her that we lost the room for the press conference and that it was probably too late to get a room at the National Press Club. I also reminded her that her sections of the report card weren't finished and that Corbett's dinner was less than three hours away. "I think we have to postpone the press conference until Friday. What do you want to do?"

"I have to go to the bathroom," she said, and out of the door she went.

Appearances be damned, I thought. I wasn't going to stand there and chat with her family. I followed her out of the room, but turned in the opposite direction – toward the elevators and the nearest exit.

When I returned to my hotel room, I received an e-mail from reporter Matt Wald of the *New York Times*. I had been corresponding earlier in the day with Wald about airline statistics. He now wrote that he wasn't interested in writing a story on the subject because he was working a different beat. He suggested that I contact Joe Sharkey.

I wrote to Kate and asked if I should call Sharkey. My phone rang a few minutes later. Kate said she didn't want me to call Sharkey. She said that it would be her "worst nightmare" and she wasn't ready to deal with that yet.

I talked to reporters often, but when I returned in September she asked me to promise that I wouldn't talk to Sharkey. To me, the reason was obvious; she must have made certain allegations about me the previous summer and she didn't want him to know I was back *working* with her.

I could only surmise that she told him that I had hacked her computers, stalked her, and heaven only knew what else. I would have liked to clear the air with him, but there was no way to defend myself or address any misconceptions he might have about my character without telling him about the affair. That was a conversation I never wanted to have with anyone.

Meanwhile, Kate conceded that it was impossible to have the press conference the next day and that we would reschedule it for Friday. She said I should come to the dinner.

"Are you sure?" I asked.

"Yes," she said, "Gotta go. Bye."

I drank a glass of Chardonnay and then went downstairs to grab a taxi. Corbett had reserved a table for ten at the M&S Grill on 13th Street. I was the last to arrive. They saved a chair for me at the end of the rectangular table, as far away as possible from Kate and her family at the other end – an enormous relief. The dinner went without incident, having the desired outcome that the diners had no idea what was really going on.

Back at my hotel, I worked until 2 a.m. to complete my sections of the report card. The most interesting thing I found was that the new reporting rules imposed on the airlines did seem to have an impact on tarmac delays. As I suspected from the moment I discovered the problem early in 2007, if we were able to get the airlines to report tarmac delays on diverted and canceled flights, that alone would reduce tarmac delays. There were 1642 three-hour tarmac delays in 2007, *not including* diverted and canceled flights. In 2008, there were 1299 tarmac delays, *including* diverted and canceled flights. By the end of 2009, the total would plummet to 868.

The next evening, Continental Connection Flight 3407, operated by Colgan Airlines, crashed near Buffalo, New York. Fifty people were killed. We couldn't have a press conference that bashed the airlines under those circumstances, so we canceled Friday's press conference. I went alone to the DOT to meet with BTS personnel to discuss new airline statistics tables they were developing for the BTS website, and then I drove home.

Back in California, Kate decided that Delta Airlines should be scored worst in the report card despite the fact that the scoring system we had used since the first report card in June 2007 placed them third to last. The worst airline would have been US Airways, but because Sully Sullenberger had become a national hero after landing a US Airways jet in the Hudson River, she didn't want US Airways to be graded worst in the report card. She wrote:

> The weighted averages must be changed to reflect the sheer numbers of strandings Delta had. Perhaps they get an F for every 25 which means they get at least 12 F's weighted in for that many strandings. But we can't give US Airways the F. F+ maybe.

She changed the scoring so that Delta would be the overall loser. It didn't matter that her 300 tarmac strandings were made up out of thin air in the first place. Apparently twelve Fs weren't enough to change the results – in the final report card, she gave them fifteen.

I resolved then and there that I would never again have anything to do with the report card, and when it was finally released in Washington the next month, I wouldn't attend. I was weary of her constant exaggerations and deceptions. It might have had something to do with finding myself on the receiving end.

On February 24, Kate flew to New York City to meet with potential publishers for her still unwritten book. She asked me to meet her there, but I declined. Had the Kate Hanni I thought I knew prior to April 2008 asked, I probably would have accepted the invitation. I just couldn't fathom how that Kate Hanni could be the same Kate Hanni I now knew. She looked, walked and talked the same, but I now saw her in a different light. I had thought her deceptions were part of a conscious plan to defeat the airlines, something one could possibly justify. But I now worried that deceit wasn't just part of an effort to mislead on behalf of the cause; rather that it was in her DNA.

MARCH 2009

Tattoos

ON MARCH 2, Kate learned that a Canadian Member of Parliament, Jim Maloway, had introduced an airline passengers' bill of rights in the House of Commons – because there was no airline passengers' rights law in Canada.

Maloway's bill was scheduled to be debated in the House of Commons on March 5. The FAA reauthorization bill was scheduled to come before the House Aviation Subcommittee for a vote on that same day. Kate thought the coincidence was newsworthy.

I arranged a teleconference for Maloway, Kate and others to discuss the issues with the media on March 4. That morning, she said she was groggy, caused by some new medication she was taking. She said she didn't know if she would be able to clear her mind enough to hold the teleconference. She asked me to write a script for her, and then she kept poking at me every few minutes.

> 12:09:44 PM   Kate: Are you there?

> 12:09:58 PM   Peace: I'm writing, leave me alone! Go away

Fifteen minutes later I sent her a script to open the teleconference and introduce the participants. After she read the script, I guided her step-by-step through the rest of the call by sending her instant messages about what to say or ask. After Bruce Cran, president of the Consumer's Association of Canada, finished talking, Kate asked if there were any questions from the press – there was nothing but silence. We only had two reporters on the line and they didn't ask any questions. It was embarrassing. She had told the Canadians we could get them a lot of media attention, however it was obvious that there wasn't much interest in the subject from the media in the U.S.

> 12:52:39 PM   Peace: do a last call for media questions - say we must be having tech difficulties and then give your cell number for media requests. thank everyone and get off (figuratively)

ON MARCH 10, Kate arrived back in Washington to release the report card that had been postponed due to the Colgan crash in February. As disturbed as I was that she changed the scoring for the report card, I still might have gone to Washington to make sure she didn't get herself into any trouble or do any damage to the cause. But a week earlier, I learned that a female reporter from a national publication would be in Washington to shadow Kate and would be staying in the same hotel. Because of that, I knew I wouldn't have to be there. Kate wouldn't do anything hazardous.

Due to the reporter's anticipated presence, Kate had spent the prior week working to get as many other people as possible to attend the press conference. In addition to Anjum Malik and Jennifer Shirkani, she arranged for three other people from the Washington area to attend. The six of them also made a record-breaking sixteen congressional appointments. She wanted me to be there too.

5:36:59 PM   Kate: You should be here for the report card tomorrow. - Can you get here?

5:38:49 PM   Peace: no

5:40:17 PM   Kate: no - just NO - No how - No way

Except for the summer of 2008, it was the first time in two years that I didn't meet her during a trip to Washington.

She held the report card press conference the next day and bestowed Delta Airlines with the dubious "When you're on the ground, they treat you like dirt" award. When she announced the award, she said, "Delta Airlines had over 300 unreported stranding events of four hours or more."

CNN covered the press conference and reported that a Delta Airlines' spokesperson said that Delta "disputes the data that this organization has come up with to make these claims."[48]

On Saturday morning, she made her second appearance on C-SPAN. I only watched for about five minutes. I changed the channel after she said, "This week we met with about thirty Senate offices and probably fifteen on the House side, and we'll be back in two weeks to do the same."

There was a time when I thought that lying to the media and the public was amusing because I was in on the gag. It wasn't amusing anymore. Even worse, in a telephone interview earlier that week, I had been backed into a corner by a CNN reporter who wanted to know how many members we had and how we were funded.

Mark Mogel, the group's research director, said FlyersRights.org has about 24,000 members, many of whom donate money, services and lobbying help.[49]

LATER THAT MONTH, Kate and I discussed how to generate publicity around airline statistics and what we should be doing in regard to pressing the DOT and Congress in regard to airline passengers' rights. As usual, we argued about a number of things during the day. I was growing increasingly impatient with her judgment, which actually seemed to be getting worse. Kate apparently interpreted my disagreeable mood as stemming from my dissatisfaction with our personal relationship. She may have been partly right.

It was nearly two in the morning and I told her I had to go to bed. She had recently told me that she was going to get a small tattoo that she would tell her husband was for him, but was really for me.

1:47:00 AM	Kate: you need to relax more and realize who you are to me and know that whatever is going on around us doesn't matter the core issue is ok for us
1:47:39 AM	Peace: k - i'll try. Maybe a tattoo on my forearm. nite - gotta go
1:47:46 AM	Kate: just learn to relax and go with the flow. I'm always going to be the figurehead and blonde bimbo media gal.
1:48:07 AM	Kate: But you are so much more and you need to know and trust that you will get acknowledged.

APRIL 2009

Out of control

BY APRIL 2009, two years and four months since her tarmac stranding in Austin, Texas, Kate's lawsuit against American Airlines was becoming a major problem, but not for American Airlines. In late 2006, before the tarmac stranding, Kate had filed a workman's compensation claim in California that asserted she couldn't sell real estate because she was too frightened to be alone in a house due to the assault she said she suffered in June of that year. She had subsequently been evaluated by a state-appointed psychiatrist.

After her tarmac stranding and the formation of CAPBOR, and because of her well-publicized travels to Washington, the state employed investigators to follow her, presumably to collect evidence that she wasn't afraid to be alone, in hotel rooms for example.

American's lawyers wanted to see the state's reports to determine how much of her damages, if any, were attributable to the stranding incident. For several weeks, American's lawyers had been trying to obtain the reports, and the judge in the lawsuit had ordered Kate to provide them.

On April 2, she called and told me that she had been honest with the psychiatrist about a variety of personal matters that she didn't want anyone, including the judge, to know about. She also said that the psychiatrist had diagnosed her as a narcissist, a diagnosis with which she disagreed. But the real reason she called, she said, was to tell me that the state's reports might include audio and video of us together in Washington – a result of the investigators the state employed to follow her.

"What kind of audio and video?" I asked.

She said she didn't know – she didn't have any details. She said she had to end the call because her husband had just come home.

I didn't get much sleep that night.

We resumed the conversation via instant messages the next day. She was worried that if she provided the state's reports to American's lawyers, it would "destroy" her.

American's lawyers already had some potentially damaging documents and they had included one of them as an attachment to one of their briefs on the online court docket. It was a partial transcript of testimony that Kate had given at a December 2006 hearing in her workman's compensation case – nine days before her tarmac stranding in Austin.

According to the transcript excerpts, Kate testified that one of her real estate clients fired her four days after her assault. Two weeks later, Kate checked herself into a facility called "Crossroads" on Antigua. She testified that Crossroads specialized in "trauma recovery and twelve-step recovery" programs and that she spent a month there. Two weeks after she returned from Antigua, her real estate firm asked her to "pull" her real estate license, which meant they fired her too.

Kate told me that the reason she had been asked to pull her license – she didn't use the term "fired" – was because the real estate firm was upset that she had lost that one client. This despite the fact that she said she had been the highest-selling real estate agent in the Napa Valley for the previous several years. That seemed possible, but the timeline that American's lawyers laid out seemed to point to a suspicious series of events. She was fired by an important client just four days after she reported the assault, and then she was terminated by her real estate firm just days after she returned from a trauma treatment facility.

I thought that the client and the people at the real estate firm either had to be completely heartless, or the story didn't add up. I also found it curious that the Crossroads website, a facility founded by famed guitarist Eric Clapton, didn't say anything about being a trauma recovery center. The website only mentioned substance abuse treatment.

Whatever the case, the pressure that American's lawyers were exerting led Kate to believe that they were playing dirty and that all of this would "destroy" her.

I was worried about my own destruction. I advised her to drop the case. I didn't know if there was really anything in the state's reports about me. It could have been a tactic on her part to draw me into the drama, but I wasn't taking any chances.

Things were disintegrating on other fronts as well. A day earlier, a judge in Arkansas dismissed Cathy Ray's lawsuit against American Airlines for her tarmac stranding in Austin, Texas on December 29, 2006 – a different airplane, but on the same night and at the same airport where Kate had been on the tarmac. The lawsuit had been filed by Paul Hudson on the same day that he filed Kate's lawsuit in California. By Ray's own admission, the flight crew had asked her twice if she wanted to get off the plane. She had decided to stay on the airplane in the hope that that flight would take off.

In his decision, the judge wrote that Ray had "admitted that Defendant [American Airlines] twice offered them the choice to deplane, however, they elected not to do so."

When the judge dismissed the case, he did so with prejudice, which meant that Ray would not be able to re-file the lawsuit. In layperson's terms, it meant there was no basis for filing the lawsuit in the first place. Kate wanted me to write a press release to spin the decision in a positive light, but the legal issues were above my pay grade. I suggested we have a conference call with Jack Corbett to talk about it.

Amiable, thoughtful, witty with a dry sense of humor, in the entire time I had known Corbett, I never heard him swear or lose his temper – a remarkable record for anyone who interacted with Kate as much as he did. But when we started the conference call to talk about the lawsuit, he was furious.

How the hell do we have a lead plaintiff that was given two chances to get off the airplane? Did anybody think to ask about that *before* the lawsuit was filed?

I listened quietly as Kate tried in vain to justify using Ray as lead plaintiff, knowing what Corbett didn't; that Ray was the only option. Finally, I asked Corbett to explain some of the legal language in the judge's decision, and then I wrote a press release that steered away from the fact that Ray had been asked twice if she wanted to deplane:

> In his April 2 decision, U.S. district Judge Robert T. Dawson wrote that the court was 'sympathetic to the plaintiff,' but ultimately ruled that the airline has no duty to provide passengers with 'a stress-free environment.'
>
> 'This decision only reinforces the need for Federal legislation to create a bright line standard for how long passengers can be kept on stranded flights,' said Kate Hanni.

ON APRIL 21, I talked to a passenger that had been on Delta flight 510 from the Turks and Caicos Islands to Atlanta. The flight was diverted to Columbia, S.C., due to thunderstorms in the Atlanta area. The passenger said they were on the tarmac for six hours in Columbia and that his two-year old hadn't eaten for eight hours by the time they got off the plane.

It was a rare hotline success story, although even in this case the passenger didn't call us until a week later, and nobody called him back for another three days.

Based on the information I had, I wrote a press release and an article for the website titled, "Stranded on the Tarmac - A Flight from Paradise to Hell." I also sent an e-mail blast to our media contacts. An article about the incident appeared in the Wall Street Journal a week later that provided a much more in-depth account from passengers, the airline and the airport, although it was obvious that my article and media release got the ball rolling.

According to the Wall Street Journal, the plane was refueled after it landed in Columbia and the crew expected to take off for Atlanta. At the same time, a second line of thunderstorms passed through the Atlanta area that further delayed their departure. By the time the storms cleared, the crew had exceeded its FAA-imposed duty hour limits by about ten minutes. It was approximately 7:45 p.m., and the passengers had been sitting on the tarmac for two hours. It took another two hours for airport and customs officials to figure out what to do, according to the Wall Street Journal:

> It took more than two hours for federal, airport and airline officials to come up with a plan to get passengers off the plane. Because the flight was an international trip, people aboard needed to clear U.S. Customs and Immigration before they could be allowed freely into the terminal.[50]

Most international flights destined for the United States were bound for one of the larger hubs in the U.S. where customs officials were on duty from early morning until late at night, sometimes 24/7. When those international flights were forced to divert to alternate airports, the alternates often did not have customs officials on duty – especially when no international flights were expected. In the case of the Columbia, S.C. airport, they had only two customs officers, and by 7:45 that evening, they had gone for the day.

After five hours on the tarmac, the 134 passengers were finally deplaned into an unfinished 1,500 square foot room with sheet-rock walls and a concrete floor. There were approximately 20 folding chairs. Guarded by TSA agents, the passengers were able to use the restroom a handful at a time.

Customs agents returned to the airport and, with concurrence of airport and Delta Airlines' officials, the passengers were allowed into an area of the terminal that was cordoned off with police tape. Meanwhile, Delta was working to get another crew to the airport to fly the passengers to Atlanta.

The customs agents processed some passengers who decided not to continue on to Atlanta. As for the remaining passengers, they arrived in Atlanta at around 3:30 a.m.

The tarmac delay task force had recommended that airports set aside a secure room for passengers from diverted international flights. This would also allow passengers to avoid another security check before re-boarding a flight to their final destination. However, the task force recommendations weren't mandatory, and only a few airports had implemented them. The airport in Columbia developed contingency plans for future events, but it's still a relatively small airport. As the deputy director of the airport told me, if they were to get just two international diversions with 300 passengers each, they would have nowhere to put them except possibly in a hangar.

ON THE MORNING of April 30, I received a Google Alert that showed that Kate had submitted an Op-Ed letter to the *San Jose Mercury News*. In it, she opposed a bill that would ban the use of electronic voice communication while a plane was in flight.

The use of cell phones while a plane was in flight was already banned by federal regulations, but this legislation would extend that ban to computer-enabled voice applications such as Skype. Airlines had recently begun to offer in-flight Internet access that made it possible for passengers to use computer applications such as Skype to make telephone calls while an airplane was in flight.

The bill to prohibit in-flight voice communications had been sponsored by Jim Oberstar and Jerry Costello, the same committee chairmen who held the key as to whether or not we would get a three-hour rule written into the House FAA reauthorization bill. Kate's letter, published in the *San Jose Mercury News,* opposed their bill:

> Wireless communication products have become an integral part
> of our everyday lives — especially when we travel.
> Unfortunately, Congress recently introduced a bill that would
> ban passengers from using wireless devices on commercial
> flights. Such a policy could place an excessive and unreasonable
> hardship on millions of Americans who travel by air.[51]

The letter was written in such a way as to leave the reader with the impression that the law would ban cell phones and all other forms of wireless communication. It didn't mention that the ban only applied when the plane was in flight, and that it only applied to voice communications, not e-mail, text messages or Web access.

At the bottom of the letter, it said that Kate had written the editorial on behalf of FlyersRights.org. That was impossible. The letter was too well written, and there was no way that Rubin, Corbett, or Hudson would have written it. It was about 4 a.m. in Napa – too early to call and find out what she was up to, so I did some investigation of my own.

A couple of weeks earlier, Kate had mentioned that yet another person who owned a public relations firm in Washington had offered to help us, pro bono, with press releases and other things. His name was Ernest Baynard. I started with him.

Baynard was the president of a public relations firm named Meridian-Hill Strategies, and a Google search showed that his firm was associated with something called the In-flight Passenger Communications Coalition (IPCC), which was headed by a Carl Biersack.

By now I had seen a number of these "consumer coalitions" emerge in Washington to support or oppose a variety of agendas. They had a recipe: 1) Set up a website; 2) Send out a press release; 3) Hold a press conference or two. Within a week, the cable news shows would have them on television to talk about their coalition and its agenda.

They were astroturf organizations, and the public relations firms behind them were obviously smarter than the producers at most of the cable news channels. Once the cable channels gave them legitimacy, the next thing I would see would be groups like this being quoted in *USA Today* or the *New York Times* as if they were grassroots organizations.

The IPCC website said that it was "organized to better inform the traveling public of new communications technologies that safely enable voice and data service while traveling in U.S. airspace." But the real purpose of IPCC was obviously to lobby against the bill that Kate's editorial, likely written by Baynard or Biersack, also opposed.

Biersack was the Director of Federal Government Affairs, a lobbyist for a Washington law firm, Balch and Bingham. Balch and Bingham's website showed that their clients included wireless telecommunications companies. Naturally, wireless companies opposed the ban because in-flight cell phone use would increase their profits substantially. At over 700 million airline passengers per year in the U.S. alone, wireless companies, particularly those in the airborne mobile connectivity business, stood to make billions.

I found a letter on the IPCC website that Kate had apparently sent on April 11 to Chairman Oberstar and ranking member John Mica in which she suggested that a study might be better than instituting the ban. The study was what IPCC was lobbying for, knowing full well that a study would delay instituting the ban, probably forever. Kate also signed that letter on behalf of FlyersRights.org.

An MSNBC poll showed that 60 percent of the public was opposed to in-flight voice communications. A Yahoo/Harris poll put the opposition at 74 percent.

From the moment she woke up that morning, we spent the entire day arguing about her editorial on the phone and in instant messages and e-mails. I wrote, "Where does this get us? How does this possibly help us? What on earth did you get for this?"

She wouldn't answer in writing. On the phone she repeated that Baynard had agreed to help us with public relations, press releases and lobbying. It was unfathomable to me that she would have taken such an unpopular and politically dangerous position in exchange for things that we were perfectly capable of doing ourselves.

In late February, she had collaborated with a Houston lawyer, Jason Gibson, on a press release that said we had joined forces with his law firm.

The release said that we had submitted FOIA requests to the NTSB to obtain safety and training records related to the Colgan crash and a Continental Airlines incident that occurred in December in Denver. She hadn't consulted the advisory board in that instance or in the in-flight voice ban controversy.

She was, in my opinion, out of control – working her own secret deals in the background. The advisory committee – primarily Corbett, Rubin and me – was already the futile entity I suspected it would be when it was formed in September.

In the foreground, we were trying to get Oberstar and Costello to change the tarmac delay language to require the airlines to set a specific time limit of three hours. In the background, she was opposing language that Oberstar and Costello favored, as well as flight attendants' unions and three quarters of the American public. And the polls showed that people were adamant in their opposition to in-flight voice communications.

By the middle of June, I had given her so much grief about it that she claimed she had written back to Oberstar and Mica to withdraw her objections, although she never showed me the e-mail. However, when later interviewed by *Congress Daily*, she did publicly switch sides:

'I absolutely don't want to be sitting next to people talking on a flight,' said Kate Hanni, executive director of FlyersRights.org, a nonprofit passenger rights group. 'I could see how it could aggravate people and cause air rage.'[52]

Baynard then chided her for her quote and told her that she should have "stuck to the talking points from the Op-Ed." She forwarded his e-mail to me thinking that it would make me happy. Instead it made me even more concerned. *How is it that a virtual stranger could reprimand Kate for her comments?* I wondered.

MAY 2009

The mantra

ON MAY 14, Kate once again waited until the last possible minute to ask me to write the testimony for her next appearance before the House Aviation Subcommittee the following week. She had led me to believe that Corbett was writing it.

> 10:58:07 AM   Peace: I don't know kate - send me what you have. jezuz - nothing like waiting until last minute

She sent me a handful of bullet points – the same bullet points I wrote for her to use during a conference call a few days earlier.

> 11:06:04 AM   Peace: that's it? - that's where we are now?

> 11:06:41 AM   Peace: that's where we were three days ago - that's not even an outline fer christ sake

During the past couple of months I had been working on airline passengers' rights issues for about eighty hours a week, including but not limited to airline statistics analysis and an extensive redesign of the FlyersRights.org website. Four hours into writing her testimony, I received an e-mail from Jack Corbett to thank me for working on it. Buried in the e-mail string was a question that Kate had written to him: "I'm wondering if we should employ Mark's help on [the testimony]? He seems to have lots of time on his hands."

> 3:23:55 PM   Peace: RU crazy - yes - answer is yes

> 3:26:52 PM   Kate: thank you

> 3:27:11 PM   Kate: RU crazy?

> 3:27:19 PM   Peace: must be

The main theme of the testimony would be to summarize the overall legislative situation and point out the pros and cons in the Senate and House bills. We still didn't have Senator Boxer's latest passengers' rights language with a three-hour rule in the Senate's FAA reauthorization bill, although we had been told earlier in the week that it would be added when the new bill was introduced in July.

In the House, the FAA reauthorization bill would still let airlines decide their own time limits for tarmac strandings. That bill was scheduled to go to a vote the following Thursday before the full House, and if we couldn't get the language changed before that, there was only a 50/50 chance that we would ever get the three-hour rule in the final legislation that would be signed by the president.

When the Senate and the House pass different versions of the same bill, such as would happen in this case, senior leaders of the relevant committees in both the House and the Senate come together in a conference. Then the horse-trading begins, with each side having to give up something in return for something else. The three-hour rule, like other differences in the bills, would be a poker chip, and it was anybody's guess how that chip would fall.

The next evening Kate asked what she was supposed to be doing in regard to the testimony.

8:07:17 PM   Peace: your section was horror stories

8:07:29 PM   Kate: OH shit. How many?

8:07:41 PM   Peace: well — some

The *horror stories* were supposed to be a collection of the worst tarmac strandings from the past several months, and they would be attached to the testimony to illustrate that long tarmac strandings were an ongoing issue.

The next day, the testimony had to be turned in by 5 p.m., and we were scrambling to get that and other things finished. With four hours to spare, Kate was finally working on the horror stories. Consumed by that task, she forwarded a press release, written by Mike Collins, to Corbett and me for approval. It was obvious that she hadn't read it.

11:57:16 AM   Peace: did you READ this release before you sent it to
               me and jack for approval?

11:57:40 AM   Kate: Yes - I figured you both wouldn't like it

12:00:26 PM   Peace: well, except for the phrase "Hanni accused
               house transportation leaders" it isn't that I don't like it,
               but it isn't correct and it isn't finished.

After I spent the next three hours working with Collins to finish the press release, Kate, possibly the most spoiled and demanding person I'd ever met, complained that Jack Corbett was giving her too much work to do.

3:02:31 PM   Peace: damn that jack - he always wants something ;)

3:02:44 PM   Kate: [expletive deleted] - going to have a heart attack
               between jack and Mike

3:03:16 PM   Peace: not much time either - less than 2 hours to make
               changes and copies and delivery

In the midst of the chaos, Kate and I got Google Alerts for an article in the *New York Times.* The article described the current state of passengers' rights legislation and some of the anomalies I discovered about the tarmac statistics for diverted flights:

> Dave Smallen, a spokesman for department's Bureau of Transportation Statistics, said the agency was planning to meet with Ms. Hanni and Mark Mogel, a FlyersRights volunteer and software engineer who has been analyzing the data, to discuss the issues they raised.[53]

Kate pasted the entire article into our instant message conversation, and then as so often would happen, I couldn't get her back on track.

3:48:38 PM	Peace: Kate! - it's almost 4pm here - where are you with the strandings?
3:49:32 PM	Kate: this article f...ing rocks
3:49:37 PM	Kate: Hang on
3:49:46 PM	Peace: u got 1 hour to get this delivered
3:50:00 PM	Peace: impossible

Fifteen minutes later, she sent me her latest version of the horror stories. She had made virtually no progress. They were terrible. She had done the same thing with the written testimony in February, but at that time neither Corbett nor I looked at them. I had attached them to the testimony and they were filed with the committee without review. There had been five of Kate's paragraphs attached to that testimony, and the first one was no better or worse than the other four:

> United flight 5309 pushed only a few feet from the gate and sits for 7 hours and 50 minutes. The airline tell the passengers they could have deplaned, the door was shut and they were pushed back from the gate, but only a few yards from the gate. United opened the door but no stairs were presented. Passengers were told 'you get off you don't get your luggage'. The passengers were hungry, angry and lost. Their flight was, after 7 hours and 50 minutes canceled. Dan Higgins from the Times Post described it as near mutiny and said that many passengers were relieved to have a law that would protect them. Since the New York Law was overturned there are still no protections and the passengers got nothing to compensate them.

A couple of weeks after the February hearing, Terry Trippler posted videos on the Internet in which he skewered Kate's stories. He concluded one of the videos asking, "How can an organization like FlyersRights.org be taken seriously when they put out garbage like this?"

Trippler was right. The February stories were an embarrassment, and her latest stories were just as bad.

4:05:03 PM	Peace: kate this still needs work. i just talked to jack and he says impossible to get them delivered today - too late. - we're both thinking that maybe we should just omit this stuff, use the articles we already have. and keep it clean - a lot of this stuff is more fodder for Trippler and unless i fix all of it, it will just be more controversy

It was after 4 p.m. and 50 copies of her testimony were supposed to be delivered to the committee by 5 p.m. It was obvious that we couldn't get it done. Despite the fact that it was she who made us late in the first place, she started hounding me every minute because she was afraid that the committee wouldn't let her testify if we were late.

4:30:31 PM	Peace: well it will be done when its done - I'm not going to include the ny times article in this version. yer not giving me a heart attack

Kate flew to Washington on a red-eye that night. The next morning, despite the fact that we weren't going to be able to do anything to change the content of the House bill, I made a couple of appointments for her to meet with congressional offices. Unlike the early days when offices would only meet with us either with or at the behest of their constituents, by now we were able to get meetings with most congressional office ourselves.

Corbett said he didn't have time to work on Kate's oral testimony, so I spent the rest of the day working on that. I also reserved a room for a press conference through Congressman Mike Thompson's office.

Jim Maloway, the Member of Parliament who sponsored the Canadian airline passengers' rights bill, and Bruce Cran, president of the Consumer's Association of Canada, had traveled from Canada to participate in the press conference and to attend the hearing. Both Corbett and I had tried to tell Kate that her continued emphasis on the Canadian law was a waste of time, but she was certain that it was an important way to influence Congress.

Kate's cell phone was dead all afternoon, so I had no idea what was she was doing until 7 p.m. when I saw that she was online. Kate was now staying at a Marriott hotel. I didn't know it at the time, but Kate had decided to stay at the Marriott because Malik was staying at the Churchill. She didn't want to risk having Malik see us together at the same hotel.

7:08:34 PM	Kate: at the bar having drinks with Danny a lobbyist for Labor unions

7:11:03 PM	Peace: ok - well, don't want to bother you while yer having drinks at the bar. When you're finished your date, you might want to deal with the testimony though.
7:11:40 PM	Peace: I'm gonna go play golf. Still have an hour of daylight.
7:13:32 PM	Kate: 'shit no
7:13:38 PM	Peace: foreeee
7:15:33 PM	Kate: you are not playing golf - No f...ing way - Fore my ass - they have left – gone - just a blip
7:15:53 PM	Kate: you should be here - shit Mark - Think outside the box

I told her there was too much work to do, but that I was trying. An hour later, I told her it was too late for me to drive to Washington. I also told her that I wouldn't make it to the press conference with the Canadians.

| 8:05:15 PM | Kate: You have to be at presser. It's at 11:30 am that's easy - Jesus Mark you have to be at the presser? Are you going to have me there all by myself? |

I told her I'd do the best I could but, in truth, I wasn't trying very hard. I hadn't seen her in three months, and I was conflicted about seeing her again.

The testimony was now in Mike Collins' hands, to add some public relations pizzazz, and he and I worked together for the next couple of hours to ensure his proposed changes were correct. While we were doing that, men were getting in line to buy drinks for Kate.

9:12:16 PM	Kate: I am now visited by a bunch of guys who are in the Private lending industry in CHicago. Very mafia
9:12:24 PM	Kate: Everyone is telling me I'm gorgeous
9:12:35 PM	Peace: great
9:12:43 PM	Kate: yeah good for me eh?
9:12:48 PM	Peace: yes

When Collins and I finished with the testimony, I sent a copy to Kate. She wanted me to call her to discuss additional changes.

10:25:46 PM	Kate: call me
10:26:07 PM	Peace: in a min - eating a sandwhcih - gimme a min
10:31:12 PM	Peace: u didn't answer
10:31:38 PM	Kate: oh I didn't hear it call again

I tried to call her again, and again she didn't answer. It was obvious that she was distracted by other things in the bar, not to mention that she had now been drinking for over three hours. I hoped she would get through the night without getting into trouble, but while her body clock was still on West Coast time, mine wasn't. I went to bed. Forty minutes later she was ready to talk.

> 11:12:22 PM   Kate: You putz. You said let's IM then you f...ing
>   disappear. And we need to finalize testimony so Mike
>   can make copies

At about 11:30 my cell phone rang. I turned it off. Then my home phone rang. I unplugged the cord. The next day, I drove to Washington and got there in time for the House Aviation Subcommittee hearing. I missed the press conference with the Canadians, but it didn't matter. Only one reporter showed up. We got one article on the MSNBC website that was picked up a few days later by the *Los Angeles Times*.

The aviation subcommittee hearing that afternoon was also a waste of time. Only two committee members stayed to hear Kate's testimony. Even Chairman Costello wasn't there. Acting chairman Boswell (D-IA) asked a witness for the ATA a question about the plethora of stories of overflowing toilets on airplanes – Kate's stories. The ATA witness answered, "A lot of these stories about non-functioning lavatories that basically have not proven to be the case when we've examined them in more detail."

By now, everyone had heard the mantra we set out two years earlier to implant in the public's conscience; "they sat for hours in a sealed metal tube with no food, no water and overflowing toilets." It didn't matter what the ATA said, and it didn't matter if it was true or not. We said it more often.

I don't remember anything else about the hearing. I had noticed Anjum Malik sitting in the gallery on the other side of the room, and found myself staring at a wall with the sound of a freight train running through my head. After the hearing, I introduced myself to the Canadians and said hello to Malik. I hadn't seen her in over a year. I wondered how she felt about shaking hands with a possible rapist.

That evening, Kate and I spent a few hours working on our laptops at a table in the bar of the hotel. Later, when we got to our room, I told Kate I had some work to do and waited for her to fall asleep before I went to bed. It didn't take long.

I hadn't slept with her since February and I didn't plan to sleep with her again. I had declined to meet her during her last two trips to the East Coast, to New York and Washington, and I had now come to Washington thinking that perhaps we could just be friends. On the other hand, I wasn't going to pay for a separate hotel room either.

The next day, we had one Senate meeting in the morning and spent the rest of the day working at a table in the cafeteria of the Senate Hart Office Building. Nearby was the same table where Kate and I sat two years earlier when she gave me her *Kate Moon* CD. I pictured us sitting there then, not knowing what lay before us. Sometime thereafter, we had fantasized about a future together working in some form of consumer advocacy or politics by day, and perhaps sharing an apartment in Washington by night. I looked at Kate, heard her nails tapping on her keyboard. She still believed that was going to happen, merrily marching forward, oblivious to the harm she had since caused.

"I'm sorry I fell asleep last night," she said, interrupting my thoughts.

"No problem," I said.

On the other side of Capitol Hill, the House of Representatives voted on their version of the FAA reauthorization bill. The yeas and nays were 277-136. The language for tarmac delays was the same as it was in September 2007. Airlines would still be able to define their own time limits for how long they could keep passengers on the tarmac. We hadn't made any progress in the past 20 months. The Senate's version of the FAA reauthorization bill had yet to be reintroduced, and we still didn't know with absolute certainty what kind of airline passengers' rights language we would get when it was.

Jack Corbett called her. "The bill passed today," she said when she got off the phone.

"That's nice," I said.

Later that afternoon, we met Jim Maloway, Bruce Cran and their wives for a meeting with a couple of officials at the Canadian Embassy. There's a protocol or custom that when a Member of Parliament is in another country, they're expected to visit their embassy. Maloway had invited Kate and me to join them.

After the embassy meeting we all went out for dinner. I tried to stay engaged in the dinner conversation, but I was preoccupied with a thought that had been running through my head since I saw Malik the day before. *I can't do this anymore. I need to go home.* When we returned to the hotel, Kate wanted to go into the bar.

"You go ahead. I'm leaving," I said.

"What about the DOT meeting tomorrow?" she asked.

"I don't care," I said.

I packed my bags and left. I couldn't get the "rape kit" thing out of my head. That led to the remembrance of everything deceptive I knew Kate had done since April 2008, and my suspicions that she had lied about everything else. As a result, I had been belligerent with her all day, which made me feel guilty and sad. I just couldn't spend another night with her.

Prostitutes and Pitot tubes

After I left Kate in Washington in late May, I began to pull away, tried to concentrate on the relationship with my wife. Ironically, while married and technically still in the midst of an affair, I couldn't have felt more alone. Other than playing golf, my wife and I had become like ships passing in the night over the past two years. Relationship building, or rebuilding, wasn't one of my strengths, and my renewed attention to our marriage hadn't gone well so far. I didn't expect, had no right to expect, that the relationship would improve overnight.

Kate was usually oblivious to my feelings, but whenever she sensed me slipping away, and this wasn't the first time, she seemed to become more attuned and would figure out a way to pull me back. It wasn't until June 9 when I heard from her again.

Paul Hudson had removed her as the lead plaintiff in her lawsuit against American Airlines. She would not even be permitted to appear as a witness if the case went forward. She was barred from appearing in her own lawsuit for the infamous December 29, 2006, Austin, Texas nine hour and sixteen minute tarmac stranding that was the genesis for FlyersRights.org.

2:17:31 PM	Kate: I'm out of the case, in fact AA threatened Paul to sue me for attorneys fees unless I were to agree never to become a witness in the case
2:18:11 PM	Peace: not even a witness?
2:18:41 PM	Kate: NO not even as a witness. I told him it was a huge mistake
2:18:52 PM	Kate: He had the f...ing nerve to say I don't make that great a witness. I told him he's full of shit.

While I went on to feign sympathy, I knew that Hudson was right. I could only imagine what was going on in her depositions. I was surprised she had lasted as long as she had.

She wanted to issue a press release to spin her removal from the case, but I was opposed. It seemed to me that there was no good way to spin this disaster, and we would be better off remaining silent. If we said nothing, the media would never know. If the media didn't know, the public wouldn't know.

Apparently, Collins gave her similar advice, and that was the end of her lawsuit against American Airlines. Paul Hudson made Kate's husband the lead plaintiff, and the lawsuit would limp along for another year before it was dismissed. Unlike the publicity that surrounded the announcement of the lawsuit, no articles would be written when it was over. According to a deposition Kate gave with American Airlines' attorneys in December 2008, she had at least one opportunity to get off the plane during her nine hour and sixteen minute tarmac stranding:

American:	And you knew that – for example, Cathy Ray testified – that twice, they – that she was offered an opportunity to get off the plane?
Kate:	Yes
American:	That did not happen on your plane?
Kate:	Yeah, it did.
American:	It did?
Kate:	It did. But unfortunately the bus that came only held 15 people. And so what happened is the people that went to the back of the plane that wanted off – and my family wasn't one of them that chose to get off. And the reason was they still told us we were going to go.

THE NEXT DAY, Kate, with the help of Mike Collins, issued a press release that criticized the FAA in regard to its handling of the Colgan crash in February and its general handling of safety matters for regional airlines. Knowing that the advisory committee would not have approved, she had worked with Collins to prepare and issue a press release that was based entirely on two newspaper articles.

This precipitated our umpteenth argument about getting involved in airline health and safety issues. Judging from a scathing e-mail he sent, Jack Corbett wasn't happy about it either. A year and a half earlier, former DOT Inspector General Ken Mead had suggested that we expand into those areas, but that suggestion was likely based on Kate's exaggeration of expertise at our disposal.

> 11:41:24 AM   Kate: Mark, since when are we NOT about passenger safety? Ken Mead made it very clear we should enter that conversation. - how many "opportunities" have you

seen lately for us? - Any?

11:42:07 AM   Peace: Yes, but he didn't say how. Question is is this the right way? I think that's what Jack is asking too. - I think if you want to enter this conversation (although I highly doubt any press will come of this) you probably should read the transcripts of the hearings that have taken place up to this point. I'm not sure reading a couple of articles provides the sort of depth necessary to comment intelligently on these subjects.

Reading transcripts wouldn't make her an expert on the complex subjects of pilot fatigue or other possible operational problems with regional airlines, but it would have been better than using articles written by the news media.

Corbett had a much stronger opinion about the press release and Kate's ongoing flouting of the advisory committee. He quit.

12:08:19 PM   Kate: He said he quit. End of story. He can't trust my judgement.

Corbett was gone. Other than Kate and me, he had contributed more to the cause than anyone – by far. I didn't know what we would do without him.

I probably shouldn't have been, but I was surprised by the coverage that the press release received. Later that day, NPR invited Kate to do an interview about airline pilots' sleep standards – one of the issues raised by the Colgan crash. We spent the rest of the day and night cramming to understand the FAA rules and regulations for pilot rest.

I found a document about pilot sleep standards on the FAA website and sent it to her. We spent the next couple of hours trying to understand what it meant. She kept asking me questions that I couldn't answer.

10:07:43 PM   Peace: good question. I wish I had done more research on this issue - I'm just not an expert.

10:07:55 PM   Kate: Mark - Why do you keep saying that?

10:08:49 PM   Peace: cause I'm not. Seriously, I want you to look good. I read that thing and think it's like a rubics cube

10:09:03 PM   Kate: So you can't cipher it either?

10:09:06 PM   Peace: nothing makes any sense - no

10:10:56 PM   Peace: I wish I was the person you could rely on to decipher all this. I'm just not - I probably could if I spent time on it, but I haven't. You need a crash course – and maybe someone like NAME REDACTED could help.

There was a pilot for a major airline who was kind enough to provide us with expertise from a pilot's perspective. He didn't agree with everything we were doing, but he was a helpful technical resource. I simply had nothing to add to the conversation. I didn't then, and I still don't understand the breadth and depth of pilot fatigue issues, and neither did Kate.

The pilot fatigue conversation was interrupted for an hour due to a call from a real person on a tarmac. Almost two years to the day from when the hotline was established, we had a live tarmac stranding. Kate and I received an automated hotline notification by e-mail.

10:11:05 PM	Kate: We have a live one on the tarmac - American Airlines
10:11:22 PM	Peace: now?
10:11:27 PM	Kate: yes
10:11:29 PM	Peace: holy chit! - flight # -where
10:11:40 PM	Kate: calling him now - just called hotline
10:11:49 PM	Peace: ok - i have that call

An American Airlines flight en route to Dallas had been diverted to an airport in Wichita Falls, Texas, due to a line of thunderstorms in the Dallas area. To complicate matters, the air conditioning system on the airplane had malfunctioned. According to the passenger who called the hotline, American was sending a mechanic to deal with the air conditioning problem, but the mechanic wouldn't be there for a couple of hours. For whatever reason, the pilot wouldn't or couldn't take the plane to a gate to let the passengers de-plane, at least as far as we knew at the time of the call.

Kate had been telling the media that we were getting several of these calls every day, and that we never failed to get passengers off the planes. The claim was something along the line that she would get lots of reporters to the airport, and the media would compel the airport or somebody to force the plane to go to a gate and free the passengers. It wasn't true, but apparently this passenger had read it or heard it somewhere and he wanted Kate to get him off the plane.

| 10:28:16 PM | Kate: wtf do I do? |

After I stopped laughing, I told her to call Terry Maxon. Maxon was a reporter for the *Dallas Morning News* and he often wrote stories about airline related issues. I don't know whether she called Maxon or not. If she had, my guess is that he would have said something like, "What the heck do you want me to do?"

We spent the next two hours working on a publicity stunt – this time it was my idea. Kate called a pizza shop and had pizzas delivered to the airport. There was no chance we could get the pizzas delivered to the airplane, but we would have a number of people who could later be interviewed by the media to verify the effort. I later arranged to have the pizzas delivered to the security gate at neighboring Sheppard Air Force Base so they wouldn't go to waste.

Back at the airport, the pilot had taken the airplane to a gate and allowed the passengers to deplane temporarily. When the weather cleared, the flight made its way to Dallas. Kate and I signed off.

12:52:45 AM	Peace: get some rest - i'm putting you on faa sleep requirements
12:53:24 AM	Kate: But since we can't understandthem here is what I'll do - I'll work for 8 hours then get an addition 8 hours of flying and i"ll "rest" 8 hours, by sitting with my compute and cathching microsleep for oh say 8 hours on and off.

The next day, NPR interviewed her on the pilot fatigue issue:

'The pilots that have reported to us are saying they're lucky to get 4 1/2 hours' sleep a night on these regional carriers,' says Kate Hanni, who runs the Web site flyersrights.org. 'And many of them are compromising where they sleep — sometimes in pilot rest lounges, not getting a hotel. It's unsafe.'[54]

ON JUNE 1, Air France Flight 447 disappeared over the Atlantic Ocean off the coast of Brazil. In the days that followed, analysis of the aircraft's telemetry indicated that the crew may have been getting inaccurate airspeed indications from their instruments. Attention focused on the Pitot tubes, which are external sensors used to measure airspeed. It had been found that the tubes could fail under extreme, icy weather conditions at high altitudes. Airworthiness directives (ADs) had been issued by the FAA as early as July 2001 to replace or repair the tubes on Airbus A300 models operated by U.S airlines.

In the past six months, Fox News had invited Kate to appear on their various news programs to talk about airline policies on scantily clad female passengers, obese passengers, and an FAA report about bird strikes. Now they invited her to appear on one of their programs to discuss Pitot tubes.

6:27:48 PM	Kate: What does Pitot mean? - I know what the tube does - But what does the word mean
6:28:10 PM	Peace: lol - some kind of guage for measuring air speed - Pitot was the inventor's name
6:31:20 PM	Kate: OK so Pitot is his name - Excited about the media coverage - Don't want to [expletive deleted] it up
6:32:13 PM	Peace: yeah - long as they don't ask you a question you don't know answer to

The next day, she was in a town car en route to San Francisco to appear on the Fox News program. Conversing with me by instant messaging, she told me that someone, an otherwise credible source, told her that congressmen who flew out of Reagan International Airport were met by "hot women" hired by the airlines to have sex with them. The airlines supposedly did this to keep the congressmen happy and thus influence their votes. She was convinced that the story was true, and she wanted us to go to Reagan to make a video.

After I dispensed with that nonsense, we discussed what we had learned over the past 24 hours about Pitot tubes and FAA airworthiness directives. We then spent several minutes talking about sound bites to use on the news program. After kicking around several ideas, we reached an agreement.

11:31:26 AM   Kate: ok - Passengers have the right to expect that safety directives have been followed by air carriers and that their government is checking to make sure these vital safety repairs are completed

11:32:35 AM   Peace: very good

11:32:38 AM   Kate: ty - I'll stick to that

I didn't see the interview, but the preparation was fairly thorough for a couple of people who had very little idea what they were talking about.

JULY 2009

We won

BY JULY, IT was clear that DOT Secretary Ray LaHood was beginning to hit his stride with consumer-friendly actions. He opposed raising gas taxes to increase spending on roads and bridges, he supported development of more mass-transit systems, and he instituted a program to entice people with gas-guzzling cars to purchase new ones. We were also getting indications that the DOT was leaning more in our direction than the previous administration with regard to airline passengers' rights. But it wasn't just LaHood. Some of our closest, consumer-friendly allies and contacts from the past few years, former staff members from Boxer's, Lautenberg's and Costello's offices, were all now in key political positions at the DOT.

FOR THE PAST several months, I had been analyzing airline tarmac statistics for diverted flights. The BTS had reinstated the new tarmac data on their website – claimed that they had reviewed it and that it was correct.

I found that the data still showed that the airlines were not reporting diversion statistics accurately. I wrote a press release that said that fifteen of the major airlines always gave passengers the option to deplane when a flight was diverted, and four airlines didn't. The implication was that an airline passenger might want to think twice about flying on those four airlines because he or she was more likely to get stuck on the tarmac with them. We could make hay out of that with the media, and I could back it up with government data. The press release was accurate, but it wasn't true. As Mark Twain wrote, "There are three kinds of lies: Lies, damned lies and statistics."

The data really indicated that it was the fifteen airlines that weren't reporting the data correctly, and thus it wouldn't make any difference whether a passenger flew with them or with the four airlines that were reporting the data correctly.

Since February, I had refused to write several other press releases knowing that the content Kate wanted me to use was untrue or half-true. She had then paid third parties to write them – third parties who would have no idea about the veracity of the content. Because of my increasing resistance to co-operate, she began to marginalize my involvement in decision making, and had gone on to make deals and alliances which she knew I wouldn't approve. I felt as though I was losing influence and control. Despite all of the personal turmoil, I didn't want to let go of the satisfaction I derived from that sense of power.

I thought if I wrote an accurate but misleading press release such as the one I had written, that maybe I could regain some of that power. She loved that release, but ultimately I realized that I wasn't going to be able to issue it regardless of what my ego wanted me to do. So I rewrote the press release to make it accurate and true. Kate didn't like that version, and she also wanted to use the first press release because she didn't understand what the data showed. She thought it made the four airlines look "sinister," when the truth was that those were the only airlines that were reporting the diverted flight data correctly. No matter how many ways I tried to explain it to her, she just didn't get it.

9:22:45 PM	Kate: Mark, no one will pay attention to this unless we really pit the 4 against the rest of them. - I'm only looking for ways to do that - salacious
9:23:40 PM	Peace: we agree on that - but if we go too far, we look silly. - and if your real point is what you said above ... that these 4 airlines are sinister in what they are doing - if you believe that, then we're off track.
9:30:42 PM	Kate: I just want to make sure this press release does YOU justice
9:30:46 PM	Kate: You fought for this law - You were meticulous
9:31:41 PM	Peace: we're not making any progress here.

There would be no press release about diverted flight statistics for now, but Kate would resurrect this subject in September.

ON JULY 14, we got word that Senator Boxer's new airline passengers' rights language was being added to the Senate version of the FAA reauthorization bill. It was a monumental achievement. Finally, there would be a three-hour rule in the bill, although the House version still would allow airlines to define their own time limits – a difference that would have to be resolved in a House-Senate conference.

There were many things that contributed to achieving that goal. Certainly, the relentless effort we had exerted over the past two and a half years was a major part of it. Also, Senators Boxer and Snowe were influential members of the Senate Commerce Committee and they had lobbied diligently for the new language to be included in the bill. But there was another reason as well. Senator Byron Dorgan was the chairman of the Senate Aviation Operations, Safety and Security Subcommittee. One of his female aides had been stranded on a diverted flight for seven hours. As Kate later wrote, "She told me we would get our 3 hour max because of her 7 hour stranding."

I wrote and issued a press release:

> Napa, CA - 07/14/2009: Today, the Senate Commerce Committee unveiled its version of the FAA Reauthorization Act of 2009 which includes important Airline Passengers' Bill of Rights provisions. Among those provisions; Passengers will have the right to return to the terminal after three hours on the tarmac if the pilot determines this can be done safely. While on the tarmac, airlines will be required to provide food, potable water, working restrooms, and reasonable cabin temperature and ventilation.
>
> 'This is a major victory for airline passengers,' said Kate Hanni, whose organization has been working for over two years for an airline passengers' bill of rights with a three-hour minimum.

THE NEXT DAY, Kate was working the phone for donations. We were broke and our fundraising letters had been bringing in virtually nothing for the past six months. Had it not been for two large donations, we would have been about $30,000 in the red. That money was long gone, although I couldn't fathom where it had been spent. Kate had made only three trips to Washington since January 1, and our year-to-date expenses shouldn't have exceeded $15,000 let alone $30,000.

Kate had maintained exclusive control over the financial records since the beginning. It was the one thing to which I didn't have direct access, although I did have enough information about expenses to know we couldn't have possibly spent $30,000. There was no point in my asking where the money went. During the e-mail war between Kate and her husband back in October, he accused her of diverting FlyersRights.org donations for her personal use and "lying to our accountant." While she had taken great care to address other allegations he made, she didn't deny either of those. Whatever the reasons, we were broke.

During her tenure on the tarmac delay task force, Kate had established relationships with a few airport managers. Separately, she had also formed a connection with an executive from COBUS Industries, a shuttle bus manufacturer. Since then, she had been hawking COBUS' buses to airport officials, the FAA, and the DOT as a solution for moving passengers from airplanes stuck on tarmacs. This is how business gets done in Washington.

One of the people she called to request a donation was the COBUS executive. The next day, an article appeared on the *Dallas Morning News'* blog about the Dallas/Fort Worth International Airport's purchase of a bus manufactured by COBUS Industries.

> 'With its six extra-large doors, a low boarding step and a flat floor, this people mover will be very efficient at loading and unloading passengers in a safe and timely manner,' said Erwin Zimmermann, vice president of sales for COBUS Industries, the vehicle's distributor for North America in a release.

> Terry [Maxon, *Dallas Morning News*] suggests they call it the Kate Hanni Memorial Bus - she's the woman behind a passenger rights movement stemming from an American Air stranding incident.[55]

WHEN I REDESIGNED the FlyersRights.org website in 2007, I hadn't anticipated the volume of press releases, articles and other materials that we would be posting on it. It had since become a cluttered mess, so I had spent the past two months on another redesign. The Senate Commerce Committee was going to vote on the FAA reauthorization bill the following week – including the new airline passengers' rights language – and I knew there would be an enormous amount of media coverage after that important event. The television news media often featured shots of our website during their broadcasts, so I had spent the previous week making a final push to complete the development effort. On the 16th, I uploaded the finished version and asked Kate to look at it. She loved it.

12:06:46 AM   Peace: it had to be done before next week - makes the org look really organized and wealthy - that kinda work don't come cheap

12:07:40 AM   Kate: Exactly. We are poor but we have great talent!

12:07:56 AM   Kate: wimpering

Five days later, on July 21, I met Kate at the Senate Russell Office Building in Washington. It was the same hearing room where we first met in April 2007. In a remarkably anti-climactic moment, with barely any debate, the Senate Commerce Committee voted in favor of the FAA reauthorization bill with the new airline passengers' rights language. *Damien* was finally out of the bathwater. The loopholes that would allow airlines to define their own tarmac time limits were gone.

I looked at Kate. "What just happened?" she asked.

"We won," I said.

After two and a half years of work, the Senate's version of the FAA reauthorization bill, with our airline passengers' bill of rights, was finally ready to go to the Senate floor for a vote. With passengers' rights language in the House version of the FAA reauthorization bill, even without the three-hour rule, it now seemed certain that we would eventually have a federal airline passengers' rights law. President Obama's healthcare initiative would suck the oxygen out of Washington for several months, and the Senate's version of the bill would not be passed by the Senate until March 2010, but it would be passed.

Later that afternoon, Kate and I walked to Union Station. I hadn't planned to stay overnight, so my car was parked at a train station about 25 miles north of Washington. She wanted to have a celebratory drink before I left, so we got a corner table at the Thunder Grille inside the station.

Two Margaritas later, I thought it might not be a good idea to drive home, that I would stay at a hotel. Kate was staying with Mike Collins for a few days to save money. She called him to see if he would put me up for the night. He agreed and said he'd come to Union Station to pick us up. Kate and I ordered another drink.

"Who do you love more?" she asked.

"What?" I asked, hoping I had misunderstood the question.

"Who do you love more?" she repeated.

Since I had last seen Kate in May, I had spent the intervening period trying to repair the relationship with my wife. It was a slow process. Because of the guilt I felt about the affair with Kate, I didn't feel worthy of my wife's love. I didn't know how it would even be possible to repair that relationship without telling her about the affair. I would either have to tell her about the affair or live a lie for the rest of my life. I was so depressed, felt so empty and so alone that I didn't know if I was capable of loving anyone, but I did know who I wanted to love *me* more, and that's how I answered Kate. I told her that I loved my wife more.

Her eyes widened, as if she was surprised.

"Well, what would you have said?" I asked.

"I would have said you," she said, "It isn't even close."

I looked at her incredulously. She seemed hurt. *I don't understand her at all,* I thought. She had made several professions of love during the past few months, but it rang hollow, seemed manipulative – was often connected to something she wanted me to do. Still, I had no way to know what was going on in her mind, and I didn't mean to hurt her feelings, if I had.

"I'm sorry, Kate," I said, "but I don't know if you've noticed – we haven't been having a relationship for months."

She said she wasn't talking about sex, she was talking about *us*. She said she was sorry that we hadn't slept together for so long, as if that had been her decision. She said she realized that I was still upset about all of the turmoil of the past, but she wanted me to let go of all of that, that it wasn't good for someone to carry around all of that negativity. She said she wanted our relationship to be like it was in the beginning. She was going to move to the Churchill on Sunday and she would be alone until Monday when Anjum Malik was scheduled to arrive.

"Come back down on Sunday, please?"

Had she asked me in an e-mail, instant message or on the telephone, it would have been so easy to say no. Sitting there in person, pleading with me with those blue eyes, she was irresistible. I wondered if it *was* possible to relive those early days. Maybe it was the euphoria of getting the Senate bill passed by the committee. Maybe the Margaritas got to me.

"OK," I said.

Soon, Collins arrived at the Thunder Grille. He drove us to another bar where we had more drinks and talked about future public relations strategy. Later at his house, he set up a mattress for me on the floor of his finished basement. Kate slept in a bedroom on the second floor.

She looked like she had been run over by a 747 when I went to her room the next morning to kiss her goodbye. We connected again later that night:

10:29:36 PM   Peace: feeling better?

10:30:14 PM   Kate: yes starting to. Was asleep until 2: 30

10:31:07 PM   Peace: felt so sorry for you. My fault. Shouldn't have been sharing my margauritas with you from the other bar.

In the days following the Senate committee vote, several prominent people and organizations in the world of commercial aviation jumped on the passengers' rights bandwagon, including two that testified against those rights during the House hearing in April 2007 – Paul Ruden of the American Society of Travel Agents and Kevin Mitchell, chairman of the Business Travel Coalition.

The political tide had decidedly turned. Also, since early in 2007, the media had focused on statistics for tarmac delays of five hours or more. Those seemed to be the most egregious, but the numbers were low. We had been trying to change the media focus to three-hour tarmac delays because the numbers were obviously higher, and on July 27, an article appeared in *USA Today* that changed the benchmark forever:

For many irate fliers, action seems overdue. ... a USA TODAY analysis of Transportation Department data shows. Between

October 2008 and May 2009, there were 577 planes that sat for
that long [three or more hours].[56]

Thirty percent of the "577 planes" was due entirely to the tarmac statistic rules that we had gotten changed. Not everyone was happy with the three-
hour rule in the Senate bill. Airlines warned that the rule would only make
things worse:

> 'There's virtually nothing good in the three-hour rule,' said
> David Castelveter, spokesman for the Air Transport Association
> in Washington, in an interview. 'It would have many
> unintended consequences that would increase delays, increase
> cancellations and add more customer inconvenience, as well as
> cost to the airlines.'[57]

AS PLANNED, KATE moved from Mike Collins' house to the Churchill
hotel on Sunday. I didn't keep my word – I didn't return to Washington. She
was furious.

In 2007, someone told Kate that General Motors had hired a woman in
the late 1960s to try to have a relationship with consumer advocate Ralph
Nader. This alleged conspiracy was supposedly intended to create or unearth
something scandalous about him and thus discredit him. Nader's automobile
safety advocacy campaigns had cost the automobile manufacturers millions
of dollars.

Ever since she heard that story, and despite the fact that she was in control of her own behavior, Kate harbored a fear that someone, namely me,
might try to do the same thing to her. This had been the subject of many conversations in the past. In the hours and days immediately following my fail-
ure to meet her in Washington, she accused me of having been engaged in a
conspiracy against her since 2007 – a conspiracy to destroy her.

This delusion would pass in a few days, but I'd finally had enough.
Kate's husband had also had enough. He found some of the e-mails about our
unfulfilled reunion on Kate's home computer back in Napa.

AUGUST 2009

End of the story

JUST BEFORE MIDNIGHT on August 4, Kate sent her husband and me a mea culpa e-mail for having an "inappropriate relationship" with me. This was somewhat ironic given that we hadn't actually been having a relationship for some time, at least not by my definition. Her e-mail also indicated that she had gotten herself into some trouble during my absence from Washington – trouble that her husband apparently wanted me to know about. A half hour after she sent the e-mail, she sent me an instant message:

12:21:37 AM	Kate:	Did you get the e-mail?
12:26:19 AM	Peace:	uh yeah - should I respond?
12:26:36 AM	Kate:	Yes you can respond. Carefully.
12:27:17 AM	Kate:	My neck is in the noose.
12:27:26 AM	Peace:	i know. ok
12:27:49 AM	Kate:	You're smart you'll think of something.

She wanted me to employ the talent for spin that I had used to get her out of so many jams in the past. I decided not to respond. Ultimately, I knew that the only way to rebuild the relationship with my wife was to separate completely from Kate. Whether or not it was even possible to smooth things over with her husband, I decided not to try. It was over, had been over for months, and it needed to stay *over*.

Two days later, on Friday, Kate called me and said that her husband was going to call my wife and tell her about the affair. If there was any sliver of a doubt that I was finished with Kate, that doubt was obliterated by the end of that call. My wife and I had just come off the golf course when Kate called, and when we got home later that night there was a message from Kate's husband on our answering machine. I erased the message the instant I heard his voice.

"Who was that?" my wife asked.

"Just some salesman that keeps calling," I said.

Her husband had also sent me an e-mail in which he asked me to call him. He wrote, "I am very concerned about our girl and need your help getting things sorted out. ... I promise a civil conversation." I replied that I would talk to him on Monday morning.

The next day, Saturday, August 8, a diverted Continental Express flight held 47 passengers on the tarmac for six hours in Rochester, Minnesota. The story was covered by dozens of media outlets including the Associated Press:

> By its sixth hour sitting on a deserted tarmac, Continental
> Express Flight 2816 had taken on the smell of diapers and an
> overwhelmed lone toilet. What should have been a 2 1/2-hour
> trip from Houston to Minneapolis had moved into its ninth hour,
> and the 47 passengers on board had burned through the free
> pretzels and drinks handed out early in their Friday night flight
> from Houston. ... it wasn't until 6 a.m. Saturday - six hours after
> landing - that Flight 2816's passengers were allowed out of the
> plane.[58]

This event sparked a national outrage over tarmac strandings. Combined with the constant barrage of tarmac stranding publicity we brought to bear over the past two and a half years, both real and fabricated, this event made it appear that these incidents were happening every day, just as she always said they were.

By Monday morning, Kate was being bombarded with requests for interviews. She went to San Francisco to appear on CNN and several other broadcasts to talk about the Rochester tarmac stranding.

Meanwhile, Kate's husband called me at 11 a.m. I told him that he didn't need to worry about me anymore, that I was "done." I confirmed that Kate sometimes engaged in self-destructive, potentially dangerous behavior when she was in Washington, which seemed to be his main concern. I urged him to ensure that somebody was with her whenever she was there, and I wished him luck. It was a civil conversation, but things were obviously not going well in Napa.

A few hours later, Kate and I connected via Skype. She was riding in the back of a town car near San Francisco after appearing on several newscasts:

3:35:59 PM	Kate: It's been aweful and I'm really tired of the drama
3:36:06 PM	Peace: yeah - me too
3:36:23 PM	Kate: My car is being turned around to go back to the city right now to pre-tape for GMA.
3:36:31 PM	Kate: I haven't eaten and I'm exhausted.
3:36:44 PM	Peace: maybe i should just go - would that be better for everyone?

3:37:47 PM   Kate: It may be at this point or I'll end up murdered by
                    an axe or in some kind of trouble because clearly I'm
                    f...ing my life up badly

Our conversation was interrupted by another call from someone in the
news media. It resumed minutes later.

3:49:35 PM   Kate: I'm so sorry. I'm a broken person.

3:49:46 PM   Peace: understand completely - we need you whole -
                    go get em

3:50:17 PM   Kate: no resentments?

3:50:25 PM   Peace: no

3:50:33 PM   Kate: TY

3:50:35 PM   Peace: yw

And *that,* as they say, was *that.* Over the next week or so, she sent me a
few e-mails to ask me to do some minor things. I complied to ensure that the
final separation was as easy and amicable as possible. Eventually the requests ended and an eerie silence commenced. For the first time in two and a
half years, there were no phone calls, no instant messages, no e-mails and no
airline passengers' rights.

I knew it was the best outcome, but I still felt sad and empty. I had
harbored a dream that I would be present for the presidential signing of the
bill, or to celebrate a rulemaking by the Department of Transportation. I now
knew there was no chance of that. As for Kate, as much as I distrusted her
and as much disdain as I had for her judgment, I still missed the daily contact
and drama that was part of our everyday, all-day routine.

I knew the adventure couldn't last forever, but I wasn't prepared for its
sudden demise. And because of the hole I had dug for myself, I grieved
alone. On a positive note, this time we had separated amicably. That was an
enormous relief because I didn't want to live through another nightmare like
the summer of 2008. Still, I was worried about what would happen to the
cause with both Corbett and me gone. Kate was a disaster waiting to happen.

Soon thereafter, I saw a press release that said Kevin Mitchell and Kate
had formed an alliance. While ironic, I felt better about the future of the
cause. Mitchell was a seasoned veteran of Washington politics and I could
only hope that he might be able to keep her on the right track. As for me, it
was time to move on. For all intents and purposes, I thought that was the end
of the story, a story I never dreamed I would ever tell.

SEPTEMBER 2009

Traitors

MY SEPARATION FROM Kate was timely for another important reason. I had exhausted the savings that I intended to use to fund business ideas I had years earlier. I needed to start making money – something that would not be easy considering how depressed I was. Even if I still had that money or could obtain venture capital, some of my best ideas had been made obsolete by the mid-2007 introduction of the iPhone and the social networking applications that now ran on that device. I had missed the market while working on airline passengers' rights.

With little else to fall back on, by early September I had started a business to develop websites for small businesses. With the economy in shambles, the idea was to provide low cost, high return websites and search engine optimization. My survey of local businesses showed an astounding absence of Web presence, and I thought my offering should be a no-brainer. I created a new website, a brochure, business cards, joined the local chamber of commerce, and I went out to try to sell websites. I went door-to-door to local businesses. With one rejection after another, my depression worsening, I wondered what would become of me.

On September 10, Kate sent me an instant message, the first in a month:

9:44:22 AM   Kate: Did you see the BTS Stats? Claiming that at every diversion airport where a flight sat for more than 3 hours all carriers state they allowed folks off of planes?

9:45:13 AM   Peace: jezuz - you trying to give me a heart attack or somthing?

For the next two days, I helped her with some airline statistics analysis, but I knew where this was headed; she was trying to pull me back in. After the second day, I changed my instant messaging status to "offline." A day later, she sent me an e-mail to ask me to do some more extensive work.

Kevin Mitchell and Kate had announced that they were going to hold a joint media event in Washington on September 22. It was billed as a stakeholder meeting, a mock congressional hearing where the grievances of airline passengers would be discussed. There was a quote from Mitchell in the announcement that said they were going to prove that the airline diversion statistics were wrong. The quote was based upon Kate's misinterpretation of the statistics analysis I had done during the summer. I had to laugh when I saw the announcement. *Mitchell is going to find himself in a lot of trouble if he lets Kate give him quotes,* I thought.

Now she wanted me to update the analysis I did over the summer to include the last few months of data – at least that's what she said she wanted. I didn't know if her motive was personal, business, or both. Regardless, I needed to concentrate on healing the relationship with my wife. I simply couldn't go backward now. I replied to Kate and told her I couldn't help her. It took me several moments to press the send button on my reply. It was difficult, but it had to be over.

A day later, Mike Fabey, the *Travel Weekly* reporter with whom I had attended the football game in December, called to ask me about the recent airline statistics reports. During that conversation, I mentioned that I had helped Kate with some statistics work for the past couple of days. There was a long pause.

"Are you sure?" he finally asked.

"Why?" I asked, suspecting that I wasn't going to like the answer.

He said that he had talked to Kate earlier. She told him that she hadn't been in contact with me since August, and she was emphatic that she would never be in contact with me again.

Oh no, please, not again, I thought.

Fabey asked if I planned to attend Kate's stakeholder meeting in Washington – two weeks hence.

"No, I'm out of the passengers' rights business," I said. "Why?" I asked.

He said that Kate told him that someone would "break Mark in half" if I tried to get in.

"What else did she say?" I asked.

He said that most of his conversation with Kate was off the record. He was only telling me about the possible physical danger because he was worried about my safety.

He didn't call me to talk about statistics, I thought. *He called me because Kate is back in character assassination mode.*

"I'm no danger to Kate and she knows it," I said.

I considered calling her to find out what her problem was, but I hoped that she would disappear if I just stayed quiet. Instead, two weeks later, three days after the stakeholder meeting in Washington, she sent me another e-mail that would extend this saga for what would seem like an eternity:

> From: Kate
> Sent: Friday, September 25, 2009 9:11 PM
> To: Mark Mogel
> Subject: Traitor. Well the FBI will sort it out.

There was no content, only the subject line. I replied, "What in the world are you talking about?"

In a series of e-mails that followed over the next five days, she wrote that a consultant named Frederick Foreman had just been fired by a company in Virginia called Metron Aviation. Metron had been hired by the FAA to analyze airport ground operations, and a report had been prepared for the FAA as a byproduct of that work. Metron had recently learned that Foreman had e-mailed that report to Kate – a report they considered to be proprietary – and they apparently fired him for that and other e-mails he sent to her.

When Metron's management met with Foreman to dismiss him, they showed him those e-mails. Foreman saw that the e-mails had been forwarded to Metron by someone at Delta Airlines. Metron Aviation also happened to be a subcontractor for Delta.

In her e-mails to me, Kate accused me of conspiring with Delta Airlines to hack into her e-mail account to forward those e-mails to Delta. In one of her e-mails she wrote, "Hope [Delta] paid you lotsa money!" In another, she accused me of hacking into her computer, changing its password and then making it crash. She said that she knew it was me because the password hint for her computer login had been changed to "peace."

I didn't know what happened to her computer or her e-mails, but I knew I didn't have anything to do with it. I also suspected that, aside from Foreman being fired, she was making the rest of it up. The scenario was eerily familiar. We exchanged other e-mails in which she made a variety of delusional accusations. I told her that her claims were "ridiculous" and that I was sure we would find the results of an FBI investigation "ironic." On the 30th I wrote, sarcastically:

> Well, hopefully you have the FBI on the case and they'll get it
> sorted out. Let me know how it turns out. I'm on pins and
> needles here.

She didn't respond to that e-mail. I assumed, wrongly, that she might have finally disappeared.

OCTOBER 2009

The Delta lawsuit

By October, I decided to resurrect the cell phone jamming idea I had during the summer of 2008 – the one that would let parents install jamming devices in the cars of teenage drivers to prevent texting or talking on their cell phones while they were driving. My heart wasn't in the website business, and I grieved the loss of my involvement in government affairs – my real passion.

Coincidentally, Secretary of Transportation Ray LaHood had recently started a federal initiative to end distracted driving, and the DOT began to hold public meetings to discuss the issue and possible solutions.

I contacted the cell phone jammer's patent owner to start a dialog about how we might be able to work together to change the federal regulations that prohibited its use. Within a week we had exchanged several e-mails and a joint venture seemed promising. He had researched my airline passengers' rights accomplishments online, and he seemed interested in having me establish a public relations campaign to advocate for his device. I was elated. I was going to get back into the game, and this was a venture that could save lives and make money. I began to work with an investment broker to help develop a proposal to raise venture capital for the campaign. This time, I intended to get paid whether the campaign was successful or not.

On October 9, Mike Fabey called me again and said that he had heard that Kate was going to file a lawsuit against Delta Airlines, Metron Aviation and *possibly* a third party for hacking her computers and e-mails. When I asked him who the third party was, he wouldn't say. Still, I assumed that the third party was me. *Why else would he have called me,* I wondered.

"Mike, I can't tell you how I know this, but she's making it up. Nobody hacked her computer or her e-mails," I said.

Four days later, on October 13, in the United States District Court for the Southern District of Texas, attorney Jason Gibson filed suit on behalf of Kate and FlyersRights.org against Delta Airlines and Metron Aviation.

Gibson was the same Houston lawyer with whom Kate had collaborated in February – without advisory board approval – in regard to an NTSB FOIA request for information about Continental Airlines and Colgan Airlines. In this lawsuit, Kate was seeking $11 million in damages from Delta and Metron. The complaint read, in part:

> Specifically, Delta conspired with Metron (or others) to obtain
> Plaintiffs' emails and computer files. Delta then provided
> Metron with the illegally obtained emails and files from
> Plaintiffs' computer and AOL account. ... As a result of the
> hacking, spreadsheets, lists of donors, e-mails, Department of
> Transportation statistics and Hanni's personal files were
> redirected to an unknown location. Additionally, all of the
> information on Hanni's personal laptop was corrupted and
> rendered useless.

She omitted me from the lawsuit, but the parenthetical "or others" was a red flag. By not naming me, she could accomplish what I now realized was her main objective with this lawsuit; to surreptitiously destroy me before I could destroy her – something I had no intention of doing. She could tell all of her reporter friends that I was the hacker, off the record, and that would accomplish two of her main objectives: they couldn't talk to me, and she would impugn my character and credibility so that, even if I contacted them, they wouldn't talk to me. I was right back where I was during the summer of 2008.

The files she claimed that were "redirected to an unknown location," spreadsheets, DOT statistics, donor lists and especially "personal files," were all directed squarely at me. I had all of those files on my computer and she knew it. Except for the personal files, I had created all of the others. If she or FlyersRights.org were truly harmed by the alleged corruption of those files, she or her lawyer could have asked me to send them. They didn't.

All she had to do now was to convince the FBI to come to my house, take my computer and voila, busted. They would confiscate all of the "I love you" videos and other personal images I had, and her problem would be permanently solved.

The U.S. Department of Justice, which oversees the FBI, had initially declined to involve themselves in the civil case, so Kate sold Senator Barbara Boxer on a conspiracy theory that the motive for hacking her computer was to undermine Boxer's passengers' rights legislation, and thus it became an issue that the government should look into. This premise, absurd as it was, was prominently featured in the complaint filed with the court, and indeed the FBI began to investigate.

When I learned about the FBI investigation, I thought for sure the whole world had gone crazy. I became paranoid. Every cable or telephone service truck parked on the street was filled with FBI agents. With every vehicle that pulled into my driveway I thought for sure I was going to be hauled off in handcuffs. My whole life, the whole story, all of the evidence to refute her nonsensical claims was on my laptop. I took it everywhere I went. I never let it out of my sight.

Fortunately, before the FBI came to knock down my door, they first set out to determine whether or not a crime had been committed. They obtained Kate's e-mail account records from her Internet service provider, they took her computer for forensic analysis, and they began to interview people at Metron Aviation and Delta Airlines.

Meanwhile, Kate and her lawyer held a press conference from his Houston law office, and soon the Internet buzzed with the news. Over the next couple of days, the hacking story appeared in every major national newspaper and online media outlet. Mike Fabey called me and said he was going to name me in a story he was writing.

"Mike, I can't tell you how I know this, but she's making it up. Nobody hacked her computer or her e-mails," I told him again.

He said there was no way for him to know if I was telling him the truth, especially since I wouldn't tell him how I knew, but Kate had filed a hacking lawsuit and she apparently told him that she suspected that her former "I.T. director" was the hacker in the Delta case. She wouldn't let Fabey use my name, although it was obvious she had identified me off the record.

She had been telling the same thing to other reporters, off the record. By using that journalistic term, she knew that they wouldn't be able to contact me to me to get my side of the story. But with Fabey, she had made a serious tactical error.

Fabey knew from working with me on other articles in the past, that it was I who managed the website and everything else related to information technology. His independent, personal knowledge enabled him to ethically talk to me and use my name, to tie me to the description Kate gave him.

I pleaded with Fabey to not print my name in his article. I repeated that she had fabricated the whole story. He said he would discuss the matter with his editors. Ironically, the press is legally justified in relying on information obtained from a "reliable source" – Kate. Fabey's story appeared in *Travel Weekly* on October 19:

> Hanni's lawyer, Jason Gibson, said Hanni believed that another person, not named in the lawsuit, was involved in acquiring the emails. He described this person as a former FlyersRights.org employee ... Hanni, however, told Travel Weekly that the party she suspected was not a former employee but a former volunteer who once served as the group's I.T. manager. She refused to name the person.[59]

Notwithstanding the obvious confusion in regard to "employee" versus "volunteer," while my name wasn't mentioned in the complaint or the article, it might as well have been. All of my former colleagues knew that I managed the website and all other information technology matters, as did many other people. I assumed that anyone who read the *Travel Weekly* article would believe that I hacked her computer and e-mails.

There was very little I could do but deny any involvement. Even that would be ineffective where Kate was concerned. I was quite sure she had launched an all-out character assassination by now, and there was no way for me to know what I needed to deny. Without references, and with this blight on my reputation, I wouldn't be able to get a job at a gas station. There was also no way that I could enter into a contractual agreement with the jammer people unless I disclosed all of this. But what could I tell them?

My dreams and my family's financial future were headed for disaster – and there was no rational reason for any of it.

A few days after the *Travel Weekly* article was published, I got a call from a complete stranger with a blocked caller-ID who accused me of "hijacking" e-mails that he said he sent to Kate earlier that day. Kate had given him my telephone number. It turned out that he had misspelled Flyers-Rights.org in the e-mail address.

On October 31, Kate sent me an e-mail and told me to remove the link to the FlyersRights.org website from my business website. "Please cease and desist from using our site as an example of your work. We have replaced the site and removed any evidence of the other site."

It struck me as odd that she would communicate directly with me at this point. I looked at the new website. It had been completely redesigned. She had removed all traces of me, my name and photographs from the new website, and she had the CAPBOR logo I designed in 2007 replaced with another.

NOVEMBER 2009

Data

On November 6, I attended a meeting that I arranged between the jammer principals and a venture capital firm. The jammer people needed money to finance the development of some of their equipment, and I had connections in that regard. When I got home, I found another e-mail from Kate that would permanently dash any dream I may have had of working with them.

The e-mail was addressed to several reporters, House and Senate staffers, DOT officials, Corbett, Rubin, Hudson and Mierzwinski. The most disturbing thing about the e-mail was that she copied the evil hacker – me.

The e-mail contained a thread between Kate and her lawyer in which they congratulated themselves for getting a Houston television station to run a story about the Delta hacking case. The basis of the story was that Kate had evidence that Delta Airlines had been accused of hacking the e-mail accounts of other people around the country.

The television station apparently hadn't done any fact checking. They certainly didn't contact me. They accepted that Kate was telling the truth. She wasn't. She had no credible evidence that Delta had hacked into anyone's computers or e-mails, but she had achieved such credibility status that reporters took her statements at face value.

I finally had enough. I replied to her e-mail, copied only Corbett, Rubin and Kate's lawsuit lawyer, Jason Gibson. I provided a nutshell version of some of her antics over the past three years, although I didn't mention any-thing about the affair or her false 2008 hacking allegations. I concluded the e-mail:

> My theory on this hacking case ... Kate got Foreman fired
> (inadvertently) and she knows it. She was probably
> corresponding with somebody who ultimately forwarded her
> emails to Delta or Metron, and the only way to ensure that she
> would be absolved of responsibility was to claim somebody else
> hacked into her computer and sent those emails from her
> account and/or computer.

Two weeks later, I was proven to be right. Thinking that Foreman might be qualified for a consulting opportunity that Kevin Mitchell had seen in an e-mail thread, Kate had forwarded some of Foreman's e-mails, including the one containing the Metron report, to a woman named Monique Sears.

Sears worked for KLM Royal Dutch Airlines which had an alliance with Delta Airlines. Sears forwarded the e-mails to Delta, who then forwarded them to their subcontractor, Metron Aviation. Metron then fired Foreman.

Delta's lawyers posted the e-mails in the online court docket. They had all come directly from Kate, and she was forced to publicly admit that she sent them. Mike Fabey wrote another article that appeared in *Travel Weekly* on November 19:

> In interviews last week, Hanni and her attorney acknowledged that she had sent the email referenced by Delta to an email address that turned out to belong to Monique Sears ... the U.S. director of government and legal affairs for KLM, which is a codeshare partner and operates a joint venture with Delta.

> 'Kate was requested to send the information by Kevin Mitchell,' said Hanni's lawyer, Jason Gibson. 'And she did.'[60]

Mitchell subsequently noted that he had not told Kate to send the e-mails – he had only recommended that Kate might want to tell Foreman to look into the opportunity. Mitchell severed ties with Kate soon thereafter.

Henceforth there would be obvious reasons to doubt her accuracy or veracity, but as far as I was concerned, the damage to my reputation had already been done. And there wasn't a damn thing I could do about it without exposing the affair – something she knew I couldn't do.

Remarkably, the ongoing story was covered only by *Travel Weekly*. While dozens of news outlets covered the initiation of the lawsuit, none of them followed up on the real story.

At this stage, everyone agreed that the e-mails that resulted in Foreman's termination were sent by Kate. One might think that those revelations would close the case, but she wasn't going to give up that easily. With her real mission to destroy me, she clung to the allegations that her computers had been hacked, and that coalition and *personal files* were redirected to an unknown location. She kept the lawsuit alive.

Just before Thanksgiving, one year to the day after the Napa County Sheriff's detective had called me to discuss Kate's false 2008 allegations, I sent a few e-mails to Kate's lawyer, Jason Gibson. I told him about the affair and her false 2008 allegations – at least the ones I knew about. I explained that Kate was lying about everything. I offered to fly to Houston on my own dime to show him all of the evidence, on the record and without my own lawyer.

Her lawyer wasn't interested. Instead, he made what sounded like a veiled threat. He replied that he wasn't interested in what I had told him, "although others might [be]."

Kate, who had only once before sent an e-mail to my wife – to wish her well when she was ill – now sent her an e-mail containing a single word; "data."

It was a warning intended to shut me up.

DECEMBER 2009

Airline passengers have rights

On December 3, I received a telephone call from a reporter for the Fox television affiliate in Philadelphia. He said he had just gotten off the phone with Kate and he was looking for someone in the Philadelphia area to go on camera to talk about the airline passengers' bill of rights. Obviously, Kate had given him my telephone number, and this was yet another way to harass me.

"Why are you calling me?" I asked.

He said that Kate was in Napa and she couldn't do the interview. He said she told him that her computer had been hacked and all of her files were destroyed, so she couldn't give him the telephone numbers of any other local FlyersRights.org members.

I told him I couldn't help him.

ON DECEMBER 21, Secretary Ray Lahood made a historic announcement. The Rochester tarmac stranding in August had been the final straw for the Obama administration, and the DOT established a rule to fine airlines for tarmac delays. Reporter Terry Maxon wrote about the new rule in the *Dallas Morning News*:

> The U.S. Department of Transportation has done what Congress has not yet done – established rules on how long passengers can be held on grounded flights before airlines must give them a chance to deplane.
>
> 'Airline passengers have rights, and these new rules will require airlines to live up to their obligation to treat their customers fairly,' Transportation Secretary Ray LaHood said in the announcement.[61]

If an airline kept passengers on a tarmac for more than three hours, they could be fined up to $27,500 per passenger. The rule was scheduled to go into effect at the end of April 2010.

It was the regulatory equivalent of the congressional legislation we had worked for since early 2007, a historic and climactic achievement. I should have been able to celebrate, but I was sick to my very core. After nearly three years of dedication working for those rights, trying to fulfill my dreams and helping Kate to achieve hers, all I had to show for it was more false accusations, more blackmail and a dismal future.

ON DECEMBER 25, Umar Farouk Abdulmutallab, a Nigerian citizen who would become known as the "Underwear Bomber," tried to ignite explosives hidden in his underwear on a Delta Airlines flight over Detroit. In the days that followed, the Transportation Security Agency announced preventative measures including a plan to increase the number of full body scanners at airports around the country.

On December 28, Kate appeared on Fox News. The host asked her what she thought about the body scanners. Kate answered:

> I've received over 2000 e-mails in the last couple of days from our members who are saying they think they are too punitive, and many people are saying they just won't fly anymore if these restrictions are maintained.

"Do *you* think they're punitive?" the host asked.
Kate responded:

> I do. I think that for a variety of reasons – obviously the vulnerabilities in the TSA have been revealed and something needs to be done to prevent explosives like this from getting through TSA, but to penalize the passengers, and this is not just my opinion, this is the opinion of our group who's coming forward – we've got 27,000 members and they are saying, Please Kate, Take this on – we already don't like to fly. [62]

It was doubtful that two members asked her to get involved in the issue let alone 27,000, but I knew where this was headed. Rightly or wrongly, Kate was going to mount a full-scale media campaign against body scanners that could ultimately affect my safety and security when I next got on an airplane.

It was time for me to either grow a pair or get mine back. This would be easier said than done because it had to begin with the most difficult part; telling my wife the truth.

JANUARY 2010

The F-B-I

IT HAD BEEN on the tip of my tongue for months; when my wife and I were driving in the car, playing golf, or watching television. I kept trying to tell her, but I just couldn't find the words. It also seemed like every talk show I saw was about cheating spouses. I had been taking mental notes – the only way to survive was to be like a picture window, an open book. On January 3, I finally told her the truth.

I showed her very personal instant messages and e-mails exchanged between Kate and me, photographs, the Churchill hotel video ... everything. It was the most embarrassing, most excruciating thing I'd ever done, but what she was feeling was even worse. She was devastated.

On one hand, it felt awful to tell her this insane story. On the other, I felt liberated. Finally, there could be no more blackmail.

Within two days, I arranged a conference call with Delta's and Metron's lawyers. I told them that I could prove that Kate was lying about everything. The only thing I wanted in return was the name and phone number of the FBI agent who was working the case. Kate's lawyer had refused to give me that information when I asked him for it in one of my November e-mails. Delta's lawyers were more than happy to oblige.

The next day, I called Special Agent James Mackey at the FBI's field office in Manassas, Virginia. Mackey was the agent in charge of the investigation. It was a remarkable conversation. Mackey said there was no evidence that anyone other than Kate had logged into her e-mail accounts, and there was no evidence that anyone hacked her computers. He was aware that Kate had already publicly admitted that she had sent the e-mails that resulted in Foreman's termination. He had concluded that the whole thing was "just a mistake," and he was in the process of closing the investigation without even having talked to me.

Oh, no you're not, I thought. I wanted to put an end to this once and for all.

I told him about the affair, the blackmail and a variety of other things. He didn't know about any of that, including, remarkably, the fact that she had made a false hacking allegation against me in 2008. I explained how the recent allegations about the loss of her personal files were a carbon copy, the same allegations and motives as 2008.

"She didn't make a mistake. She lied to you," I said. "Lying to the FBI is a felony, isn't it?" I asked.

He said that it was a felony, and he asked me to send him some evidence via ground delivery. I created a compact disc with several e-mails and other files, and sent it to him. I never heard from him again. The FBI closed their case, but the Delta lawsuit went on for another nine months. I don't know why. Maybe none of the lawyers talked to the FBI agent.

Later in January, I made several attempts to get the Napa County Sheriff's Department to reopen the investigation into the false 2008 allegations against me. The only thing I could get from them was a document that showed the case number and the charge against me. When I received the document by e-mail, I almost had a heart attack. The charge on the document said "Felony Extortion."

"Extortion!" I yelled at my computer screen. "Where the hell did that come from?"

All this time I had thought the detective had called me to talk about computer hacking. He never said anything about extortion. Despite sending them numerous e-mails and leaving several voice messages, I couldn't get the sheriff's department to reopen the investigation or send me any additional information. *What the hell is going on?* I wondered.

MARCH 2010

Airline safety and security

FEBRUARY WAS A blur. I may have been in a coma. If the stress and strain of defamation and false accusations wasn't enough to send me close to the edge, seeing the effects that the affair had on my wife, something for which I had no one to blame but myself, made me wonder if I deserved to live at all. I couldn't believe how far I had fallen. Two years earlier I was flying high, had tens of thousands of dollars in my checking account, was meeting with politicians in Washington, setting policy, writing sound bites and speeches, and having the time of my life. Now I was broke, deep in depression, and I wanted to die.

Unable to just go kill myself, I began to drink heavily, smoke four packs of cigarettes a day, hoped I would contract lung cancer and die under the influence of heavy doses of morphine. This behavior did not make the prospect of reconciliation with my wife any better.

Remarkably, she recommended that we get some counseling, and so we began the slow process of trying to climb from the depths of despair to some sense of relative stability and normalcy. Unfortunately, ongoing current events kept interrupting that process.

On March 4, Kate sent a newsletter that was particularly disturbing:

> I secured a coveted meeting with Randy Babbitt, the FAA
> Administrator. Those present included 9 elite FAA staffers. Mr.
> Babbitt answered all questions asked and emphasized that his
> agency was diligently working on safety protocols pertaining to
> U.S. regional airline carriers. He requested the Coalition's input
> once the protocols are out for comment.

This is a nightmare, I thought. *What is my moral responsibility – my legal responsibility?*

I had long agonized over what to do about Kate's entrance into airline safety and security issues. Three years earlier I set out to help her get a three-hour tarmac law passed – a law that I believed in, and one for which she was certainly entitled to advocate. But Kate, in my opinion, was by no means qualified to advocate for airline safety and security issues. Even if she had ten thousand airline safety and security experts at her disposal, she was now the final decider of policy and her judgment was unsound to say the least.

In January, I learned that Kate had, at least twice, generated thousands of letters using the names in the passengers' rights petition. I already knew that she had done that in May 2007, but I now knew that she had done the same thing in September of that year. Just before the Strand-In, she had again generated thousands of letters using names of people without their permission, and faxed the letters to Chairman Rangel and the House Ways and Means Committee.

The May 2007 campaign was likely influential in getting airline passengers' rights language added to the House version of the FAA reauthorization bill, and the September campaign explained why Rangel thought that his committee had been "inundated by complaints from airline passengers." That campaign had been the impetus for him to insist that deplanement language be added to the bill.

I wondered what else Kate might have done that I didn't know about.

Every citizen has a right to advocate for whatever grievance they may have. But I don't think they have the right to manufacture data and letters to support their issues, no matter how well-intentioned their goals might be.

Where would we be if everyone were to go to Congress and lie to them about substantive facts? Why doesn't Congress ask people to substantiate their claims? Why aren't there deterrents in place? Why doesn't Congress administer an oath to every person who testifies before them? I don't know if that would have made any difference to Kate, but at least there would be no room for ambiguity. How many others in Washington use the same tactics to work on less noble goals?

There were plenty of examples of long tarmac delays that were wrong and needed to be addressed. *But what if Kate's forays into airline safety and security have an influence on policies in those areas?* I wondered. I couldn't bear the thought of Kate having any kind of say in the safety and security of airline passengers, mainly because sometimes I was one of those passengers. I had thought that I could rely on the collective intelligence of people in the government to do the right thing, but the fact that FAA administrator Randy Babbitt and his staff would meet with Kate to discuss safety protocols for regional carriers was beyond belief.

The Senate was to debate the FAA reauthorization bill, including airline passengers' rights language, in a couple of weeks. In December, the Obama administration had announced that the three-hour tarmac rule would go into effect in April. *What if I do something that derails that? Should I?*

On March 13, I was sitting in my living room recliner, laptop suspended by the polyethylene tray I had fabricated in the basement four years earlier. The television was tuned to CNN. Suddenly, I heard Kate's voice. I looked over my laptop and there she was. The CNN host asked her if she was happy with the progress on airline passengers' rights.

> 'And airline passengers can – and we have 27,800 members
> who have helped us get to this point. It's been three years and
> two months of 4:00 in the morning till 11:00 at night work
> every day for not only myself but many of our members. And
> we're very grateful that the Senate is finally taking our bill to the
> floor for a vote.'[63]

I thought I had been desensitized to drama, but she operated on a supernatural scale. I felt sick, numb. My brain had been like mush for months. I had threats and blackmail and hacking charges and stalking allegations and rape kits and restraining orders and extortion and lawsuits and FBI agents and detectives and reporters and my devastated future and people still getting stuck on tarmacs and on and on all banging around in my skull when I was awake and in my dreams – nightmares.

Later in March, I told the cell phone jammer people that I wouldn't be able to work with them. Kate had robbed me of any possibility that I could run a public relations campaign or lobby on behalf of that technology or anything else for that matter. There was no way I could explain everything to the jammer people, and I wouldn't enter into an agreement with them under false pretenses.

BY THE END of March, I thought for sure I was going to die. There were days when I couldn't get out of bed. I couldn't sleep at night and I couldn't stay awake in the daytime. I had heart palpitations and I didn't have the strength to open a water bottle. My skin broke out in rashes. Strange bumps appeared on my arms. I'd never had a rash in my life. They would appear for a few hours, disappear, and then reappear later. At the insistence of my wife, I went to see my doctor. I hadn't seen him in two and a half years.

I told him that I'd had an affair with a woman who was vindictive, spiteful, manipulative, possibly criminally insane, and who had accused me of a variety of crimes to cover up her own infidelity and other deceitful, if not illegal, acts.

"She's also one of the most revered women in the country," I said.

"So, you're under some stress?" he asked.

"Uh, yeah," I said.

APRIL 2010

Mission accomplished

I SPENT THE first week in April getting blood tests, an ultrasound and a nuclear stress test. I was tested for everything my doctor could think of: heart disease, Lyme's disease, human parvovirus, and dozens of other maladies. When I met with him to go over the test results, he said my health issues were physical manifestations of extreme stress. He prescribed a skin cream, a stomach acid reducer and less stress.

A week later, the Napa sheriff detective's September 5, 2008 e-mail appeared as Exhibit A on the online court docket for Kate's lawsuit against Delta Airlines. As near as I could tell from the documents that were attached to the exhibit, Kate's lawyer was trying to get the judge to block me from providing "personal information" to Delta's lawyers, information that I knew was central to the entire case.

I couldn't believe what I was reading. The Napa detective had recounted a conversation he had with Kate during which she had alleged that I had hacked her computer, stolen a sex video and that I tried to extort her. The tone of the e-mail made it sound like I was an obsessed, crazed stalker. I had long suspected she might bring up those false hacking accusations again, but I did not expect this. And this was the first I had heard about a sex video. She was like a box of Cracker Jacks – a surprise in every package. But, I finally understood how all of the pieces fit together.

When Mike Fabey saw the detective's e-mail on the court docket, he called and asked me if I was ready to talk about Kate. He knew I knew more than I had been willing to tell him up to this point. Ironically, by posting the detective's e-mail on the court docket, Kate and her legal team had provided the stimulus for me tell everything I knew, and she had left me no choice. Still, it would be one of the most difficult things I had ever done.

On the telephone, I told Fabey that the computer hacking, sex video, extortion and obsession allegations paled in comparison to something else I was told a few days earlier; that Hanni had alleged that I drugged and raped her in a hotel room near Washington in 2008.

Fabey asked if I would be willing to talk to him about all of this in person. I agreed. He said he would drive up from Virginia.

When he arrived at my house, I thought I was going to die. My heart was pounding. I was dizzy and could barely talk. An hour into the interview, I looked around my dining room and out of the windows. It had seemed cold and dreary earlier. Now everything seemed warmer, brighter. My heart attack symptoms had subsided. I felt like I had just emerged from a confessional.

"Your color is returning," Fabey said.

"Was I pale before?" I asked.

"No, you were red," he said. He said that I looked so bad at the outset that he came close to stopping the interview.

I had told Fabey everything I could think of; character assassinations, misleading Congress, doctoring report cards, and exaggerating the size of the coalition and the number of hotline calls. I showed him evidence along the way; e-mails, instant messages, spreadsheets and news articles. I didn't tell him about Kate's relationship with LMG, or some of the potentially more serious acts such as generating letters using the petition signatures. Even still, he recognized the importance of what I had told him.

"This is serious stuff," he said. "There's a great possibility that you and I will end up in a witness chair."

Fabey turned to the e-mail from the Napa detective. My basic ground rule for the interview was that I would cover as much as possible, but the personal relationship between Kate and me was off the record. I agreed to explain her allegations, but he wouldn't be able to use any of it in his article.

Based upon what Kate had already told him, Fabey was still skeptical that there was ever a personal relationship between Kate and me. I didn't know it at the time but, just as she had with the Napa detective, she had portrayed me as a stalker, an obsessed volunteer of whom she had always been fearful. She had also written to Fabey the previous fall that she was afraid I would try to harm her physically. She wrote to him: "Sorry I'm so emotional. I'm just living in a lot of fear right now."

"I need to know, do you have, or have you ever had a sex video of Kate?" Fabey asked.

"Absolutely not," I said.

"Why would she say you did?" he asked.

I explained to Fabey that I had several risqué pictures of Kate, but that none of them were from a video. Her husband had found one of those pictures on her computer during the summer of 2008. However, Kate's picture was only part of the image he found. The image also contained a portion of a very personal instant message conversation between Kate and me – all part of the same image.

To explain how that image and conversation could exist sans the affair, Kate told her husband that I had stolen a video that she made for him, that I extracted a frame from the video, fabricated the instant messages, and then planted the composite image on her computer. She also told him that I erased the original video from her computer. I would have to be obsessed and crazy to do all of that, so that's where all the mentally deranged allegations came from. That image was what she used as evidence when she filed her complaint with the Napa County Sheriff's Department. She couldn't have shown them a matching video, because there never was a video. The whole thing was a lie to cover up the affair, I said. She was paranoid that I would use that image and others to embarrass her publicly.

Fabey pointed out that I had worked in the computer industry for my entire career, so it was plausible that I could have hacked Kate's computer. He also said that it might have been possible that I tried to blackmail or extort her over those pictures, regardless of where I got them.

I explained to Fabey that, despite all of those years in the computer industry, my knowledge didn't include the technical skills necessary to hack into computers. I had succeeded in the computer business primarily due to my ability to manage projects and people. Website development, the IT-related things I did, require relatively simple technical skills. The programming skills I used in my younger days are now as extinct as the dinosaurs.

"I wouldn't be able to remotely hack into someone's computer if my life depended on it," I said.

I showed Fabey several e-mails and instant message conversations that proved Kate lied about the hacking and extortion allegations. Some of those e-mails were from Kate's husband to me, and it was obvious that even he knew that she lied to both him and the police. I didn't realize what he meant at the time – in October 2008. It wasn't until I saw the Napa detective's e-mail that I realized that Kate's husband actually thought that I had conspired with Kate to come up with the hacking story.

I also told Fabey that I tried to get the Napa detective to reopen the case in January – to clear my name with them.

"I hit a brick wall with him, but maybe he'll talk to a reporter," I said.

I showed Fabey the contents of the compact disc I sent to the FBI in January, knowing full well that it would be a felony to lie to them or provide them with falsified evidence.

"All of it, including the lawsuit against Delta, is all part of the same elaborate lie," I said. "Nobody hacked her computer or her e-mails."

I also asked Fabey, rhetorically, why I would go to the trouble of hacking her computer remotely when I had access to it dozens of times in the hotel rooms Kate and I shared. The existence of the affair was still a matter in which Fabey was apparently not yet convinced. I couldn't blame him. I was only able to imagine what Kate had already told him.

Fabey asked to see the video I made with Kate and me at the Churchill hotel. I showed him the video.

"Unbelievable," he said.

It was obvious that the video definitively proved she had been lying about me all along. Fabey asked me to tell him more about the rape allegation. He wasn't going to put anything in the story about that either, but he said it was important to my overall credibility.

After the Napa detective's e-mail was posted on the court docket a week earlier, I sent an e-mail to all of my former colleagues, except Kate, and told them about the affair. I explained the folly of the restraining order episode, Malik's rape concerns and Kate's computer hacking allegations. Two of those former colleagues contacted me almost immediately. One of them was Anjum Malik. Malik said she hadn't said anything about rape that morning – it had been Kate.

I explained to Fabey what Malik told my wife and me on speakerphone; that when Kate returned to her room that morning, she told Malik, frantically, that she suspected I slipped something into her drink and raped her in my room. Kate then used her cell phone to call a doctor, but Malik had the impression that she wasn't really talking to anyone. Then, after she hung up the phone, she told Malik that it was too late to call the police because we had a press conference scheduled at the Capitol that morning.

"I have reason to believe that Kate told Burt Rubin a similar story after I dropped her and Malik off at Senator Boxer's office," I said.

"Will either Rubin or Malik confirm that?" Fabey asked.

"You'll have to ask them," I said.

Fabey asked when I recorded the video at the Churchill hotel.

"In December 2008, ten months after the restraining order episode, eight months after the rape allegation, four months after she filed the complaint with the Napa County Sheriff's Department, and one week after she dropped that complaint." I said.

We had talked for about three hours when Fabey said he'd heard enough. He said he knew from years of experience when someone was lying to him. He called it the "bullshit factor," and he knew I was telling him the truth, but he'd had to see me in person to make that determination.

"Is there anywhere to eat around here," he asked.

"There's a pizza shop about two minutes from here," I said.

"C'mon," he said. "I'm going to buy you lunch."

After lunch, as he got into his car to return to Virginia, Fabey looked at me sideways and asked, "Was it worth it?"

ON APRIL 29, 2010, Kate Hanni held a press conference at the National Press Club in Washington to applaud the three-hour tarmac rule that went into effect that day.

She had achieved her dreams – she was famous and she was a star – she was *The Ralph Nader of the Skies*. The article published by most news outlets was written by the Associated Press. Attached to that article was a photograph of Kate Hanni at the Strand-In on September 19, 2007 – holding court inside the Mock-I.

The Strand-In, September 19, 2007, Copyright © 2007 Associated Press
Second row, right: Jennifer Shirkani and her two children.
Third row, left: Anjum Malik.

Four of the people visible inside the Mock-I, including Kate Hanni, Anjum Malik and Jennifer Shirkani, were members of FlyersRights.org. Burt Rubin and Annette Hagan are visible in the sunlight beyond. The others are tourists, cameramen and reporters.

EPILOGUE

ON JULY 26, 2010, three months after he interviewed me and after an extensive investigation, Mike Fabey's article was published in *Travel Weekly*:

> Today, just weeks after new Department of Transportation rules went into effect limiting tarmac delays to three hours, FlyersRights.org should be celebrating a hard-won victory. Instead, in a series of interviews with Travel Weekly, current and former members of the group's inner circle have criticized Hanni's leadership, questioned her motives and impugned her credibility.
>
> Among other complaints, as detailed below, they say Hanni has: Misled Congress; Manipulated her group's 'report card' data in a vendetta against Delta, an airline she is suing for allegedly hacking her computers; Inflated her membership numbers; Leveraged her group's influence to encourage lawmakers to award contracts to a financial supporter; Publicly maligned people she considers threats to her own influence in the travel industry and on Capitol Hill.[64]

Fabey's article was later named as a top three finalist for the 2010 Jesse H. Neal Awards, regarded as the Pulitzer Prize for business journalism. In an attempt to be fair to Hanni, and perhaps to limit their exposure to a lawsuit, Joe Sharkey was invited by *Travel Weekly's* editors to supply a quote for the article. The article concluded with a quote from him:

> I wish Kate had not later become involved in what I told her on numerous occasions was 'mission creep,' getting into areas beyond passengers rights. But I nevertheless think that Kate Hanni, whatever her flaws in later strategy, is an American hero. As I have told her again and again, she should be a movie.

I couldn't agree with you more, Joe, I thought.

DESPITE HER ATTEMPTS to block my voluntary cooperation with Delta's and Metron's lawyers, I was scheduled to give a deposition for that lawsuit at a hotel in Collegeville on October 4, 2010. I hadn't bothered to retain a lawyer – I knew she could never let that deposition happen. Two weeks before my deposition, Hanni dropped her lawsuit against Delta Airlines and Metron Aviation. She publicly acknowledged that neither Delta nor Metron had been involved in any hacking, although she continued to insist that her computers had been hacked.

I was so disappointed that the lawsuit had been dropped and my deposition canceled that, at the originally appointed time, I went to the hotel anyway. I still had a story to tell and I had wanted to tell it under oath. While Fabey's story had exposed Hanni's lack of credibility, it hadn't exonerated me from her false allegations – something that was impossible to do without getting into the subject of the affair. I sat in the hotel lobby and thought about the past three and a half years. We had accomplished so much. She had then set out to destroy me – for no rational reason that I could ascertain. It was all so sad, so unnecessary, and so tragic.

A few months later, Burt Rubin and Jack Corbett formed their own airline passengers' rights organization. Hanni subsequently issued a newsletter to inform her members, as well as news media and government recipients, not to trust the new organization that "we believe to be a front group for the airports and possibly the airlines." The newsletter also said, "The founders of this new group were once part of our organization, but have parted ways with us because they disagreed, for some reason, with the ways in which we achieved our incredible success."

Anjum Malik also abandoned FlyersRights.org and joined ranks with a new organization created by Chris Elliott and Kevin Mitchell.

In late 2010, Hanni appeared on several newscasts to inform the news media that she had called on her 30,000 members to stage a national protest at airports against the use of body scanners. Like the 2007 holiday program, in which she claimed she had members handing out brochures at all of the major airports, the body scanner protest was to occur on the eve of Thanksgiving 2010. Unlike the 2007 holiday program, reporters from several news networks were staked out at many of the major airports to capture the protest on camera. No outraged FlyersRights.org protesters showed up – not one.

TEN MONTHS AFTER it went into effect, people began to ask me if I thought the DOT's three-hour rule was working.

"It depends," I usually answered.

In an article published in *USA Today* on January 11, 2011, the author noted that there had been only 12 tarmac delays of over three hours since the rule was introduced:

> Federal data show that the rule may be having an impact. There
> have been only 12 total tarmac delays of more than three hours
> reported from May (the first full month after the rule went into
> effect) through November 2010. That compares with 550 during
> the same seven-month period of 2009.[65]

If you measured success by the numbers, then obviously the rule was working. But there were other sides to the story.

There was no single root cause for the tarmac stranding problem. Gate availability, airport operational capabilities and capacity, air traffic control issues, flight crew contracts and FAA duty-time rules, airline over-scheduling, weather, diverted flights, international flights and customs issues, all contributed in some way to tarmac strandings. Many of these factors were embodied in a single incident on February 12, 2008.

United Airlines Flight 195 departed its gate in Philadelphia at 6:40 p.m. during an ice storm. Weather conditions worsened and the aircraft returned to the gate about 40 minutes later. They were probably fortunate to get a gate because most gates were usually occupied by other arrivals or departures. Nevertheless, all of the passengers elected to remain aboard. They wanted to go to Los Angeles.

Flight 195 was just one of dozens of other flights that were scheduled to depart or arrive during the prime time evening period. Airline schedules are designed primarily to cater to business travelers, so most flights are scheduled during the early morning and late afternoon, often exceeding the capacity of the airport even during good weather conditions.

United 195 left the gate again a half hour later and proceeded to a deicing pad where it took an hour to be deiced. Because of the continuing inclement weather, air traffic control increased spacing requirements for all arriving and departing aircraft, so after it was deiced, the flight joined a long line of other planes waiting to take off.

Deicing fluid has a limited effective time, and after waiting in line for too long, the plane had to get out of line to be deiced again. The flight finally took off a few minutes after midnight after four hours and 23 minutes on the tarmac.

FAA regulations limit the amount of time pilots can be on duty during a 24 hour period. Unfortunately, the delay in Philadelphia, combined with strong headwinds, forced Flight 195 to divert to Las Vegas to refuel. The flight crew could not resume the flight because they had exceeded their FAA time limits. Passengers and crew deplaned at approximately 2:00 a.m. in Las Vegas. At 6:30 a.m., a fresh flight crew flew the passengers to Los Angeles. The passengers arrived about twelve hours later than originally scheduled. If the flight had been canceled in Philadelphia, it could have been three or four days before all of those passengers found seats on flights to Los Angeles.

The crew and the airline made every attempt to get the passengers to their destination. Should they have done that? According to United Airlines, only two of the passengers later contacted the airline to complain.

After the DOT's three-hour rule went into effect in 2010, the airline wouldn't have considered trying. They would have canceled that flight and most likely all of the other flights out of Philadelphia that night.

According to industry consultants, the average revenue for a domestic flight is $7,000. The proposed DOT fine of $27,500 per passenger could cost the airline up to $2.75 million on a flight with 100 passengers.

On February 10, 2011, Bloomberg reported that almost 90,000 flights were canceled between November 1, 2010 and February 4, 2011.

> The industry's net revenue loss for the period may be $629 million, using the average estimate of $7,000 for each scrapped flight from consultant Vaughn Cordle of AirlineForecasts LLC.[66]

MarketWatch reported that December 2010's cancellations were the second highest in history.

> 'Airlines are pre-cancelling simply to avoid a potential tarmac delay,' said Terry Trippler, a travel analyst at Rules to Know, a consultancy, in an interview. Starting in April, airlines face fines of up to $27,000 [sic] a person on aircraft sitting on a tarmac for more than three hours. Lawmakers passed the rules following a string of horror stories of passengers being stuck on planes for long periods of time without food, fresh water or clean lavatories. Pre-cancelling flights have helped airlines avoid such costly fees ... [67]

Remarkably, Joe Sharkey wrote about the inflexibility of the three-hour rule and its consequences – in an interview with airline pilot Bruce Hedlund:

> Once upon a time, [Hedlund] said, pilots and airlines would try to bull their way through weather disruptions like the East Coast blizzard that shut down the New York area airports. But last spring, a new federal law imposed heavy fines on airlines for keeping airplanes full of passengers on tarmacs.

'Now they're often not even trying to take off. They're just
going straight to wholesale cancellations,' said Mr. Hedlund
...[68]

On January 26, 2011, I was scheduled to fly to Florida for a golf trip
with friends – my first airline trip since the three-hour rule went into effect.
The airport in Philadelphia got about a half-inch of snow that morning. By
the time I got to the airport at around noon, I could barely tell that it had
snowed at all. Nevertheless, my airline canceled all of its flights in and out of
Philadelphia that day. With a larger winter storm bearing down on the East
Coast that night, many airlines also pre-canceled all flights for the next day.

I had two choices: cancel my vacation, or pay five times the cost of my
original ticket to get to Florida on one of the airlines that were still operating.

The answer to whether the DOT's three-hour rule was working may
depend upon how much money you have and how necessary it is to get to
your destination on time – to make an event like a vacation, a wedding or a
funeral. When I had a six-figure income, I was ready, willing and able to pay
five times the price of a ticket to get where I was going, as long as I didn't
have to sit on the tarmac.

Now that I was barely eking out a living building websites, I would have
happily traded a few hours on the tarmac for the extra $500 I charged to my
credit card, plus monthly interest, to get to Florida. On the other hand, I
wouldn't have wanted to sit on that airplane for nine hours and sixteen
minutes.

KATE HANNI HAD written to me in August 2007:

> One commitment you have from me is no matter what I'm loyal
> to a fault and you can count on that I will never forsake you for
> any glory that may come my way. ... I will endeavor to include
> you in all the glory and have you experience the kudos you so
> justly deserve ...

There is no glory for me in this story, and perhaps that's because I don't
deserve any. Indeed, karma can be a bitch. But there is a happy ending for
airline passengers. The protections and rights that were adopted include, but
are not limited to:

1. On domestic flights, airlines face a fine of up to $27,500 per
   passenger if they hold passengers on the tarmac for over three hours.
   The same fine applies to international flights with a four hour limit.
   In the first fine levied against an airline for violating the rule,
   American Eagle was assessed $900,000. Nearly 25 percent of that

was refunded to the affected passengers through travel vouchers or frequent flyer miles.

2. Passengers are entitled to proper ventilation and working lavatories any time a flight is delayed on the ground for an extended period of time, including "adequate food and potable drinking water" for delays of more than two hours.

3. Compensation for being involuntary bumped from a flight (over-booking compensation) was substantially increased.

4. Airline and third-party websites are required to prominently display all optional, ancillary fees and taxes at the time of ticket purchase.

5. Airlines are required to return baggage fees if bags are lost.

And airlines are required to report more tarmac stranding statistics than ever before. All of these consumer rights and protections were issued by the U.S. Department of Transportation. It would take until February 2012 before Congress would codify these and other rights into permanent law.

A comprehensive list of airline passengers' rights can be found on the DOT's website: http://airconsumer.dot.gov/publications/flyrights.htm.

AFTERWORD

AFTER I LEARNED that Kate Hanni alleged that I drugged and raped her in April 2008, I wondered, again, if she might have also lied about her June 2006 assault incident – her survival from which had so inspired me when she first told me about it in 2007.

It seemed to me that any thorough author, or any *Chief Research Director* worth his weight in salt, should talk to the people who might know. For my final interview for this book, I called the Napa Police Department – a separate entity from the Napa County Sheriff's Department – and talked to the detective who had been in charge of Hanni's 2006 assault investigation. He had never heard of me. We talked for about 30 minutes, some of it off the record, but the beginning and end of the conversation was also interesting.

"You're writing a book about Kate Hanni?" the detective asked.

"Yes," I said.

"You've got to be kidding," he said.

I assured him that I wasn't kidding. I recounted that Hanni had told me that the police had lost valuable DNA evidence and that they hadn't fully investigated her case.

"We didn't lose any evidence, and we thoroughly investigated everything," he said.

"Hanni told me that she gave the police the name of a suspect, but that the police never questioned him," I said.

The detective said that wasn't true either – they did interview him.

"He was so innocent that we were sorry we dragged him into the case," he said. "There were no other suspects." he added.

He said that the case was technically still open, but that there was no active investigation. Apparently, the police can't close a case until they reach a definitive resolution. He also said that Hanni had registered other allegations that I might want to look into; one with the local sheriff's department, and another in San Diego several years earlier.

He obviously didn't know that I had been the subject of the complaint she filed with the sheriff's department, and I already knew about the San

Diego incident. The police in San Diego had long since closed that case – an incident in which Hanni claimed she had been kidnapped at knifepoint. I had heard enough. I felt ill, sullied. I was – at long last – *done*.

I thanked the detective for talking to me but, before I hung up, he renewed his incredulity that anyone would write a book about Kate Hanni.

"Are you a friend of hers or something?" he asked.

"No," I said – *and perhaps I never was,* I thought.

BY AUGUST 2011, do-it-yourself websites offered by Google and other companies had all but put my website company out of business. I had applied for project management positions through online job sites, but didn't get more than a couple of telephone interviews. It wouldn't have mattered if someone had been interested in hiring me. Technology firms routinely conduct background investigations, and a simple Google search would turn up many of Hanni's false allegations against me. I also had no references for anything I had done since I started working with her five years earlier, and I had spent the past year writing this book – a book I didn't know if I had the courage or will to publish.

Having limited options, I applied for a part-time job as a liquor store clerk. On New Year's Eve, December 31, 2011, my first day of work, I found myself stocking shelves and bagging champagne for customers. One of those customers was an English gentleman with whom I had often played golf and dined at the private club where I had been a member. Years earlier, he had told me that he had been amazed to read about me in *Time* magazine.

"What are *you* doing here?" he asked in surprise as I bagged his holiday cheer. He then bowed his head, looked away, and apparently thought he shouldn't have asked and that I didn't need to answer.

There's no need to feel sorry for me, I thought. I had come a long way since sleeping in cars and cheap hotels 35 years earlier. I had risen and fallen, gained and lost much since then, but I never forgot from where I had come. I was grateful to have the job and I had much else to be thankful for. I still had my health and, more importantly, I still had my wife. For the first time in five years, I felt grounded, like I was back where I belonged.

"Happy New Year," I said.

"Happy New Year to you too, Mark," he said.

Five weeks later, Congress finally passed the FAA reauthorization bill. In addition to a long list of airline passengers' rights, the bill called for the establishment of an aviation advisory committee that would include, among other experts in the aviation industry, one consumer advocate. The bill was signed into law by President Barack Obama on Valentine's Day 2012, exactly five years from the date of the infamous JetBlue tarmac strandings. No one from FlyersRights.org was invited to attend the signing ceremony.

ACKNOWLEDGMENTS

I wish to thank my publishing lawyer, Lloyd Jassin of New York City. Lloyd's accomplishments in the publishing and entertainment industry are too wide-ranging to attempt to list here, but I encourage prospective authors and journalism students to visit his informative website at CopyLaw.com to learn about his firm, its services and copyright law. I am deeply grateful for the time and personal attention he gave to my manuscript and to me.

I'd also like to thank book editor Susan Leon of Larchmont, New York. Her patience, encouragement and editorial advice were instrumental in my ability to breathe life into what was, early on, a DOA manuscript. I was unable to retain her for the entire project, and I hope she isn't disappointed with the final result. Readers can find Susan on the Web at BookDocs.com.

BIBLIOGRAPHY

[1] Dorgan, Marsha. "Real estate agent assaulted in vacant home." *Napa Valley Register*, June 23, 2006. http://napavalleyregister.com/news/local/article_3192e8d2-768b-5991-ae95-6c564be88193.html

[2] Sciutto, Jim. "Mom Crusades for Airline Passengers' Rights." *ABC News with Diane Sawyer*, 04/20/2011. http://abcnews.go.com/WNT/video/mom-crusades-airline-passengers-rights-kate-hanni-airport-refunds-13422563

[3] "Airline Passenger Rights." *C-SPAN*, February 1, 2007. http://www.c-spanvideo.org/program/196401-4

[4] "Chances of Long Airport Delays Slim." *Associated Press*, March 6 2007. http://www.register-mail.com/stories/030607/BIZ_BCIOPRJE.G01.shtml

[5] Levin, Alan. "Revised fliers' bill of rights draws fire." *USA Today*, May 21, 2007. http://www.usatoday.com/travel/flights/2007-05-21-passenger-rights_N.htm

[6] Sharkey, Joe. "Stuck on the Runway, Thinking Rebellious Thoughts." *New York Times*, May 15, 2007. http://www.nytimes.com/2007/05/15/business/15road.html

[7] Bailey, Jeff. "An Air Travel Activist Is Born." *New York Times,* September 20, 2007. http://query.nytimes.com/gst/fullpage.html?res=9400E3DB103BF933A1575AC0A9619C8B63&pagewanted=2

[8] Stark, Lisa. "Airlines vs. Congress: Passenger Bill of Rights Needed?" *ABC World News with Diane Sawyer,* June 13, 2007. http://abcnews.go.com/WN/story?id=3275928&page=1

[9] Loose, Cindy. "Upright and Locked – Held Against Your Will." *Washington Post*, June 17, 2007. http://www.washingtonpost.com/wp-dyn/content/article/2007/06/15/AR2007061500747.html

[10] "Airline Passenger Bill of Rights." *Harris Online*, June 22, 2007. http://paulharrisonline.blogspot.com/2007/06/airline-passengers-bill-of-rights.htm

[11] "Aviation Consumer Groups Decry Misleading Statistics On Flight Delays; Groups Call For Congressional Investigation." *Aero-News.net*, June 22, 2007. http://www.aero-news.net/index.cfm?contentBlockId=af62ef64-ea80-4ec3-a6bc-e1c64ba1ca78

[12] Teague, Don. "Trip to Dallas turns into flightmare." *NBC Today Show*, January 11, 2007. http://www.msnbc.msn.com/id/16565583/#storyContinued

[13] Hughes, John. "Buffett Battles Bush as Corporate-Jet Owners Fight Tax Increase." *Bloomberg*, May 14, 2007. http://www.bloomberg.com/apps/news?pid=newsarchive&sid=a_weVSOX_Ito

[14] Schmidt, Tracy Samantha. "Flight Delays: Worse than Reported?" *Time*, July 5, 2007. http://www.time.com/time/nation/article/0,8599,1640183,00.html

[15] Raine, George. "One Woman's Flight or Fight Response." San Francisco Chronicle, July 31, 2007. http://articles.sfgate.com/2007-07-31/business/17255115_1_airline-passengers-bill-passenger-bill-kate-hanni

[16] Lytle, David. "How you can stand up to the airlines." *Frommers.com*, September 9, 2007. http://www.frommers.com/articles/4640.html

[17] Sharkey, Joe. "The Ralph Nader of the Skies." *Portfolio*, September 18, 2007. http://www.portfolio.com/business-travel/features/2007/09/18/Kate-Hanni-Profile/

[18] "Creating a Passengers' Bill of Rights." *National Public Radio*, April 10, 2009. http://www.npr.org/templates/story/story.php?storyId=102962279&ps=cprs#commentBlock

[19] Wilber, Del Quentin. "Anger Over Airline Delays Spurs Passengers' Coalition Into Action." *Washington Post*, September 17, 2007. http://www.washingtonpost.com/wp-dyn/content/article/2007/09/16/AR2007091601571.html

[20] *Rotor News,* September 20, 2007. http://www.rotor.com/Default.aspx?tabid=2631&mid=3977&newsid3977=56369

[21] "The Messy Skies." *Washington Post* (Editorial), October 9, 2007. http://www.washingtonpost.com/wp-dyn/content/article/2007/10/08/AR2007100801425.html

[22] Sharkey, Joe. "In the Crowded Sky, change is approaching." *New York Times*, December 11, 2007. http://www.nytimes.com/2007/12/11/business/11road.html

[23] Zumhagan, Brian. "Airline Passengers' Group Fights for Bill of Rights." *WNYC*, November 18, 2007. http://www.wnyc.org/news/articles/89066

[24] "Club 33: The most influential people in the travel industry." *Travel Weekly*, November 20, 2007. http://www.travelweekly.com/article3_ektid163386.aspx

[25] Kovner, Guy. "She's not giving up." *Santa Rosa Press Democrat*, March 16, 2007. http://www.pressdemocrat.com/article/20070316/NEWS/703160305

[26] Sharkey, Joe. "On Time? Late? Here We Go Again." *New York Times*, November 18, 2007. http://www.nytimes.com/2007/11/18/business/18bug.html

[27] Adams, Marilyn. "Two fliers seek class-action suit against American." *USA Today*, January 1, 2008. http://www.usatoday.com/money/industries/travel/2008-01-01-class-action_N.htm

[28] CNN *Larry King Live*. July 16, 2008. http://edition.cnn.tv/TRANSCRIPTS/0807/16/lkl.01.html

[29] Oldham, Jennifer. "Air traffic controllers' labor tactics raise concern." *Los Angeles Times*, January 17, 2008. http://www.latimes.com/news/local/la-me-airtraffic17jan17,0,2032871.story

[30] Adams, Marilyn. "Pair of flier advocates fight for airline passengers' rights." *USA Today*, May 19, 2008. http://www.usatoday.com/money/industries/travel/2008-05-18-passenger-rights-airline_N.htm

[31] Hensel, Bill Jr. "Passenger group, union team up. Machinists and rights advocates oppose mergers." *Houston Chronicle*, February 25, 2008. http://www.chron.com/disp/story.mpl/business/5569788.html

[32] Weiner, Eric. "Attention Airlines: This is your passenger speaking." *National Public Radio*, November 19, 2007. http://www.npr.org/templates/story/story.php?storyId=16352567

[33] Compart, Andrew. "Passenger rights group flunks airlines on tarmac delays." *Travel Weekly*, February 28, 2008. http://www.travelweekly.com/article.aspx?id=169732

[34] Author unknown. "Pilots: Weapon rules are too strict." Source Unknown, March 29, 2008. http://www.tradingmarkets.com/.site/news/Stock%20News/1272864/

[35] Rosato, Donna. "Money's 100 Best; The rest of the best; Best defense against airline angst." *CNNMoney.com*, April 2008, http://money.cnn.com/galleries/2008/pf/0804/gallery.best_rest.moneymag/8.html

[36] Pae, Peter. "Industry defends air travel safety." *Los Angeles Times*, April 10, 2008. http://articles.latimes.com/2008/apr/10/business/fi-airsafety10

[37] Adams, Marilyn. "Pair of flier advocates fight for airline passengers' rights." *USA Today*, May 19, 2008. http://www.usatoday.com/money/industries/travel/2008-05-18-passenger-rights-airline_N.htm

[38] Elliott, Christopher. "Another worthless passenger bill of rights heads to the runway." *Consumer Traveler*, June 25, 2008. http://www.consumertraveler.com/today/another-worthless-passenger-bill-of-rights-heads-to-the-runway/

[39] Lovitt, Rob. "Preview of a passengers' bill of rights." *MSNBC.com*, September 23, 2008. http://www.msnbc.msn.com/id/26838562/

[40] McCullagh, Declan. "Corn farmers take anti-Google fight to Washington." *CNET News,* June 11, 2008. http://news.cnet.com/8301-13578_3-9965555-38.html?tag=mncol;txt

[41] McCullagh, Declan. "Wanted: Writers for D.C. tech lobby group, secrecy mandatory." *CNET News,* August 14, 2008. http://news.cnet.com/8301-13578_3-10016960-38.html

[42] Stauber, John and Rampton, Sheldon. "Toxic Sludge Is Good For You." *Common Courage Press*, 1995. http://www.prwatch.org/books/tsigfy10.html

[43] Lowy, Joan. "Tarmac Task Force To Passengers: Sit Tight." *Associated Press*, November 11, 2008. http://www.cbsnews.com/stories/2008/11/11/national/main4594206.shtml?source=RSSattr=U.S._4594206

[44] Trippler, Terry. December 3, 2009. http://my.videobloom.com/video/view/b409712a0e2b37cc0102423d00b034c3

[45] Kaufmann, David. "A champion for America's airline passengers." *Financial Times*, December 6, 2008. http://www.ft.com/cms/s/2/8553d16e-c0d3-11dd-b0a8-000077b07658.html#axzz1FepLfDuX

[46] Fabey, Michael. "DOT acknowledges flaws in data on tarmac delays." Travel Weekly, December 22, 2008. http://www.travelweekly.com/print.aspx?id=186156

[47] McCartney, Scott. "DOT Yanks New Stats on Tarmac Delays After Flaws Found in Data." *Wall Street Journal*, January 8, 2009. http://blogs.wsj.com/middleseat/2009/01/08/dot-yanks-new-stats-on-tarmac-delays-after-flaws-found-in-data/tab/article/

[48] The Situation Room with Wolf Blitzer, *CNN*, March 11, 2009. http://transcripts.cnn.com/TRANSCRIPTS/0903/11/sitroom.01.html

[49] "Delta one of top airlines to get an 'F' in report." *CNN*, March 11, 2009. http://articles.cnn.com/2009-03-11/travel/airlines.report.card_1_tarmac-delays-american-airlines-delta-air-lines?_s=PM:TRAVEL

[50] McCartney, Scott. "From Paradise to Perdition on the Tarmac ." *Wall Street Journal*, April 28, 2009. http://online.wsj.com/article/SB124087571331061425.html

[51] Hanni, Kate. "Opinion: In-flight wireless ban needs more study." *San Jose Mercury News*, April 29, 2009. http://www.passengercommunications.com/_pdf/04.29.09_Hanni_MERC_oped.pdf

[52] Hatch, David. "In-Flight Cell Phone Ban Causes Static." *CongressDaily*, June 19, 2009.

[53] Stellin, Susan. "Passengers' Advocates See Progress." *New York Times*, May 18, 2009. http://www.nytimes.com/2009/05/19/business/19passenger.html

[54] Hochberg, Adam. "Buffalo Crash Puts Focus On Regional Airlines." *All Things Considered, National Public Radio*, June 15, 2009. http://www.npr.org/templates/story/story.php?storyId=105438574&ft=1&f=1003

[55] Torbenson, Eric. "D/FW gets a bus for bad weather." *Aviation Blog; Dallas Morning News*, July 16, 2009. http://aviationblog.dallasnews.com/archives/2009/07/dfw-airport-gets-a-bus-for-bad.html

[56] Stoller, Gary. "Stranded on the tarmac." *USA Today*, July 27, 2009. http://www.usatoday.com/travel/flights/2009-07-27-travel-runway-delays_N.htm

[57] Hughes, John. "Trapped U.S. Airline Passengers May Get a Rescue From Congress." *Bloomberg*, July 21, 2009. http://www.bloomberg.com/apps/news?pid=newsarchive&sid=a9UWI3Zb18RQ

[58] Merchant, Nomaan. "Passenger recounts night spent trapped on Rochester runway." *Associated Press*, August 10, 2009. http://minnesota.publicradio.org/display/web/2009/08/10/continental-flight-2816/

[59] Fabey, Michael. "Hanni credibility at risk in lawsuit over stolen email." *Travel Weekly*, October 19, 2009. http://www.travelweekly.com/article3_ektid205142.aspx

[60] Fabey, Michael. "Delta: We stole no emails, the plaintiff made them public." *Travel Weekly*, November 19, 2009. http://www.travelweekly.com/article3_ektid206634.aspx?

[61] Maxon, Terry. "DOT sets rules on tarmac delays." *Dallas Morning News,* December 21, 2009. http://aviationblog.dallasnews.com/archives/2009/12/dot-sets-rules-on-tarmac-delay.html

[62] *Fox News*, December 28, 2009. http://video.foxnews.com/v/3957586/punitive-guidelines

[63] CNN Newsroom. *CNN*, March 13, 2010. http://transcripts.cnn.com/TRANSCRIPTS/1003/13/cnr.01.html

[64] Fabey, Michael. "Airline passenger advocate's credibility under fire." *Travel Weekly*, July 26, 2010. http://www.travelweekly.com/article3_ektid218036.aspx?

[65] Yu, Roger. "Airlines go second straight month with no long tarmac delays." *USA Today*, January 11, 2011. http://www.usatoday.com/travel/flights/2011-01-11-airline-on-time-performance-november_N.htm

[66] Credeur, Mary Jane. "U.S. Airlines Cancel Second-Most December Flights on Snowstorms." *Bloomberg*, February 10, 2011. http://www.bloomberg.com/news/2011-02-10/u-s-airlines-cancel-second-most-december-flights-on-snowstorms.html

[67] Hinton, Christopher. "Airlines scrub flights and avoid tarmac fines." *MarketWatch*, February 10, 2011. http://www.marketwatch.com/story/airlines-scrub-flights-and-avoid-tarmac-fines-2011-02-10

[68] Sharkey, Joe. "Blizzard, and Inflexibility, Knock Out Air Travel." *New York Times*, December 27, 2010. http://www.nytimes.com/2010/12/28/business/28road.html?_r=1